INHERITANCE

A PSYCHOLOGICAL HISTORY OF THE ROYAL FAMILY

By the same author

Behind the Facade: A Psychiatrist's View
Darling Georgie: The Enigma of King George V
Ladies of the Bedchamber: The Role of the Royal Mistress
The Lonely Hearts Club
An Unsolicited Gift: Why We Do What We Do

INHERITANCE

A PSYCHOLOGICAL HISTORY OF THE ROYAL FAMILY

Dennis Friedman

PETER OWEN
LONDON AND CHICAGO

PETER OWEN PUBLISHERS
81 Ridge Road, London N8 9NP

Peter Owen books are distributed in the USA and Canada by
Independent Publishers Group/Trafalgar Square
814 North Franklin Street, Chicago, IL 60610, USA

First edition published in Great Britain by Sidgwick and Jackson, 1993
This revised and enlarged edition published 2014 by
Peter Owen Publishers

PAPERBACK ISBN 978-0-7206-1594-4
EPUB ISBN 978-0-7206-1833-4
MOBIPOCKET ISBN 978-0-7206-1834-1
PDF ISBN 978-0-7206-1835-8

A catalogue record for this book is available from
the British Library

Typeset by Octavo Smith Publishing Services

Printed and bound in the UK by
CPI Group (UK) Ltd, Croydon, CR0 4YY

For Rosemary, our family and future generations

ACKNOWLEDGEMENTS

In the first edition of *Inheritance*, published in 1993, family interactions within the British monarchy from Queen Victoria and Prince Albert to Prince Charles and Princess Diana were used as a backdrop to highlight family life.

This new edition, while doing this, in addition looks at how the present generation of the Royal Family, up to the birth of Prince George of Cambridge, third in line to the throne, is coping with the daily disclosures of the print and digital media.

Published material, including biographies and letters, has been the sole source of information. No member of the Royal Family or any of their confidants has been interviewed, and hearsay, including unsubstantiated rumour, has generally been excluded from comment. All interpretations are my own, while acknowledgements are due to Susan Hill who researched and contributed to the writing of this book and the previous edition.

My original publisher, William Armstrong, had faith in the project from its inception and took a keen personal interest in it, as has Peter Owen, the publisher of this new edition. Hazel Orme brought the added dimensions of an historian's approach to her skilled copy-editing and intuitive understanding of the subject matter. Her role has been taken over by Antonia Owen.

Thanks are due to my wife, Rosemary, for her advice and help with the manuscript and to Debbie Lennard who has patiently and painstakingly typed and retyped it as events overtook its progress with bewildering rapidity.

CONTENTS

ILLUSTRATIONS

Idealized painting of Queen Victoria and Prince Albert with five
   of their children in 1846 by Franz Winterhalter (*Hulton-Deutsch
   Collection*)
Queen Victoria with her son Edward, Prince of Wales, and
   Princess Alexandra of Denmark on the day of their marriage in
   March 1863 (*Hulton-Deutsch Collection*)
Edward, Prince of Wales, demonstrates his hunting skills with a
   wild white bull at Chillingham Castle, Northumberland,
   c. late 1879 (*Hulton-Deutsch Collection*)
King Edward VII with his son Prince George and two of his
   grandsons in Highland dress (*Hulton-Deutsch Collection*)
King Edward VII with Queen Alexandra on the royal yacht
   at Cowes about four months before his death in 1910
   (*Hulton-Deutsch Collection*)
Princess May of Teck aged three, photographed in 1870, forty years
   before she became George V's Queen (*Hulton-Deutsch Collection*)
A bejewelled Queen Mary at her daughter Princess Mary's marriage
   to Henry, Viscount Lascelles, 1922 (*Hulton-Deutsch Collection*)
Eddy, Duke of Clarence, heir to the throne before his premature
   death in 1892, photographed with his younger brother Prince
   George, later George V (*Hulton-Deutsch Collection*)
The Duke of York with Lady Elizabeth Bowes-Lyon soon after
   she consented to marry him in January 1923 (*Hulton-Deutsch
   Collection*)
The Duke and Duchess of Windsor photographed in 1937 in
   Nazi Germany with Dr Robert Ley, leader of Hitler's Labour
   Front (*Hulton-Deutsch Collection*)
A teenage Princess Elizabeth with her younger sister Princess
   Margaret Rose gardening at Royal Lodge, Windsor, in 1940
   (*Hulton-Deutsch Collection*)
King George VI's wife Queen Elizabeth with her children
   Princess Elizabeth and Princess Margaret Rose in costume,
   photographed in 1941 while performing in *Cinderella* at
   Windsor Castle (*Hulton-Deutsch Collection*)
An unusually relaxed Prince Philip at his stag party in November
   1947 (*Syndication International*)

Princess Margaret photographed at London's British
   Industries Fair with Group Captain Peter Townsend, 1953
   (*Hulton-Deutsch Collection*)
Prince Charles aged six waving regally from his chauffeur-driven
   limousine in 1954 (*Hulton-Deutsch Collection*)
A teenage Prince Charles fails to live up to the expectations of his
   father the Duke of Edinburgh on the polo field at Windsor
   Great Park in 1965 (*Syndication International*)
Princess Anne on horseback at the Windsor Horse Trials in 1975
   (*Hulton-Deutsch Collection*)
Queen Elizabeth II posing for her official portrait to commemorate
   her Silver Jubilee in 1977 (*Hulton-Deutsch Collection*)
Diana Spencer on the day of the announcement of her
   engagement to Charles, Prince of Wales, in February 1981
   (*Hulton-Deutsch Collection*)
Prince Charles saying goodbye his fiancée Diana before leaving her
   for a five-week foreign tour in 1981 (*Syndication International*)
Queen Elizabeth reacts to her horse losing at the 1985 Epsom
   Derby (*Syndication International*)
A rare instance of inadvertent sartorial impropriety by Princess
   Diana (*Rex Features*)
Princess Diana competing for attention with her husband's
   sports car (*Syndication International*)
Princess Margaret smoking after major lung surgery in 1985
   (*Syndication International*)
The newborn Princess Beatrice with her parents, the Duke and
   Duchess of York, in 1988 (*Syndication International*)
Queen Elizabeth at Windsor Castle after it was severely damaged
   by fire in November 1992 (*Press Association Photo Library*)
Prince William with his brother Prince Harry and girlfriend Kate
   Middleton at a rugby match at Twickenham, London in
   February 2007 (*Associated Press/Press Association Images*)
The Duke and Duchess of Cambridge leaving St Mary's
   Hospital, London, with their newborn son, Prince George of
   Cambridge, 23 July 2013 (*DPA/Press Association Images*)
'The Firm' assembled on the balcony of Buckingham Palace to
   watch the Trooping the Colour in 2012 (*Doug Peters/EMPICS
   Entertainment*)

PROLOGUE

On 26 March 1819 Her Royal Highness the Duchess of Cambridge gave birth to a son christened George. The recently born son of the present Duke and Duchess of Cambridge, also named George, is the earlier Duke of Cambridge's first cousin seven times removed. At the time of his birth in 1819, for eight weeks only, Prince George William Frederick Charles of Cambridge was, like his 2013 namesake, destined to be the future King. The birth of Princess Victoria put paid to this. No one, other than himself, is likely to put paid to the destiny of the son and heir of William and Kate, the present Duke and Duchess of Cambridge. Will that please Prince George when he reaches the age when children begin to consider their future? What will he feel when he discovers that he does not own his future? His future belongs to his family. No future can be more preordained than that of the heir to the English throne. He may disqualify himself only by failing to satisfy the necessary criteria, while exploring his ancestry may provide clues to the outcome.

On 3 December 2012 St James's Palace announced that Catherine Middleton, the Duchess of Cambridge, wife of Prince William, the grandson of the reigning monarch Queen Elizabeth II, was expecting her first child. In the early months of the pregnancy Catherine, generally known as Kate, suffered from severe morning sickness. She was admitted under the watchful eye of the media to the King Edward VII Hospital in London for treatment of *Hyperemesis gravidarum*, a severe and unremitting form of morning sickness, not usually life-threatening but thoroughly unpleasant for the sufferer. The condition gradually resolved, and the pregnancy proceeded smoothly.

Six months later the media, determined not to miss any event connected with the birth of a royal baby, moved its operations to the private Lindo Wing of St Mary's Hospital, Paddington, London, where both Prince William and his younger brother Prince Harry had been born, to await the baby's birth.

On 22 July 2013 at 4.24 p.m. a royal prince was born to the Duchess of Cambridge and Prince William Arthur Philip Louis, her husband of fifteen months. It heralded the beginning of a new chapter for the British Royal Family.

Within a week the baby had been named George Alexander Louis, possibly to commemorate the 300th anniversary of Prince George of Hanover's enthronement as King George I in March 1714 which heralded the beginning of the Hanoverian dynasty or, more likely, to please his great grandmother Queen Elizabeth II since George was not only her father's name but one of the names bestowed by her on her firstborn son Charles, the baby's grandfather and heir apparent to the throne.

Will it be possible to predict what the future will have in store for this baby boy destined to be King of England? Can any conclusions about his future be drawn from the life patterns of his ancestors on both his father and mother's side? *Inheritance* looks to Queen Victoria, her consort Prince Albert and their descendants for clues.

George's destiny is to inherit the throne and possibly become England's seventh King George. He is third in line of succession to the throne after his grandfather Prince Charles and his father Prince William.

He can do very little to change his destiny other than refuse to accept it. It is waiting to embrace him like a bespoke overcoat. When his time comes he will wear it. It has been made to fit him by his past, and it will shape his future. It will be a perfect fit. Only his destination is unpredictable.

He is expected to accept the duties of Head of State and opt for continuity and stability in the role of monarch, stumbling only if his path is obstructed or if he emulates his great-great-uncle King Edward VIII who abandoned his inheritance because he put love before constitutional duty – or if his country elects to become a republic.

It is possible to gain some understanding of Prince George's life options by investigating his ancestral and personal past. We are all victims of our inheritance, but few of us know how our ancestry has shaped us. The Prince will grow up to carry a burden of choice of which for a while he will be unaware. He will seamlessly embrace unchanging tradition and be drawn into social customs to which he will have been introduced. The behavioural changes that some of his forebears have made are little different from how his subjects might behave when exposed to similar social pressures. What differences there are will be based on the influence of the media. When a member of the Royal Family's private life is exposed we realize that he or she is more one of 'us' and less one of 'them'. Traditional barriers that for centuries have represented privilege and privacy begin to crumble. The monarchy influences families in the United Kingdom and the Commonwealth, rewards achievement and aspiration, values social graces and dislikes publicity.

In 1861 a Prince of Wales, son of Queen Victoria and Prince Albert and a future king, strayed from the royal path by having a clandestine affair with Nellie Clifden, an actress. In 1936 a Prince of Wales, son of King George V and Queen Mary, abandoned the throne for Wallis Simpson, the one woman he felt truly understood him. In 1992 a Prince of Wales, son of Queen Elizabeth II and Prince Philip, married to Diana, Princess of Wales, thought twice about his inheritance when it came to light that both he and his wife had compromising friendships. They divorced in 1996.

Can it be that a fatal flaw runs through the Royal Family like the San Andreas Fault, contaminating relationships and severing marriages? Were the first rumblings of this felt in the nursery of Queen Victoria? Did it continue to affect her descendants – hostages not only to their genetic inheritance but to ancestral patterns of upbringing – as they played out their psychodramas against a privileged background of English palaces and Scottish castles?

Could hints of this have been detected 150 years earlier when Prince Albert looked for a mother in Queen Victoria and she for a father in her consort? Was it their unresolved conflicts that made them unwittingly neglect the emotional needs of their nine children, passing on to their royal descendants an ever-widening chasm of psychological problems?

Inheritance examines the complex interpersonal relationships of the Royal Family from when the ten-year-old Victoria, on hearing that she would be Queen, promised, 'I will be good', and her cousin Albert, her future husband, confided to his diary at almost the same time, 'I intend to train myself to be a good and useful man.' The result of their rigid upbringing, with its emphasis on duty rather than on love, has been to produce in the Royal Family – just as it would in other families – unhappy adults destined to seek compensation in alternative forms of gratification including such risk-taking activities as extramarital relationships, gambling at casinos and racecourses, and involvement in high-arousal sport and other activities.

Some activities are life-enhancing and involved with issues of protection and rescue; others are concerned with service to the country. Both Prince William and his brother Prince Harry have been engaged in the armed services, serving Queen and Country. Prince William was a search-and-rescue pilot until he gave it up soon after the birth of Prince George to concentrate on 'royal duties and charity work'. Prince Harry, still a bachelor in 2013 but said to be highly sought-after, was until lately in active duty in the Army Air Corps but is in the process of transferring to SO3 (Defence Engagement) in the Horse Guards headquarters, London.

Royal tradition has it that duty comes before family. Diana, Princess of Wales, the virgin bride of the Prince of Wales and the grandmother of Prince George, was not the first to cast a stone on to the smooth surface of the royal pond but probably the first victim of twentieth-century media inquisition that ensured her personal life would receive worldwide prominence. Scandals involving royals before the age of mass communication remained hidden, mainly because of the secrecy and sycophancy of royal courtiers. Revelation of Princess Diana's marital problems in the course of a BBC *Panorama* interview with Martin Bashir in 1995 came as a shock to many, but feminists and others accepted it as a woman's right to speak out; a right men had always exercised.

Princess Diana was dubbed the 'People's Princess' after her death, and the country warmed to her common touch and disclosures of her vulnerability. Her untimely death in a car crash in 1997, after her divorce from Prince Charles, provoked an unprecedented outpouring of grief from the British people.

Will Prince George inherit his grandmother's capacity to understand and empathize with the British public? Has the Royal Family relaxed its rigidity, become more open and aware that the lifestyle of its members is more visible than ever? Does media intrusion feed into and sanction social change that has already evolved? Prince George may be at an evolutionary crossroad. As time passes he may see gradual changes in an institution that has remained the same for centuries. Will he welcome these changes or opt to live in the past?

An understanding the dynamics of the Royal Family might just help us recognize how our own psychological inheritance has affected us. Can a loving grandparent, an absentee parent, a supportive teacher or an antagonistic sibling influence our emotional development and eventual choice of life partner? *Inheritance* looks at the public behaviour of one of the world's most private families. Through historical records and, more recently, digital intrusion it has been forced to share some of its secrets with us.

Is the wall that encloses the Royal Family beginning to crumble? There have been several attempts at escape. In recent times Edward VIII succeeded with the help of Wallis Simpson, while the family closed the door firmly behind him. The door also slammed on Princess Margaret when she tried to marry an outsider. Princess Diana did escape but died in the attempt. Others downgraded their status and hoped that no one would notice.

The baton has been handed to Prince George. What will he do with it?

1

QUEEN VICTORIA AND PRINCE ALBERT

'The hand that rocks the cradle . . .' – John O'London's *Treasure Trove*

Queen Victoria and her consort Prince Albert were both psycho-logically disadvantaged in that neither was brought up by two caring parents. Franz August Karl Albert Emanuel was the younger son of Ernst, Duke of Saxe-Coburg-Saalfeld, who later became Duke of Saxe-Coburg-Gotha. His mother, Duchess Louise, was the daughter of August, Duke of Saxe-Gotha. Queen Victoria's father, the Duke of Kent, died when she was just eight months old, while the four-year-old Albert was deprived of his mother, Duchess Louise of Saxe-Coburg-Saalfeld, when she was banished from the Court following her illicit relationship with an Army officer. As a result, both Victoria and Albert left legacies of emotional damage, handing down through the generations their unresolved conflicts and disturbed behavioural patterns together with the Crown.

Several of Queen Victoria's descendants have been seriously depressed, compulsive gamblers or have had problem with alcohol misuse. Some have had difficulties in making and maintaining com-mitments and others in bringing up their children. In three out of the five generations, from Queen Victoria to the present Prince of Wales, certain family members seem to have experienced confusion about their sexual orientation, and at least one has turned for solace to illegal drugs. Every generation has experienced marital crises, reflected particularly in certain twentieth-century events that many feel brought the future of the monarchy into question.

Victoria and Albert, two deprived children born within three months of each other, were destined to seek attention and love to compensate for the absence of the parent of the opposite sex. Destiny also played a role in their betrothal and subsequent marriage.

Princess Victoria was born in 1819, the only child of an arranged marriage between Prince Edward, Duke of Kent, and Princess

Victoria Mary Louisa of Saxe-Coburg-Saalfeld.[1] Prince Edward's parents, George III and Queen Charlotte, had produced thirteen children, yet the succession was a matter of concern. Their eldest son George, the Prince Regent, was unlikely to have further children with Caroline of Brunswick, whom he hated – his only legitimate daughter Charlotte died in childbirth in 1817 – so his younger brothers were encouraged to produce legitimate offspring.

Edward, Duke of Kent, was living in Belgium with a French-woman – Julie, Madame de St Laurent – who was slightly older than he. At the age of forty-eight, and with some initial reluctance, he terminated this long-standing relationship and married the thirty-year-old Princess Victoria of Saxe-Coburg-Saalfeld. Although the relationship was not, at first, a romantic one, Edward and Victoria later grew fond of one another. At any rate the couple settled into apartments in Kensington Palace, which had been grudgingly offered to them by the Prince Regent, where Victoria, their only child, was born ten months after the marriage. She was delivered by Fräulein Siebold who, coincidentally, also delivered her cousin Albert three months later.

The Princess was christened in June, but several of her parents' chosen names were rejected by the Prince Regent. He did not, however, object to the name Alexandrina, after the Tsar of Russia, Alexander I. Victoria was called by the diminutive Drina until she was twelve. Although the Duke of Kent may have been hoping for a son, he was not displeased by the arrival of his daughter – 'The decrees of Providence are at all times wisest and best,' he wrote – and he had no reason to suppose that Princess Victoria would accede to the throne. He, after all, had brothers who might yet produce sons, and Victoria's mother was still relatively young and fertile.

By the end of the year Victoria's parents were considering returning to Germany where life would be cheaper and the atmosphere warmer. The Prince Regent, who was still distraught over the death in 1817 of his daughter Charlotte, not only regarded Victoria as an intruder but resented the continuing presence at Court of her uncle Prince Leopold, who was also Charlotte's widower and a constant reminder to her grieving father of his beloved daughter's death. Before deciding on their move to Germany, however, the Duke of Kent took his wife and just-weaned daughter to Sidmouth in Devon for Christmas. By the sea he caught a cold that developed into pneumonia. On the advice of Dr Stockmar, a young friend of Prince Leopold, the Duke made his will. Among his executors was his equerry Sir John Conroy.

The Duke died on 23 January 1820, six days before his father George III. Accepting the generosity of a small allowance from her brother Leopold, the Duchess of Kent, together with Princess Victoria, returned to Kensington Palace, where Victoria grew up without a father and with a mother who was not only a poor relation of the Royal Family but a foreigner. The two men in her life were her Uncle Leopold and Sir John Conroy.

King Leopold of the Belgians, brother of the Duke of Kent, was born in 1780, Prince of Leiningen, the son of Francis, Duke of Saxe-Coburg. He had married Charlotte, the cherished daughter of the Prince Regent, in 1816, against her father's wishes. That the Duke of Kent had encouraged the courtship may partially explain Leopold's later fondness for Victoria. He remained on the fringes of the English Court after Charlotte's death and, until accepting the crown of Belgium in 1830, was a frequent and welcome visitor at Kensington Palace, although he was absent for four years following his accession.

Victoria responded warmly to this flamboyant uncle. Elizabeth Longford tells us that he sported a wig, three-inch soles on his shoes and a feather boa. This outward effeminacy may have primed the Princess to feel comfortable with such men, and an attraction to the effeminate, to men dressed as women, was to remain with her for the rest of her life. Leopold displayed consistent kindness and generosity towards Victoria and her mother, and his affection for them both contrasted sharply with the *froideur* accorded the Duchess by George IV, who appeared to think it was something of an impertinence for her to have given birth to the heir to the throne and associated this, all too painfully, with the death of his own daughter. That he had never liked Leopold made it inevitable that he would feel hostility to those with whom his son-in-law was aligned. On her uncle's departure for Belgium, however, Victoria wrote, 'I look up to him as a Father, with complete confidence, love and affection. He is the best and kindest adviser I have. He has always treated me as his child and I love him more dearly for it.'

By contrast, Captain John Conroy, whose influence over her

mother increased after Leopold's departure, seemed a scheming, ambitious intruder. Upon her accession Victoria banished him from Court, and at his death in 1854 she wrote to her mother, 'I will not speak of the past and of the many sufferings he entailed upon us by creating divisions between you and me which could never have existed otherwise.'

An Anglo-Irishman, Conroy was married to Elizabeth Fisher, a relative of the Duke of Kent's former tutor, which connection might have led to his appointment as the Duke's military equerry in 1817. After the Duke's death Conroy took it upon himself to serve his widow with particular diligence. He moved, with his family, into Kensington Palace where he became Comptroller of the Duchess's Household. He was knighted in 1827.

If Conroy had ambitions to establish and wield influence over Victoria, by now clearly destined to be Queen, through her mother, he failed. Victoria referred to his 'personal affronts', 'slights and incivilities' and to her 'hatred' of him. Her dislike of Sir John certainly contributed to her later estrangement from her mother whom she perceived as being overly close to him. Later she was ruefully to refer to the enmity that had existed between the Duchess and herself at the time.

Victoria and her mother had a curious mutually dependent relationship. The Duchess owed her place at Court to the existence of Victoria, and Victoria needed her mother's approval and the reassurance of her presence. They slept in the same bedroom until the daughter was eighteen. The Duchess of Kent's mothering of Victoria alternated between extreme protectiveness – until she had become Queen, Victoria was not allowed to walk downstairs without someone holding her hand – and zealous expectation.

Victoria collected male and female dolls, compensation perhaps for her lack of brothers and sisters. (Fond as she was of her two maternal half-siblings, Charles born 1804 and Feodora 1817, children of Victoire, widow of Prince Erich Charles of Leiningen, they were occasional playmates rather than family.) She quickly learned to respect authority and the importance of duty. Writing in her fifties, Queen Victoria described her earliest memory, that of being admonished as a two-year-old: she had been crawling on a yellow carpet at Kensington Palace and was warned that if she made a noise her Uncle Sussex – Augustus, Duke of Sussex – would punish her. Early memories tend to have a particular significance: memory encapsulates feelings and attitudes that are never forgotten and which current behaviour continues to reflect.

Victoria continued to suppress her own needs and never ceased trying to please authority. She remained for ever dependent on the approval of her ministers and of the public. She was dedicated to duty, and family life inevitably took second place. Her early years were both over-controlled and lacking in childhood pleasures. Later, with little or no experience of happiness, she had little to offer her children.

Victoria, indeed, thought of giving birth with distaste. 'I think, dearest Uncle,' she wrote to Leopold – by now King of the Belgians – with ill-concealed impatience, 'you cannot really wish me to be the "mama d'une nombreuse famille" . . . men never think, at least seldom think, what a hard task it is for us women to go through this very often.' Her dislike of pregnancy and babies, whom she thought 'frog-like', was not conducive to a benevolent attitude towards young children. 'Having children is the only thing I *dread*,' she remarked, soon after her first pregnancy threatened to disturb her newly married idyll with Albert. All but the last of her nine children endured their childhoods while their mother was in that state of pregnancy she found so disagreeable or in its aftermath when she showed little interest in her new baby.

Children learn early on to suppress feelings they sense will be unacceptable, because they fear the loss of parental approval upon which they are entirely dependent. Disapproval, expressed in body language – the warning finger, the stern glance – may come to be as threatening as anything verbally expressed. Victoria's need to please her mother through compliant behaviour was, as with all children, based on fear of being abandoned, a concern strong in Victoria since she had already lost one parent. Victoria's remark 'I will be good' reflects both a precocious sense of duty and a need for the approval of the parent on whom she was still heavily dependent. When parents impress on their children the importance of duty and obedience rather than showing them unconditional love, negative feelings in the child are obliged to be suppressed, often only to reappear inappropriately in adulthood. Such children over-emphasize pleasing at the expense of acquiring self-esteem and self-confidence and adopting assertive behaviour.

If Victoria felt threatened by the attention her mother showed Sir John Conroy, she was happy in the company of Fräulein (later Baroness) Louise Lehzen. The daughter of a Lutheran pastor, Lehzen was brought from Germany when Victoria was five to be her companion and governess and had previously taught Feodora. While Lehzen's presence maintained her charge's familiarity with things German, she was diligent in her efforts to interest Victoria in British history. Victoria had lessons from numerous teachers, but it was her relationship with Lehzen that most shaped her character. Although severe, Lehzen was loyal and protective, and Victoria understood that her reprimands did not imply diminished devotion. One of Lehzen's habits was to pin a sprig of holly to Victoria's collar, so that her small, sloping chin would always be raised. Had Victoria not been fond of her, some complaint about this might have been found in the daily diary that Lehzen herself had encouraged her to keep.

As Victoria grew into womanhood she retained affection and respect for Lehzen. Even as Queen, she wrote in her journal, 'Walked with my *angelic*, dearest Mother, Lehzen, who I do so love! . . . the most estimable and precious treasure I possess and *ever shall possess*.'

Perhaps, in the light of such freely expressed affection, it is not to be wondered that Prince Albert resented Lehzen's continuing presence in the royal household and, in particular, the influence she had on his wife. In 1842 she finally left the household and returned to live in Germany on a pension of £800 a year. Lehzen's departure was engineered by Albert. He described the governess as 'a crazy, common, stupid intriguer, obsessed with lust of power'. Victoria deferred to him in Lehzen's dismissal, having found her 'other half' in her husband and therefore less in need of a surrogate parent. She continued to correspond with Lehzen, though, and visited her until the Baroness's death in 1870.

For the young Victoria it must have been distressing to have had a mother who bonded with her during breastfeeding but who had probably given this up abruptly on the death of her husband. This would have been her first experience of the pain of separation that reappeared so dramatically on the death of her own husband. A more gradual separation from her mother and breastfeeding would have allowed her to cope better with the losses, forty years later, of her mother and husband. Her confusion would have been compounded by the presence of Fräulein Lehzen, another 'mother' who was not only affectionate but who imbued her with a strong sense of self and impressed on her her place in history. From her biological mother Victoria learned 'negligent mothering', but from her surrogate mother she learned how to be a queen. In the event, because of her remoteness and her melancholy aura during her bereavement she became the mother that her people wanted rather than the one her children needed.

Queen Victoria's grief when her mother died in March 1861 was greater than she might have anticipated. After a period of estrangement shortly after Victoria's accession, mother and daughter had grown closer as Victoria's family increased and mutually enjoyed discussion of her children's progress. It is not surprising that Victoria felt regret that her mother's affection for her had not been acknowledged by the Duchess. Victoria had told Lord Melbourne, 'I don't believe Ma ever really loved me.' After the Duchess's death she was moved to find many fond references to herself among her mother's papers, which could well have caused her to feel both remorseful and guilty about her interpretation of her mother's behaviour. On Albert's birthday in August – normally a day to be celebrated – and four months before his unexpected death, Victoria wrote, 'Alas! so much is different this year, nothing festive . . . I am still in such low spirits.' She also wrote to her Aunt Augusta of her 'immeasurable loss and grief', which caused her loss of appetite, headaches, irritability and what Lord Clarendon referred to as a 'morbid melancholy' – or what we would now term depression. Finally Albert heard of reports circulating in Germany that the Queen was being attended by several doctors. He denied the 'horrid, vile rumours' but set about persuading Victoria to end her mourning for her mother and return to some semblance of public life. But shortly afterwards he, too, was dead, from typhoid fever, leaving Victoria a widow at the age of forty-two. In 1861 she experienced one loss too many, and her melancholy demeanour remained for the rest of her life.

The death of Victoria's father had led her mother to try to play the role of both parents for her daughter. That this had not worked for Victoria was demonstrated by her continuing dependency on her mother until her marriage to Albert. She may have hoped that Albert would come to replace her father, but in reality she needed him to be both father and mother to her – her mother may have felt herself a good parent, but Victoria's perception of her would have been influenced by the Duchess's reaction to her bereavement when Victoria, as a tiny baby, was entirely dependent on her. That both her mother and her husband died in the same year reactivated Victoria's dependent needs.

In 1848 she lost Viscount Melbourne, who died six years after his stroke. Victoria had relied upon him as she would on a father, and he had spent much of his time at Windsor acting as her private secretary and mentor as well as her first Prime Minister. Happily, at the time Albert was able to take his place.

Victoria's feelings had always to be suppressed. Her earlier losses were denied, but this defence eventually broke down at Albert's death. The Queen's sadness was as much to do with unexpressed, and now inexpressible, childhood grief (since there was now no one to whom she could relate) as it was for the loss of a mother whom she had come to feel she may have misjudged and a husband on whom she had been heavily dependent.

Victoria had grown up a lively and spirited child. She was not intellectually gifted but was full of curiosity and imagination. Like other members of the Royal Family down the generations she drew well, had an ear for music, a gift for mimicry, and she enjoyed the make-believe world of ballet, theatre and opera. However, when it became clear that she would eventually become Queen new responsibilities meant that she had much less time for the things she enjoyed, especially when she embarked on a series of tiring journeys around Britain. These provided visible evidence to the populace that the monarchy was continuing, but at the end of one tour she wrote, 'Here is the end of our journey, I am happy to say. Though I liked some of the places very well, I was much tired by the long journeys and the great crowds we encountered.' Her travelling companion and only friend was Lehzen, and communication from her mother was largely admonishing; she exhorted her daughter to 'Avoid stepping out of your room an unknown and untried person . . . shew a promise of character – let the People hope for something worth having, free from all the faults of former reigns.'

It was a great joy for her to be reunited with Uncle Leopold in 1835 after the four-year separation. Letters, however kindly and frequently exchanged, were not as satisfactory as meetings. 'What happiness was it for me to throw myself in the arms of that dearest of Uncles who has always been to me like a father,' she wrote in September. King Leopold had married Louise of Orleans who became at once 'very dear' to Victoria.

Because Victoria's childhood and adolescence almost totally lacked the companionship of her peers, she never learned how to communicate with children and became drawn to animals as soon as she had outgrown her dolls. Her favourite pet, a King Charles spaniel called Dash, came into the household, ironically as a present for her mother from the loathed Sir John Conroy. Victoria commandeered the little dog, giving him presents at Christmas and dressing him in little jackets and trousers. Dash in his turn was devoted to her, refusing to leave her room when she was ill.

The dog was something that she could openly cherish and pet in the absence of fulfilling human contact. Horses, too, symbols of strength, power and masculinity, were important to her all her life, from the ponies she rode as a child to the great beasts upon which Landseer and others painted her, dressed in her widow's weeds, the bridle frequently held respectfully by a gillie.

The Princess was given firm lessons about the significance of the Crown – and her destiny to uphold it – and her own importance. By the time she was twelve she merited a 24-hour bodyguard, and was very much aware that when her uncle William IV died she would be Queen. She was addressed as 'ma'am', treated with deference by courtiers as well as servants and the breadth of her education stressed the magnitude of her future role. Victoria was pleased to observe in her own features a resemblance to those of the King and had been inconsolable when the Duchess of Kent decided that her daughter should not attend his coronation: it had been decreed that Victoria's royal uncles should take precedence over the heir presumptive. The child was a state treasure yet lacked family life and grew to be wilful. The diarist Charles Cavendish Fulke Greville, who was as spiteful as he was amusing, described her as 'hard-hearted, selfish and self-willed'. If this was so, much can be attributed to the baffling paradox that confronted her. While being trained for the throne, she was denied the unqualified 'personal' acceptance from loving parents that would certainly have made her a better mother and would scarcely have made her a lesser Queen. When she complained that years later William Gladstone addressed her as if she were a public meeting, it was perhaps an unconscious declaration that, rather than being seen as a person, she symbolized an institution.

Comfort eating is a well-known phenomenon. Those who eat to excess may be expressing a wish for gratification hitherto denied them and possibly unfulfilled childhood needs. At the age of seventeen Victoria was barely five feet tall but weighed almost nine stone. Shortly after she became Queen it was reported that she was ordering her dresses a size larger. According to Elizabeth Longford, she resolved to eat only half a biscuit at lunch and then, later, to miss the meal altogether. These resolutions were broken, however, and Victoria may have taken comfort from Lord Melbourne's remark that the best figure for a woman was 'fine and full with a fine bust'. Soon after, however, he told her that she was in danger of becoming very fat, but he sweetened the pill by attributing her weight to her age. Victoria's weight gain may be interpreted as compensation for insufficient emotional nourishment from her mother and a prelude to another frustrated appetite – the sexual – that was to become apparent later.

William Lamb, Viscount Melbourne, Victoria's Prime Minister at her accession, was to become as important to the young Queen as her uncle Leopold had been to her as a princess. He was not merely a scholar, consummate politician and wit but was attractive, charming and affectionate to Victoria, whose regard for him was not reduced by his having scraped through two scandalous divorces. Their devotion was entirely mutual, and in Melbourne Victoria found the support, kindly advice and almost flirtatious regard that she might have wished for from a father. He dealt expertly with all her self-doubts, reassured her that her nervousness denoted 'high and right feelings' and comforted her when she bemoaned her short stature and the shape of her nose. Her height, he said, was 'great enough', and people with small features 'never did anything'. To have Melbourne at her elbow, guiding her invisibly, eased Victoria's transition from Princess to Queen.

Two of Melbourne's favourite names for girls were Alice and Louise, and Victoria duly gave these names to two of her daughters. She was highly entertained by his waggish epigrams: of wife-beating, he remarked, 'It is almost worthwhile for a woman to be beat, considering the exceeding pity she excites', and, of cheating, 'No people cheat like the English.' His influence might have been of dubious value, although amusing, but he treated Victoria as a person and a woman as well as his Queen, and she responded accordingly.

It was just as well that Victoria was able to confide in her Prime Minister and that he was generally sympathetic and wise. When she admitted to him that she had become lazy about dress, Melbourne replied, 'That's the feeling of a sensible person, but I shouldn't encourage you.' She disliked getting up in the morning, took her bath last thing at night instead of before dinner, so that she could cut down on the time spent dressing and undressing, and even disliked brushing her teeth. Melbourne reminded her of the Four Commandments enumerated by a prominent politician's wife to her children: 'Fear God. Honour the King. Obey your parents. Brush your teeth.'

It may be that Victoria's lack of interest in washing and dressing can be attributed to her dislike of the Mistress of the Robes, the Duchess of Sutherland, but it is more likely that the depression which was to affect her throughout her life was beginning to show itself. Because she could not face the day she neglected both her appearance and her personal hygiene. In the light of her childhood losses, new responsibilities, political pressures and the burden of duties for which she was only half prepared, a change in behavioural patterns was inevitable.

Lord Melbourne became one of Victoria's few trusted confidants. She leaned on him, relied on him and felt able to be herself in his presence. When Melbourne resigned, albeit temporarily, in 1839 she despaired. 'All my happiness is gone! That peaceful life destroyed, that dearest kind Lord Melbourne no more my Minister,' she wrote in her journal on 7 May. She wept at the idea of either the Duke of Wellington or Sir Robert Peel forming an administration. However, her spirits lifted when Melbourne unexpectedly formed a new government and Sir John Conroy resigned from her mother's household. (She found herself able to dance until a quarter to four at a ball held for the visiting Russian Tsarevitch.)

Victoria dreaded the thought of marriage at this time in her life and wrote to her uncle Leopold, whom by now she knew desired a match between herself and her cousin Albert, requesting that Albert's proposed visit be cancelled. The King of the Belgians was shrewd enough to remain calm and persuaded Victoria to agree that

Albert's visit should not be forgotten but merely delayed for a few months. On 18 April 1839, after a discussion during which Lord Melbourne had advised against marrying a foreigner or a commoner, marriage seemed to have been staved off. She wrote in her journal, 'Why need I marry at all for 3 or 4 years? Did he see the necessity? I did not think so, still this & certainly the present state is dreadful; always, as he says on the verge of a quarrel; I said I dreaded the thought of marrying; that I was so accustomed to have my own way, that I thought it was 10 to 1 that I shouldn't agree with anybody.' The 'dreadful' state to which Victoria alluded was her uncomfortable relationship with her mother. Until and unless she married, Victoria would remain stifled by the Duchess's suffocating presence.

Victoria had first met her cousin Albert in 1836 when he and his brother had visited London. She was unaware that this was an early move in Leopold's long-cherished plan to see his niece and nephew married and was no more impressed with Albert than she had been with other glamorous European male cousins who had been presented to her.

As a frequent visitor in court circles Leopold was better placed than anyone to see the political benefits of a match between Albert, younger son of his brother Ernst (Duke of Saxe-Coburg-Saalfeld), and his niece Victoria. His long-nursed wishes were realized late in 1839 when the brothers visited Victoria again. Mindful perhaps of the infancy and thus fragility of his own dynasty, Leopold was keen to replicate through his nephew and niece the union between the houses of Hanover and Coburg that his own first marriage had represented. After her cousins' first visit Victoria dutifully and probably unconsciously colluded with Leopold's plans by writing of Albert to her uncle in terms certain to please him. 'He possesses every quality that could be desired to make me perfectly happy. I have only to beg you now, my dearest Uncle, to take care of the health of one, now so dear to me . . .'

Yet the eighteen-year-old Victoria's admiration of Albert did not prevent her from delaying a return visit for three years. That she experienced one of history's great *coups de foudre* when she saw Albert again speaks of several things: her wish to be freed from her mother's lowering influence and to replicate in her personal life the power she had come to enjoy as Queen, Albert's startling loss of weight since 1836 and the lean beauty which was consequently clear, and her helpless desire to please her uncle.

After Albert's mother Duchess Louise had been banished from Court, she had subsequently married her Army officer. In the seven years before her death Albert never saw her again. Although his father was kindly he was also remote, and Albert came to lean heavily on his older brother, also named Ernst. He grew up without the influence of women, and it is likely that he was not only ignorant and suspicious of them but hostile to them. It was inevitable that, as an adult, he would unconsciously try to replace the irreplaceable and seek a woman who understood his loss. No seeking was necessary, though. Albert knew that his marriage was preordained and that he had little choice in the matter. 'I intend to train myself to be a good and useful man,' he wrote, uncannily reiterating his Cousin Victoria's vow to be good.

Albert was as assiduous a diarist as Victoria, although he mainly recorded details of his illnesses. His preoccupation with loss, unlike Victoria's, showed itself in hypochondriasis, the loss of his health, his *élan*. Illness and a fear of death, the ultimate separation, echoed anxieties relating to the loss of his mother. Having been deprived of the source of life at the age of four, he inevitably remained concerned about loss of life through illness. The renewal of life through birth was important to both of them, but it was life they sought, not children. Albert, like Victoria, had looked to a series of tutors for companionship and mothering. One in particular, Herr Florschütz, known to Albert as 'Thus', provided him with an emotional prop. As a youth in Venice, plagued by an abscess on a tooth, he wrote of his longing for Thus's comfort, 'but nowhere could I find my beloved Thus to sob out my pain in his arms'.

At the University of Bonn Albert's interests were artistic and intellectual. He studied natural sciences, languages, music and painting. He fenced, developed a deep love for the beautiful but melancholy music of Mendelssohn and played chess, often against himself. He seems to have been a natural scholar but had difficulty in relating to others: he was content in solitude and neither sought nor encouraged friendship. This did not seem to trouble him – loneliness for him was a way of life. Thrown upon his own resources at an early age, he had had limited opportunities to rely on others or to trust them: his mother probably would have had little time for him while she was involved with her lover before Albert was four, and after that he never saw her again.

Albert's shyness affected his behaviour when he returned to England in 1839. He knew almost no one and was hampered in conversation by his heavy German accent. After the all-male society of the university and knowing that he was to be judged by a young Queen – not to mention her Court – he vowed that he would not be 'corrupted'. In German, the word meaning 'to corrupt', *bestecher*, may also be translated as 'bribed': a strange reaction to a proposed commitment to a woman. But his first commitment, that to his mother, had ended badly, and it seems likely that he would have reservations about involvement with another woman. It was clearly his duty to marry, but a one-to-one relationship with a female was not something to which he was looking forward: Melbourne noted that he showed a marked reserve with ladies and made tactless and premature remarks about 'moral codes'.

From the moment that Victoria indicated her enthusiasm for their marriage in 1839, Albert was denied any wish to return to his studies, his music or his Rhineland. His life was determined for him, but, by nature shy and withdrawn, it was not easy for him to adapt to it. Since role-playing often reflects an uncertainty about one's own role in life it was not surprising that one of his few diversions was his talent for mimicry, a talent shared by his wife.

Victoria was perhaps fortunate that her attraction to 'beautiful people' such as Lord Melbourne was not shared by Albert. Resigned to his fate, and probably indifferent to it, Albert was not put off by her plumpness or homeliness, and anyway it is possible that since she was in love she had acquired the radiance that love can bring to the plainest of women. We are told by Elizabeth Longford that at times Victoria was worried by Albert's quiet wistfulness, particularly during occasions which were supposed to be social. 'When she introduced him to her ladies for the first time he found it very tiresome and could not remember which was which.' In General Grey's account of Albert's early life, written with Victoria's approval and published in 1867, it is asserted that Albert 'never took kindly to great dinners, balls, or to the common amusements of the fashionable world'. Victoria was enchanted by his appearance and seems to have been sexually attracted to him. 'Albert's beauty is most striking, and he is so amiable and unaffected – in short, very fascinating,' she wrote during his second visit. Albert's 'beauty' (a term more usually held in association with women) rather than his 'good looks' appealed to Victoria, probably because once more she had found a father in a 'woman'. But her infatuation with him stopped short of leaving him in any doubt as to who would be the senior partner in their marriage. Victoria always wore the trousers, just as her mother before her. After their betrothal Albert mooted plans for a long honeymoon, but his fiancée replied, adoringly but firmly, 'You forget, my dearest Love, that I am the Sovereign and that business can stop and wait for nothing.' Later on, in the early days of their marriage, Victoria recorded that after she had dealt with some state papers, 'Albert helped me with the blotting paper when I signed.'

Paradoxically it had been at the Queen's insistence that the word 'obey' was retained at their wedding service. Her resolve to delay marriage had dissolved during Albert's autumn visit. Victoria proposed to him within three days of his arrival, and they were married on 10 February 1840.

The diarist Charles Greville queried Albert's sex drive and physical desire for his bride when he observed that the couple took a walk early in the morning after their wedding night. 'Strange that a bridal night should be so short; and I told Lady Palmerston that this was not the way to provide us with a Prince of Wales.' Yet Albert's need to be reunited with a lost mother was quickly satisfied by Victoria's first pregnancy and the birth of their daughter Victoria (known first as Pussy and then as Vicky) and by eight further pregnancies over the next sixteen years. Since Albert had never felt loved by a woman in his childhood he welcomed the birth of his daughter. He adored her – but, more importantly, he expected her to adore him.

No child should be expected to please a father by filling the vacuum created by an earlier bereavement. In certain circumstances a daughter may gradually come to replace a wife, with all the inevitable incestuous and damaging consequences to the child. It is improbable that the 'replacement' of Albert's mother with his daughter led to sexual abuse, and in any event Albert would have been unlikely to have found physical contact with a woman particularly agreeable since his early life experiences would have ruled against it. Vicky would, none the less, have been emotionally exploited if Albert's demands of her were such that the normal parent–child transaction was distorted. (Albert's affection for Vicky was not repeated with any of his other children, and, at times, it was a source of friction between him and his wife.)

When Vicky (married to Prince, later King, Frederick, 'Fritz', of Prussia) was pregnant for the first time, and about to present a shortly-to-be-reunited Germany with the future Kaiser Wilhelm, Victoria admitted that she resented pregnancy because it came between her and Albert.[2] This would suggest that Albert avoided his wife sexually during this time and probably in the postnatal period. Albert had once again satisfied his need to create another 'mother', but Victoria, having enjoyed the physical union with him, regretted its consequences, namely the children. She described herself as being 'wretched', 'low' and 'depressed' during and after her pregnancies. However, 'Can I have no more fun in bed?' was her response to news from one of her doctors that her ninth pregnancy must be her last. The remark adds weight to the suspicion that Albert's sexual attentions were procreational rather than recreational and that Victoria now anticipated, reluctantly, fewer approaches from her husband. Victoria must have suffered from Albert's sexual indifference, and the transfer of her resentment to the infants, who had resulted from his need to make a mother of her, was sad but understandable. She would have envied them having a father, since she had not had one herself.

Early in their marriage Victoria and Albert restored and enlarged Osborne House, an Italianate villa on the Isle of Wight. More intimate than a palace and relatively informal, it became their favourite residence; Victoria hung their bedroom with paintings of male nudes – perhaps instinctively hoping that her husband would find them visually erotic.

Albert and Victoria were certainly united by bonds other than parenthood. Victoria, delighted with her husband, gradually conferred upon him the status reserved for men she loved and trusted. As Albert became a father figure as well as a husband, Lord Melbourne's influence gradually faded.

Soon after their marriage Albert had complained to Prince William of Lowenstein that he was 'the husband, not the master of the house'. 'I alone must be her adviser,' he wrote to Melbourne in the politician's declining years. Victoria was happy or at least willing to defer to Albert, as she did over Lehzen's dismissal. But it was she and not he who had been trained to be a monarch. Although she worshipped Albert, regarded him as head of the family, gave him access to the red dispatch boxes and gazed at him adoringly in every official portrait, it was not enough for him.

Albert seldom gave vent to his helplessness: there were few people in whom he could confide. On one occasion, however, after he and Victoria had quarrelled over Lehzen's influence in Pussy's nursery, he wrote to Baron Stockmar, 'Victoria is too hasty and passionate for me to be able to speak of my difficulties. She will not hear me out but flies into a rage and overwhelms me with reproaches of suspiciousness, want of trust, envy, etc., etc.' His dissatisfaction with life at home, his lack of friends at Court, a persisting language barrier and ongoing frustrations concerning his lack of official purpose led him to take upon himself an advanced and scientific concern in industrial and agricultural matters. He had many interests, travelled widely and achieved much, but, by addressing himself to Britain's problems rather than to its people, he earned respect but little affection.

One of Albert's concerns was the state of the drains and sewerage at Osborne, Windsor and Balmoral. Advances in technology in the royal palaces helped to improve public health generally in that people became aware that disease could be caused by inadequate waste disposal. However, this and other crusades failed to make Albert popular. He noticed that the hundreds of candles in Buckingham Palace were snuffed half burned and discarded – perhaps because a low-glowing candle casts an unflattering light on a lady's throat. Albert, however, saw no reason why so much candle-wax should be squandered every year and put a stop to the practice. His motives might have been commendable, but generations of palace servants had seen the half-candles as an extra source of income, and Albert's economy provoked an indignant reaction below stairs.

With time on his hands, and satisfying his obsessional needs, Albert took it upon himself to catalogue, restore and hang the many valuable pictures that lay stacked and neglected in the royal archives. Like Sir Anthony Blunt a hundred years later he became Keeper of the Pictures. He worked hard both socially and politically, and although the British people might later have had good reason to thank Albert for his Teutonic diligence and precision, at the time they evinced little interest. He was embraced neither by society nor by the nation but only by the plump arms of his wife and by the trusting Vicky, the one woman he loved for herself who in return was expected to love him for himself. Albert was lonely and unhappy for much of his life. William Gladstone's comment upon his 'stillness and chillness' suggests depths of internalized misery and frustration. He was friendless at Court, intellectually thwarted, sufficiently insecure to resent his wife's enduring affection for Baroness Lehzen and for some of her Prime Ministers and able to communicate only in a disciplinary way with most of his children.

Feared by them, disliked at Court and misjudged and misunderstood by the British people (even though he contributed to an industrial and cultural flowering that significantly improved millions of lives), Albert adopted distanced behaviour as a defence against his feelings of rejection and turned to the familiar past: Germanic music, customs from home (including the Christmas tree he introduced to Britain), the celebration of nature in the woods around Balmoral, the 'Swiss Cottage' he had constructed in the grounds of Osborne and the intimacy of conversations in German with his wife. As he grew older Albert identified more and more with those who supported unpopular moral stands and felt at one with minority opinions. By the age of forty-three Albert must have felt completely isolated. Even his only friend, Baron Stockmar, had returned to Germany and was now geographically closer to Albert's beloved Vicky than Albert himself would ever be.

Although Victoria and Albert were united in their disappointment with their son and heir Prince Albert Edward, born on 9 November 1841, they were divided by quarrels and disagreements about him. At first his birth was celebrated: the Queen had produced the desired male heir, and he was a strong, attractive baby. Before long, however, Albert displayed his preference for Pussy, and Victoria showed marked indifference to the son who was to succeed her.

Between the nurseries and the Queen's apartments at Buckingham Palace lay a vast maze of chilly corridors. Although Victoria could have altered these arrangements, she chose not to do so. A belated interest in him on the part of both his parents must have come too late for Edward. He spent much of his adult life attempting to deal with the consequences of having been dismissed by his mother almost as soon as he was born. Since neither Albert nor Victoria was temperamentally suited to parenthood, it is ironic that they had such a large family. As we have seen, both Victoria and Albert had been married for twenty-one years when in 1861, shortly after the birth of their ninth child, Albert contracted typhoid fever and died. Sick and feverish, he had asked to be buried in Germany, but the woman at his side was to deny him his last wish, just as his mother in leaving him had denied many of his earlier ones.

Albert had spent over twenty years in emotional isolation, imprisoned by his obsessional needs just as his daughter-in-law Alexandra was later to be by her deafness. He had not embraced the British people, only their problems. The child who had kept a diary of his aches and pains yearned always for his mother. Perhaps Albert hoped that he would return to her in the afterlife in which he so deeply believed. 'We do not know', he had written, 'in what state we will meet again; but that we shall recognize each other and be together in eternity I am perfectly certain.' Indeed, so strongly did Victoria concur with the notion that their spirits would be reunited that she attempted to communicate with Albert through mediums after his death.

His marriage to Victoria could not have been very happy, despite the desperate attempts at communion through sex. He had been withdrawn and introverted throughout his adolescence, but he was drawn to Victoria, as she to him, out of a need that they shared for emotional fulfilment. He was crushed by the affections of a woman on whom he depended but whom he could not have loved – because dependence and hostility go hand in hand – and from whom he was unable to escape other than by dying.

Queen Victoria virtually beatified Albert both within their marriage and after his death. His monument in Kensington Gardens, the plans for which she approved, has him seated beneath a sharply steepled spire – pointing him, as it were, to heaven – and surrounded by ecclesiastical architectural features.

Victoria's demeanour during the thirty-eight years of her widowhood, and especially the first decade, suggested to her children and grandchildren that little mattered without her spouse. Her children were a painful reminder to her of Albert's absence and even less important to her now than they had been before. But for Victoria, too, the marriage must have been less than satisfactory. Hungry for love, she had married a man of probably confused sexual orientation with a fixation on his mother's passion for another man. This would have made of him a partner who fulfilled her 'expectations of neglect' based on the absence of her father and subsequent ineffectual mothering.

Women with cold or distant husbands often direct their emotional energies into their children or work. Victoria did neither. She did have some insight and knew that there was room for improvement in her behaviour – she encouraged Albert to write reports to her on her progress. Nevertheless it was she who proposed marriage, it was in her palaces that they lived, and it was her crown that symbolized the balance of power in the relationship.

Victoria was the first Queen Regnant of England since Anne. From the insecurities of her childhood had come the certainty that she, as guardian of the Crown, could, like her forebear, demand love and loyalty. She assumed that she had Albert's love, just as she expected love from her children. She was happy with Albert, and she expected him to be happy with her. Victoria believed that her children were fortunate to have such a perfect man as their father, but by the time of his death, much psychological damage – unrecognized by either parent – had already been passed on, most notably to their heir Albert Edward, who had become an angry and emotionally impoverished young man.

At the time of Edward's birth his sister Vicky was ill, and Victoria may have experienced an early pang of jealousy at her husband's concern for their little daughter. Because of her need for Albert, she would have had difficulty in blaming him for this, so her resentment would have been displaced on to her new baby whom she saw as yet another rival for Albert's love. It is significant that Victoria referred to Edward as 'the Boy' until her next child, 'Fat Alice', was born. Such dismissive and depersonalizing nicknames are hurtful, derogatory and humiliating. The woman whose name has become synonymous with the virtues and values of family life was unable to express affection for her children until long after they needed it most.

There are many portraits of Queen Victoria painted during and immediately after her childbearing years. In most of these she is depicted as melancholy despite being surrounded by her apparently adoring husband who stands, or leans, by her side, and children who gather, like puppies, around the folds of her skirt. A listless hand will touch the ruffled shoulder of a younger child, but the seated

Queen never smiles, and the eyes are glazed behind the bulbous stare and above the drooping chin.

Victoria had always been parsimonious. She knew that the Crown represented the ultimate source of national wealth, and she was careful not to squander it. Having been given so little parental love as a child, she had a profound sense of inner poverty. She inherited her mother's debts and insisted that these be paid off out of her own allowance. Living mentally in her past, she was slow to pay for the modernization of her homes, and gas and electricity were not installed in Buckingham Palace or Balmoral until 1846. Single bulbs dimly illuminated vast rooms as if to underline the Queen's reluctance to expose cracks or stains in the fabric of her castles. Paradoxically, in her role as Empress of India, the Queen upheld a large staff of Indian chefs and servants to prepare the curry that was invariably served as an alternative at dinner and which was almost never sampled. She deplored decadence but had a bottle of whisky brought to her room every night. This was seldom touched, but in its reassuring and potentially comforting presence the bottle at least might have been a ghostly reminder of the maternal nurturing she had been denied.

The Queen, who had always been fat, began putting on even more weight in her widowhood, but compulsively satisfying oral needs could hardly make up for her losses. William Gladstone noted in 1863 that the Queen weighed over eleven stone. Today this would be regarded as obese for a woman of less than five feet in height. After Albert's death she became depressed for some years, virtually retiring from public life until her Golden Jubilee in 1887. For her children this seclusion was another reminder that she had always been more concerned with their father than she had been with them. Her prolonged grief reaction included the discouragement of any kind of pleasure within the family and a determination that Edward in particular should be married as quickly as possible to a suitable princess. Victoria expected to be dead within a year of Albert's demise and had informed King Leopold of this conviction. Years later, in 1888, having been deprived of a rapid reunion with Albert, she told Vicky that she had contemplated suicide. Something, however, had restrained her. 'A voice told me, for His sake – no, Still Endure.'

As a child Edward had disappointed his parents with his lack of scholastic achievements and even with his looks. He was now, in addition, being used by his mother as a scapegoat for her deep and lasting distress at the death of his father. In January 1862 his mother wrote to Vicky, 'I doubt if you could bear the sight of the one who was the cause; or if you would not feel, as I do, a shudder . . . I feel daily, hourly, something which is too dreadful to describe. Pity him I do . . . But more you cannot ask. This dreadful, dreadful cross kills me!' Perhaps belatedly experiencing guilt about the distanced mothering that her upbringing had compelled her to adopt with her own children, Victoria treated her grandchildren more kindly. She was demonstrative and affectionate with them and took an extraordinary interest in the progress of each one. The depth of her concern was to be queried and resented by her daughter-in-law Alexandra who knew, both directly and indirectly from Edward, what a bad mother Victoria had been.

The paradoxes of Victoria's marriage to Albert are manifold. Despite her avowed devotion to him, her many references to 'I and Albert' reflect vanity and conceit that were defences against feelings of inferiority and worthlessness. An arrogant self-sufficiency, the legacy of her dead father, covered her sense of being unworthy of love. The curious association of veneration with domination that characterizes Victoria's relationship with her husband epitomizes similar patterns found in later manipulative women in the Royal Family, such as Queens Alexandra, Mary, Elizabeth the Queen Mother, Wallis Simpson and the late Princess of Wales.

We know that Victoria and Albert had difficulty in expressing their feelings face to face. On paper Victoria found possible an intimacy with Vicky after her daughter's marriage which is unlikely to have developed had they remained in the same house. Such communication might have been somewhat artificial and distant, but at least a fondness existed and was expressed. The same cannot be said of Victoria's feelings towards her eldest son.

As a widow Victoria resumed her lifelong search for the kindly man of authority. The three she lighted upon were Benjamin Disraeli, who was effeminate, the gillie John Brown, who wore the kilt, and her Indian servant, the Munshi, who dressed in long androgynous robes, perhaps all of them reflections of the original care-giver, the mother who had to be both mother and father combined. Before her marriage Victoria had relied on the affection and advice of older men, notably her first Prime Minister Lord

Melbourne and King Leopold. During her marriage her husband came to meet almost all her emotional needs. One important result of this was that she was able to perceive her politicians with an objectivity that would hitherto have been impossible and thus to develop political opinions and diplomatic skills yet to be surpassed by any British monarch.

In widowhood Victoria formed new attachments. Her beloved Albert was no longer available to guide her, and the Queen reverted to the patterns of her youth. The men she chose to advise and support were all of an age that reflected her need for a father figure, even if by now she was older than they were.

Victoria's relationship with John Brown, her chief gillie, is the most widely speculated on. Years before his death Albert had appointed Brown to take particular responsibility for the Queen's ponies when she was at Balmoral. After Albert's death, because Brown had received the blessing of the beloved deceased, he came to represent a continuity with Albert himself. Brown was allowed to address Victoria as 'wummun', chided her if she was inappropriately dressed for a chilly ride and would lace her tea with whisky. It was not long before this servant's presence was required at Osborne where the Queen was in danger of becoming a permanent recluse.

Within five years of the Prince Consort's death Brown's salary had increased fivefold, he had been given a cottage at Balmoral and 'Esquire' rank, which raised him far above any ordinary servant's status. The Queen's dependency upon him even led to rumours that they had married. Yet despite fondly addressed New Year greetings and an affectionate remembrance of him in her will, there is no evidence that Queen Victoria had any more, or any less, than the most innocent emotional dependency on this uncultured Highlander. However, her people and, indeed, her family might not have appreciated fully how much John Brown had helped the Queen to cope with the loss of her husband and gradually to return to the public life she might have otherwise eschewed.

On Victoria's death the new King, Edward VII, ordered that all the busts and other relics that his mother had collected after Brown died in 1883 should be destroyed. The former Prince of Wales would have resented the displays of trust and affection towards a gillie when his mother had been unable to show them to him.

Victoria had first met Benjamin Disraeli in 1844 and disliked him. By the time he became her Prime Minister in 1868 Victoria saw him in a kinder light. He was married to an older woman and related to women in a seductive and flirtatious manner. He seemed to need the approval of an older woman and referred to the plump and plain Victoria as his 'Faery Queen'. He sent her early copies of his novels, and when in 1868 the Queen privately published her *Leaves from the Journal of Our Life in the Highlands* he referred to Victoria and himself as 'we authors'.

Disraeli explained his rapport with the Queen by saying that he spoke to her as a woman. As astute with his monarch as he was with politicians, Disraeli hoped that the widowed Queen would respond to his approach more readily than she had to some of her previous ministers. Victoria would have had little notion of the implications of effeminacy in men or lack of conventional femininity in women. She took her 'Dizzy' at face value – as a man who made her smile, treated her with respect and yet had the confidence to advise her when her opinions were questionable.

The importance of John Brown and Benjamin Disraeli in Victoria's life contributed to her recovery from her ongoing bereavement reaction. For years she had shown no sign of interest in her family, her people or her empire, but she was encouraged back into public life by the attentions of these men. Brown and Disraeli might have gained personally from their relationship with her, but the greater gain – that of the re-emergence of the Queen as an active leader of her people – might have ensured the continuation of the monarchy.

The third and last of Queen Victoria's most devoted servants was known as the Munshi. His name was Abdul Karim, and he came into her service around the time of her Golden Jubilee, aged twenty-four. His father, he said, was a doctor in Agra, but others in the Queen's household at pains to dispute his origins tried in vain to challenge his story. The Queen, however, appointed him as her secretary to help her with papers and documents relating to matters in India, gave him a cottage at Windsor and a staff of his own and resisted plots to discredit him as a spy.

He clearly treated her with a fondness and respect she did not receive from her children. She would not listen to their criticisms or those of political advisers who were concerned about her association

with a 'black man' – a phrase Victoria abhorred. None of the suspicions of espionage against the Munshi were ever supported. When
he died, however, the new King, Edward VII, arranged for all his
papers to be burned. This act, which echoes Edward's order that all
evidence of his mother's attachment to John Brown should be
destroyed, suggests the jealousy he felt towards the few friends she
had made. No one could blame him for scapegoating others who
had received the kindness and loyalty from his mother that she had
denied to him.

Victoria reigned for sixty-four years. She involved herself in the
complex diplomacies of the Crimean War, the long-drawn-out
unification of Germany and the escalation of hostilities in Ireland.
She was as well, if not better, informed than any previous monarch
about affairs of state and had simultaneously dealt as best she could
with the demands of a large family and a husband who was often
melancholy.

In allowing her seventeen-year-old daughter to live in Germany
after her marriage to Prince Frederick, having, indeed, agitated for
the alliance with Prussia, Victoria was yielding to both personal and
political expediency and therefore exploiting Vicky. No amount of
tearful remorse as the day of Vicky's departure drew nearer could
alter the fact that her main rival for Albert's affections was shortly
to be removed and that Victoria was not displeased at this. Equally,
it was desirable for England that the inevitable unification of the
disparate German states should be achieved under the leadership
of Prussia and that a close bond, created by marriage, should foster
British interests.

The match between Vicky and Frederick had been encouraged
by Albert for slightly different reasons. If his favourite child resided
in his homeland he would, vicariously, be there, too. Albert wanted
to strengthen the links between his birthplace and his adopted
country and as early as 1851, when Vicky was only ten, had
promoted the idea that his daughter would eventually marry his
cousin. Frederick was ten years her senior, but in 1855, when Vicky
was not quite fifteen, he was invited to spend the summer at
Balmoral. To her parents' delight she accepted his proposal.

As a 'Victorian' the Queen lent her name to a new valued lifestyle
and an expansive industrial age. As a woman she loved her husband
but failed to understand him. As a mother she produced nine

children but failed to communicate with them. She indulged her own griefs but was unable to tolerate the problems of others.

In a revealing letter to her seventeen-year-old granddaughter, Princess Vicky – warning her against same-sex friendships – the now elderly Queen hinted at sexual liaisons between women that in those days were rarely acknowledged. 'You are right to be civil and friendly to the young girls you may occasionally meet, and to see them sometimes – but never make friendships: girls' friendships and intimacies are very bad and often lead to mischief . . .'

Victoria had a 'blissful' marriage, a large family, world power and an empire. Not one of these, however, could compensate her for her primary loss. Through the absence of a male role model she had learned only to relate to distant men, such as Albert, and authority figures, such as her uncle King Leopold. The full burden of Victoria and Albert's emotional problems was to be passed on to the next runner in the royal relay race, their eldest son, Albert Edward, Prince of Wales, eventually to be King Edward VII.

2

EDWARD, PRINCE OF WALES:
HIS CHILDHOOD AND ADOLESCENCE

''Tis better to have loved and lost . . .'
– Alfred, Lord Tennyson, 'In Memoriam A.H.H.'

King Edward VII, as he became, was named after his father but always known within the family as Bertie. He was the first heir born to a reigning British monarch for eighty years, and his arrival was widely celebrated. His life was to be dictated by his search for the love that childhood had denied him, which contributed to, among other proclivities, his promiscuity, his compulsive eating and his gambling.

Edward was born prematurely. He was, however, a large baby, and Victoria had a difficult confinement. Before his birth his mother was already depressed, and Edward's arrival did nothing to lift her spirits. Her beloved Lord Melbourne was out of office and had had a severe stroke, leaving him paralysed and unavailable. In addition, trouble was brewing in the nursery. Pussy was unwell. Lehzen had advised Victoria not to worry unduly about her daughter, but Albert accused her of neglect. A furious row broke out. Albert wrote to his wife, 'Dr Clark has mismanaged the child and poisoned her with calomel and you have starved her. I shall have nothing more to do with it. Take the child away and do as you like, and if she dies you will have it on your conscience.' He wrote to his friend, Baron Stockmar, that 'Lehzen is a crazy, common, stupid intriguer, obsessed with lust of power, who regards herself as a demigod.' Victoria was 'naturally a fine person but warped in many respects by wrong upbringing'.

Victoria displayed her usual contrition in the face of Albert's anger, but the tensions between husband and wife led to Lehzen's return to Germany and, more significantly, illustrate how Victoria, in striving to recapture Albert's approval, was showing more concern at the well-being of her daughter than that of her new baby.

Albert had stayed with Victoria during her confinement. She was pleased to have produced the male heir for which the country had been waiting since the death of George III, but the delivery exhausted her. She handed over the baby to the wet nurse Mrs Roberts and did not see him again for six weeks. After Vicky's birth Victoria had been depressed, and the arrival of Edward again provoked this response. (It recurred after the births of all her children.) He was a placid baby, caused no trouble, making few demands upon his mother. When this 'good baby' grew up to become a 'bad child' it must have come as some surprise to his parents, unaware that a passive, undemanding, docile infant is unknowingly colluding in its own emotional deprivation. Had Edward been more demanding or Victoria more nurturing, his life might have been happier and healthier.

Few opportunities were given to Edward to develop that trust which is based on the certainty of freely available affection. If he seldom cried in his mother's presence, there was no need for her to comfort him. If he slept most of the time, she was not required to soothe him with lullabies or stimulate him with baby-talk. It is ironic that the child's failure to make his presence felt contributed to his parents' failure to communicate with him. Negligent parenting is tragic in any family; in one in which the children are expected to secure royal dynasties the repercussions will echo through the generations.

The tensions that existed within the royal household during the heir's first weeks, coupled with Albert's unequivocal worship of his older sister, would have left Edward with the conviction that his father loved Vicky more than he loved him and that his cold, distant and indifferent mother cared for him not at all. It was not until he was a grown man and had affairs with a succession of loving women that he was in a position to redress the balance. That his lovers were mainly married women with children fulfilled his earlier need for a mother's love.

The kindest words that his mother could find to say of 'the Boy' after his christening at Windsor were that at least 'he now had his dear father's name'. But he was for ever denied the honour of using the hallowed name and always known in the family by the diminutive 'Bertie'. And, although he resembled his father a little, he did not have the same delicacy of feature. His appearance was *lumpen*, and he was slow by nature. Despite all of the recent ructions, harmony was restored in the household, and by July of that year Victoria was again pregnant, and gave birth to 'Fat Alice' in April

1843, simultaneously dislodging Edward from his status as baby of the family after just seventeen months.

When Edward had outgrown the ministrations of his nurses, his mother felt that 'the Boy' would more easily acquire his father's virtues if he were supervised by a person of more noble character. Someone of superior standing was required to look after the future King of England, and Edward was assigned to the care of Lady Lyttelton, one of the Queen's ladies-in-waiting, the first in a long line of tutors.

Edward's life was burdened from the start both by the millstone of his destiny and his awareness that his sister Vicky was preferred by his parents. Later he was to suffer from the inequality of the treatment received by his younger siblings. It was not that they escaped the harsh punishment meted out by Albert, but it was Edward who seemed to bear the brunt of it: the others were spared the pressures of the high expectations placed on the shoulders of the heir to the throne. Nursery sounds disturbed Prince Albert, and he would frequently use corporal punishment on his children. Among other 'crimes' that invited his attention were disobedience and laziness. Edward, for whom higher standards had been set, was punished more often and more severely than the other children, although Albert saw no harm in whipping them – his daughters as well as his sons. Charles Wynne Carrington, who became a true friend to Edward, wrote of his early acquaintanceship with Prince Albert when, as a boy, he was one of a very few youngsters selected as suitable companions for the royal children. Albert seemed 'a proud, shy, stand-offish man, not calculated to make friends easily with children. I was frightened to death of him'. But Frederick Gibbs, one of Edward's tutors, later noted in his diary that he agreed with Albert, who advocated the boxing of ears and the striking of knuckles with a stick should Edward fly into one of his rages.

Albert deplored the laziness and untidiness he observed in the younger children and would bind their hands together in punishment for minor transgressions. The use of physical restraints was recommended by the German paediatrician D.G.M. Schreber as a means of controlling the 'wilfulness' of children. He had introduced various harnesses and braces to encourage them to sit upright at the table and to correct their posture; Albert would seem to have followed the advice given in Schreber's notorious book *The Harmful*

Body Positions and Habits of Children, Including a Statement of Counter-acting Measures published in German in 1853. He seems to have carried restraint even further than Schreber, whose dangerous advice was to influence more than one generation of German parents; as each generation of child victims grew up, they became the persecutors of the next generation and could have contributed to Teutonic authoritarianism. Views like this were spreading throughout Europe: control and restraint, directed towards the breaking of a child's spirit, were recommended as an essential ingredient in encouraging compliancy. Victoria attributed God-like qualities to her husband. In so doing she was echoing Schreber's advice that fathers must be as 'gods in the family' and that children should be devoted to God's divine authority. Schreber believed that if the child's father is his God, then the father's power over the son increases. On 26 August 1857 Victoria wrote, 'You may well join us in thanking God for joining us all to your dearest, perfect Father . . . None of you can ever be proud enough of being the child of *such* a Father who has not his equal in this world – so great, so good, so faultless. Try, all of you, to follow in his footsteps and don't be discouraged, for to be really good in everything none of you, I am sure, will ever be. Try, therefore, to be like him in some points, and you will have acquired a great deal.' She might have directed this exhortation to all her children, but it was certainly Edward who felt its full weight.

By the time Edward was four he had developed a stammer. Lady Lyttleton, who was firm but not unkind, was forced to report that he was 'uncommonly averse to learning, not like his sister'. Edward quarrelled with Pussy and bullied his younger brother and sister. When he was six Victoria wrote that he was backward compared with his elder sister.

Labelled as stupid, he was punished for his parents' failure to respond to his rare early signals for attention such as crying or showing a desire to be picked up, which would have made learning easier for him and allowed his intellect to develop. He was forced to fit into a mould of their devising, with no recognition of his individuality and finer qualities. Helpless, frustrated and miserable, the child was fated to become the adult whose appetites were never satisfied.

'The Plan', which was systematically to govern the heir's education and moral development, had been worked out by Victoria and Albert, with the help of Baron von Stockmar (who had come to

England as Albert's companion upon his marriage to Victoria). In January 1848 the diarist Charles Greville wrote, 'the hereditary and unfailing antipathy of our Sovereigns to their Heirs Apparent seems thus early to be taking root, and the Q. does not much like the child'.

It was unfortunate for Edward that Lord Melbourne no longer exerted strong influence on the Queen. 'Be not over solicitous about education,' he wrote, in December 1841 when the Prince was only weeks old. 'It may be able to do much, but it does not do as much as is expected from it. It may mould and direct the character, but it rarely alters it.'

Even six years after Melbourne had made his remarks hope still remained that Victoria and Albert intended their son to learn about affairs of state and come to understand his destiny. 'We talked about Vicky and Bertie, Albert saying the latter ought to be accustomed early to work with and for us, to have great confidence shewn him, that he should early be initiated into affairs of State . . . the more confidence we shew him the better it will be for himself, for us and the country,' wrote the Queen, in her journal on 12 December 1847. Not long afterwards, she began to fear that Bertie would never be fully capable of dealing with his future responsibilities. Several tutors had been engaged for particular subjects, but Edward's education was supervised first by Henry Birch and then by Frederick Gibbs, the first of whom the boy came to like and trust, the second less so. Lessons in French and German continued; religion, music, arithmetic, geography, history and English were included in his curriculum. But many of the masters could not easily adapt to the shifting domestic arrangements of Victoria's Court, and so, despite the continuity of Birch and Gibbs and his parents' wish that he should study almost every day, Edward was deprived of the chance of forming the relationships with his masters that might have made learning seem less of a chore. By the time he was eighteen, in April 1859, Victoria felt gloomy enough to write to Vicky in Germany, 'Oh dear, what would happen if I were to die next winter! One trembles to think of it. It is too awful a contemplation . . . And all from laziness! Still, we must hope for improvement in essentials; but the greatest improvement, I fear, will never make him fit for his position. His only safety – and the country's – is his implicit reliance in everything on dearest Papa, that perfection of human beings!'.

Despite the rigours of Edward's education, nothing was to convince Victoria that her 'backward' heir had progressed. She may have felt that she encouraged Bertie when she wrote to him in praise of his father, but it is more likely that the boy was disheartened by remarks that could only suggest an unfavourable comparison. Despite Edward's initial dislike of Henry Birch, he was a kind man to whom his pupil later became attached. Birch revised his first impression of a boy 'impertinent, lazy, inconsistent, moody, selfish and ignorant' and came to see Edward's qualities of humour and enquiry. The Prince of Wales, according to Birch, did not respond well to the devising of his lessons because 'he was so different on different days'. This may have been a euphemism for the rages and dumb insolence the Prince exhibited. Birch, anxious to be fair, also remarked that he 'always evinced a most forgiving disposition after I had occasion to complain of him to his parents, or to punish him'.

It is likely that Edward's parents regarded Birch as an inadequate disciplinarian, for they were not satisfied with his progress. A new tutor was engaged, Frederick Gibbs, who was stricter and more formal. Gibbs recorded that the Queen had noticed that the Prince would hang his head in contrition only, within a short time, to have 'one of his fits of nervous and unmanageable temper'.

Two other tutors formed differing views. Dr Voisin, who attempted to teach Edward French, warned Gibbs, 'You will wear him out too early . . . Make him climb trees! Run! Leap! Row! Ride! . . . In many things savages are much better educated than we are.' Edward's German master, Dr Becker, also recognized the Prince's honesty, saying he had 'a great straightforwardness and a sense of truth . . . as I scarcely ever witnessed in a child of his age'. Dr Becker went further and suggested that the strains imposed on the Prince by the severity of his educational regime could cause 'a nervous condition of total prostration and collapse'. These views went unheeded, but Gibbs failed to recognize or nurture any of Edward's intellectual capabilities such as his gift for languages.

By the time he was thirteen Edward became unhappy at his brother Alfred's departure to Royal Lodge in Windsor Great Park. Initially their parents had been pleased to have the two boys brought up together, but now they considered separation more desirable given Edward's special educational requirements as heir to the throne. Edward's loneliness was further compounded when he was sent with Gibbs for an intensive two-month study period at Balmoral, but he continued to disappoint his parents academically and to irritate them in other ways: he argued, interrupted adult conversation and remained prone to tantrums and rages.

By 1852 so worried were his parents at the flaws they perceived in Edward's character that they felt the answer must be to step up his lessons to seven hours a day six days a week and to ensure that he was exhausted by an even more rigorous programme of physical exercise. Ever obedient, Frederick Gibbs obliged. The Queen had noted of her son that 'First, he hangs his head and looks at his feet, and invariably within a day or two has one of his fits of nervous and unmanageable temper. Secondly, riding hard, or after he has become fatigued, has been invariably followed by outbursts of temper.' She had also observed that Edward had a strained relationship with his elder sister and was crushed by her clever articulate dismissiveness.

The Prince of Wales suffered from a lack of friends and companionship, especially after he had been parted from his favourite brother, further reinforcing his awareness of human inconstancy. (He was never as close to the other six younger siblings.) Moreover, his parents had stressed that there was a difference between 'companions' and 'friends' and that Princes could not expect to enjoy the latter. It was perhaps perspicacious of them to warn the royal children about the attentions of sycophantic courtiers and realistic to point out that the friendships available to others would be hard for them to make. It made it difficult for their children to feel, however, that they were capable of being loved for themselves.

While warning them of the dangers of 'friendship' Victoria and Albert at the same time instilled into their offspring that they were not superior to other children. Against the background of this conflicting advice, however, a companion, Charles Wynn-Carrington, later Marquess of Lincolnshire, was engaged for Alfred but also played with the other royal children at Buckingham Palace or at Windsor.

Having been ignored throughout his infancy, Edward began to draw attention to himself as an adolescent. The 'good baby' had long been the 'bad child', and his parents used ever more forceful measures to suppress his outbursts. He began to rebel against the tyranny of his upbringing and to express negative emotions – including jealousy of his siblings – that had been suppressed in the nursery. He gave vent to his anger at being ignored by his care-givers and his resentment at being humiliated and victimized by his parents. Soon he would be getting his own back by taking 'mothers' away from 'fathers', seeking a substitute for love through sex, food and cigars – under the illusion that they could replace it – and taking risks at the gaming tables to provide himself with the stimulation he had not received from Victoria and Albert as a child. Few children pass through puberty without feeling misunderstood. Bertie's bewilderment was compounded by his receiving no approval or encouragement from his parents, who seemed blind to his strengths, or from his teachers, who disagreed about his potential. In a rare admission of Prince Albert's severity (with which she invariably colluded), the Queen wrote to Vicky in 1861 that 'You say no one is perfect but Papa; but he has his faults, too. He is often very trying in his hastiness and over-love of business.' Prince Albert, conversely, complained that 'the disagreeable office of punishment' had always fallen on him even though his wife had been anxious that the errant child be reproved.

Things began to improve a little for the Prince of Wales when he was fifteen. He was allowed to choose what he would eat from items in a prescribed diet; until now, his needs, even for food, had always been controlled by his parents. Suddenly to be allowed to satisfy a long forbidden appetite would have encouraged overemphasis on his appetite not only for food but also for other 'life enhancers'.

Yet before long, even more drastic measures were deemed necessary to improve Edward's character, including another new diet which, it was hoped, would also stimulate his brain. A light breakfast of bread and butter and the occasional egg was prescribed; lunch of meat and vegetables and seltzer water and a slightly more substantial dinner with a little claret or diluted sherry. Any beneficial effects were not immediately obvious.

When Edward was seventeen Gibbs left and was replaced by a 'governor', Colonel Robert Bruce. Edward was not to leave the house without explaining where he was going and why, and Colonel Bruce chose his friends for him throughout his short stays at Oxford and Cambridge. Even now that he was away from home Victoria, usually able to express affection on paper, could still bring herself to write only of Edward's shortcomings: his head was too small, his nose too large, his chin receded as did his hairline; he was too short and too stout. In the manner of those who criticize in others the faults of which they are aware in themselves, this catalogue of her son's physical imperfections could equally have been applied to herself.

Always having been solitary, even preferring in games of chess to play with himself –the type of self-gratificatory activity seen often in those who are products of a lonely childhood – Albert had no understanding of 'team spirit' or of being a 'good sport'. Edward could not have learned from his father how to relate to others, since companions had been discouraged, and even his brother had been sent away in spite of their closeness. He had not the least idea how to be a 'good loser'. At the gaming tables he put his fate in the hands of 'Lady Luck' who – as his mother had earlier – very often disappointed him.

When Edward was taken to Paris in 1856 he was enchanted by Empress Eugenie, who turned down his request to be allowed to stay a little longer, telling him that his parents would be unhappy without him. Any hopes that the Prince might have entertained about the truth of her remark would have been dampened had he seen a letter written by his mother to the Queen of Persia in October of that year shortly after his visit. 'When Albert is away all day long, I find no especial pleasure or compensation in the company of the elder children . . . only very occasionally do I find the rather intimate intercourse with them either easy or agreeable.' Once again Victoria was demonstrating that she believed it the child's duty to please the parent, not that of the parent to care for the child. But Bertie's life continued to brighten somewhat. He now had a personal allowance and was permitted to choose his own clothes. After the Paris trip he travelled to the Rhine and to Switzerland with courtiers, and these new freedoms brought out the best in him. One of his companions, Colonel Henry Ponsonby, described him as 'one of the nicest boys I ever saw, and very lively and pleasant'.

Edward wore his hair in an 'effeminate' way, to which his mother objected, and began to develop an idiosyncratic style of dress. He had come to believe that females – perhaps from the example of his sister Vicky – were favoured. By adopting a hairstyle more appropriate to a woman Edward was taking the first step towards envy of all things female. Although his features were never delicate, he was described in 1857 as being slim and handsome by Prince

Metternich who entertained him in Austria. Most boys of his age with a personal allowance and some limited freedom of choice would assert individuality, even express rebellion, through their appearance and would want the cut of their suits and their hair to differ from that of their fathers. However, 'A gentleman does not indulge in careless, self-indulgent, lounging ways . . . He will take nothing from the fashions of the grooms or the gamekeeper, and whilst avoiding the frivolity and foolish variety of dandyism will take care that his clothes are of the best quality.' Prince Albert's advice could scarcely have made more inevitable his son's liking of countryman's clothes for shooting and stalking and fashion-setting details for his more formal wardrobe.

In 1858 his mother could still write to Vicky that 'I feel very sad about him. He is still so idle and weak.' Later that year, in another letter to Vicky, the Queen lamented, 'Unfortunately, he takes no interest in anything but clothes, and again clothes. Even when out shooting he is more occupied with his trousers than with the game!' Vicky, however, disagreed with her mother about Bertie's 'dullness'. 'He is lively, quick and sharp,' she wrote – before, perversely, going on to enumerate his shortcomings. She had been deputed to help her parents find a suitable bride for Edward and was probably anxious to stress his good points before acknowledging his lesser ones, about which she generally agreed with her mother. The years of tension in the nursery were not conducive to sibling solidarity between them. However, Vicky played her part, and it was she who suggested Alexandra of Denmark as a possible wife for her brother.

'The Boy' was overweight and, had he been the scion of another family, would not have been regarded as much of a catch. But he had become proficient in three languages, had some knowledge of economics, science, drawing, riding and – oddly – bricklaying and carpentry. His expanding girth was not entirely his own fault: at Oxford, forbidden to live in college as he would have preferred, he maintained a household, Frewin Hall, outside the town where, at his father's insistence, he was required to host regular dinners for selected academics, fellow undergraduates and distinguished visitors to Oxford. A first-class chef had been engaged to prepare the food, and after years of being forced to eat from a restricted range of unappetizing foods Edward overindulged. His father, as yet unaware that his son would receive moderately good results from Oxford, was ready to criticize him to Vicky, castigating Edward for enjoying 'rich and indigestible foods' and adding, in another letter, 'I never in my life met such a thorough and cunning lazybones . . . it does grieve me when it is my own son, and when one considers that he might be called upon at any moment to take over the reins of government in an Empire in which the sun never sets.'

Edward's introduction to the Empire, however, was a triumph. In 1860, shortly after his time at Oxford and Cambridge, he toured Newfoundland in Canada and then went to the United States. To the surprise of his parents, he displayed a charm and diplomacy that endeared him to the people. Like many another unloved child, Edward had developed techniques designed to encourage positive responses. Charm, like seductiveness, is used to manipulate others to provide concern and interest which, it is believed, would not otherwise be available.

Edward's short periods at university and the promise he displayed gave his parents the inaccurate impression that he could have been the scholar for whom they had wished. When he joined the Grenadier Guards in Ireland his ever-hopeful father expected that the Prince would learn the duties of an Army officer within ten weeks. In this unrealistic plan he was to perform in every regimental rank, being promoted every two weeks so that he would take charge of a battalion after ten. This process would normally take some years, even for unusually able and ambitious soldiers. Edward was indeed allowed to wear a colonel's uniform at the end of the ten weeks but complained that he was expected only to perform the duties of a subaltern.

Just before leaving Ireland he had a short relationship with a young camp follower, Nellie Clifden, rumours about which began to circulate in London shortly afterwards. In November 1861 word of his son's indiscretion reached Prince Albert, who realized that if it were made public it would jeopardize the proposed plans for Edward's marriage to Princess Alexandra of Denmark. Family pressures made it inevitable that once again the young Prince of Wales would be accused of a 'crime' – his infatuation with the young actress – and castigated for this youthful lapse by his parents for the rest of their lives. It was more likely that Albert's horror at learning of Edward's sexual adventure was less to do with politics than with his own sexual prejudices. Many fathers at that time would have welcomed their son's initiative and, had he not taken such a course, might well have introduced him to a brothel. Albert behaved more as if a beloved daughter had lost her virginity or a son been caught *in flagrante delicto* with another man. Certainly overt premarital heterosexuality seemed to outrage him unduly.

Although Albert was suffering from a feverish illness, he went to Cambridge to discuss the sorrowful and chastising letter he had already written to his son. He arrived at Madingley Hall, where Edward had been lodged to keep him out of harm's way. The weather was cold and damp, but father and son walked for several hours – largely because Edward got lost – until Albert felt confident that he had shown Edward the folly, danger and moral turpitude of his behaviour. He then returned to London and resumed work, but his health deteriorated. Victoria was reassured by his doctors who told her that there was no cause for alarm, but it soon became clear that Albert's condition was critical. On Friday 13 December 1861 the Prince Consort died from typhoid fever.

Queen Victoria always maintained that her eldest son had caused her husband's death, and she never forgave him for it. A leading expert of the day confirmed 'that great worry and far too hard work had led to his death'. Although the probability is that Albert was already in the early stages of the disease when he visited Edward at Cambridge, Victoria chose to believe that the long conversation in the damp and chill air of their walk was the direct cause of his death. Edward spent the next forty years underemployed and under a cloud.

Plans for the Prince of Wales's marriage now proceeded with increased urgency. The Prince had been in no hurry and had insisted that he wanted to be sure he was in love before any marriage took place. Victoria, feeling perhaps that Bertie had forfeited his right to be consulted, was not prepared to let him dither. What other scandals could be lurking to demolish the chances of such a suitable match? It was not only that the Queen thought marriage would be stabilizing and character-forming for Edward but her conviction that her son was to blame for her husband's death and her desire to see him as infrequently as possible.

Victoria spent the first few months of her bereavement at Osborne. She expected and perhaps hoped to die within the year and was anxious that Edward's life should be under control when he succeeded her. She wrote of Edward's misdemeanour to Vicky, who passed on to Alexandra's parents Victoria's message that Edward had been encouraged by 'wicked wretches' and had had something of a scrape, but that both his parents had forgiven him, lest there be any suggestion that Alexandra did not know exactly what she was taking on. It was Vicky also, visiting Coburg with her brother at the same time as the Danish Royal Family, who effected the introduction between him and Alexandra. Tactfully she left before her brother, leaving him to his duty and his destiny. Edward knew what his duty was – and how he might redeem himself in his mother's eyes. He proposed to Alexandra and was accepted with alacrity in September 1862.

There were few things to cheer Victoria in the months after her husband's death, although she managed to take some gloomy pleasure in her son's betrothal. Before the marriage in March 1863 Alexandra spent ten days with the Queen, at Osborne. Victoria would have preferred a longer visit, but Alexandra wanted to be with her own family for her eighteenth-birthday celebrations. Victoria found her future daughter-in-law enchanting, with most of the qualities the Queen regarded as necessary for the wife of the heir: beauty, a good nature and what Victoria perceived as 'character'. She would have wished Edward's bride to have had a better education and a little more culture, but Alexandra was young enough to learn – and certainly young enough to be indoctrinated and influenced.

The Queen could not bring herself to sit in the main part of St George's Chapel, Windsor, where the wedding took place. She watched the ceremony from the little gallery above the altar, known as Katharine of Aragon's Closet, managing only a wintry smile for Beatrice, her youngest daughter. Afterwards, she ate alone in her apartments, then visited her late husband's mausoleum rather than join her son and daughter-in-law and their guests for the wedding breakfast.

The day should have been one of optimism for Edward, on which he might have hoped for the past to be forgiven, but it had been blighted, once again, by his mother who, from the moment he was born, had made her priorities clear: that her husband was more important than her children.

3

KING EDWARD AND
QUEEN ALEXANDRA

'That which we call a rose by any other name would smell as sweet.'
  —William Shakespeare, *Romeo and Juliet*

'No one who knows the character of the Queen and of the Heir Apparent can look forward to the future without seeing troubles in that quarter,' wrote Sir James Clark in 1865.

Alexandra Caroline Marie Charlotte Louise Julia of Schleswig-Holstein-Sonderburg-Glücksburg was born in Denmark on 1 December 1844. Like many other women who have since married into the Royal Family she was, in comparison with her husband, poverty-stricken and obscure, but the British people have always had a soft spot for Cinderellas or, better still, commoners. Princess Alexandra was, in fact, neither of these, but her background was different to that of her husband.

Her father Prince Christian was not in direct line to the throne until his elder brother contracted a morganatic marriage which constitutionally precluded him from reigning, and, decades later, made poor relations out of the Teck branch of the Danish Royal Family. (Victoria took pity on them, bestowing on them grace-and-favour accommodation in London and, on the marriage of May of Teck to the future George V, the Dukedom of Cambridge.)

Alexandra, in contrast to Edward, had been brought up with warmth and informality. Until the marriage of her uncle and the consequent elevation of her father's status she lived in a fine, rather than grand, house, the front door of which opened directly on to a peaceful Copenhagen street. She shared a bedroom with her sister, made many of her own clothes, was able to go into shops without restriction and travelled about the city unaccompanied – much as did Lady Diana Spencer before her marriage to Prince Charles. Her education was not so much neglected as considered irrelevant. She had music lessons, learned to draw, acquired social graces and some French and English but little else. She could barely read. However, she grew up in an affectionate family home, which gave her a strong sense of her own worth that later stood her in good stead.

Denmark had been financially impoverished by the Napoleonic Wars, during which its Navy was all but destroyed. Alexandra grew up against a background of wounded national pride in which her country, now politically and economically weak, lived in constant fear of its neighbour, Prussia, which was anxious to annexe the Danish territory of Schleswig-Holstein. Although Alexandra came to suspect and abominate all things German, she married into the world's most powerful family – which was of German origin. Her marriage could not have been anticipated by her family. Years earlier her father Prince Christian had hoped to marry Victoria (before she became Queen), but his suit had been dismissed. That Alexandra was able to marry Queen Victoria's heir in 1863 is an indication, perhaps, that Europe was running out of suitable princesses. Alexandra was by no means the first choice for Edward, but she had several advantages. She was willing, whereas others had turned him down, she was Protestant, and the alliance with Denmark would create a useful political bridge. Alexandra's father must have seen a satisfying irony in his daughter being found so eminently suitable by the son of the woman who had rejected him some twenty-five years earlier. Alexandra herself, aged seventeen, was thrilled and excited at the prospect: she would never again have to sew on a button, let alone make her own clothes.

Her arrival in England in 1863 was celebrated by the Poet Laureate, Alfred Tennyson, in 'A Welcome to Alexandra' with verses that began:

> Sea King's daughter from over the sea,
>   Alexandra!
> Saxon and Norman and Dane are we,
> But all of us Danes in our welcome of thee,
>   Alexandra!

It was a true reflection both of Alexandra's immediate popularity and Britain's joy at the anticipated union with a Nordic country. Prussian territorial ambitions were well known, and an alliance between Britain and Denmark would enhance the latter's security. The proposed union, however, placed Victoria and her government in a somewhat delicate situation because of Vicky's position as

Crown Princess of Prussia. Whether Victoria was motivated by a wish to see her eldest son married at any cost, or by the forlorn hope that perhaps at last 'the Boy' could be happy, is open to debate. Possibly she felt that the family links between Britain and Prussia were so strong that any serious political friction between the two countries could be avoided. Either way she seriously misjudged or perhaps underestimated her future daughter-in-law.

By the time of his marriage the Prince of Wales seemed to be genuinely in love. He wrote to his mother after his betrothal, 'I cannot tell you with what feelings my head is filled, and how happy I feel. I only hope it may be for her happiness and that I may do my duty towards her. Love her and cherish her you may be sure I will to the end of my life.'

Queen Victoria needed no convincing: after Alexandra's first visit to England she wrote, 'Can't say how I and we all love her! She is so good, so simple, unaffected, frank, bright and cheerful . . . This jewel! She is one of those sweet creatures who seem to come from the skies to help and bless poor mortals and lighten for a time their path!'

The honeymoon period of the marriage (not the pleasant days away that Edward and Alexandra enjoyed after their wedding or the London Season that followed) was short-lived. It was not long before the Queen was complaining to her son that he and Alix were tarnishing the dignity of the Crown by being seen publicly and socially too often. Edward's reply was that the Queen's seclusion gave him little choice – someone within the family had to be reassuringly visible – but this remained a source of tension between them until the Queen's Golden Jubilee in 1887.

Victoria even wrote to Vicky that Alix and Edward looked ill and that her son and daughter-in-law were 'nothing but puppets, running about for show all day and night'. Once again she made an unfavourable comparison between her husband and her heir. 'Oh, how different poor foolish Bertie is to adored Papa, whose gentle, loving, wise motherly care of me when he was not yet twenty-one exceeded everything!'

In the middle of the nineteenth century fashionable women were well built and statuesque. Alexandra, by contrast, was tall, slender and elegant with a pale, grave beauty that did not conform to the fashionable stereotype. Her simplicity and good humour countered the smallness of her mouth and rather bulbous eyes. She had grace and style and, like the late Diana Princess of Wales, became a leader of fashion. She wore pearl and diamond chokers – probably to hide a small scar on her neck – a style that immediately became popular. When rheumatic fever left her with a limp, limps were sometimes affected by her admirers as was her occasional use of a cane. She was undoubtedly cherished by the public, and although this might have pleased her it did not compensate for the deafness that affected her relationships with her husband and children.

A woman who must abandon her native tongue on her marriage is disadvantaged. Edward spoke German and French, as did Alexandra; she also had a little English, but they were able to communicate with each other only at the most superficial level. The subtleties and nuances of the English language – in which humour and cynicism as well as metaphors are expressed – were lost on Alexandra, and her hearing impairment would have exacerbated this. She was able to comprehend neither her husband's anxieties nor his needs, so he eventually ceased to burden her with them. Because of her deafness she was unable to hear her own voice clearly, which tended to become strident – tolerable in some situations perhaps but hardly conducive to private exchanges. Her husband had had a mother who did not listen to him, and now he had a wife who was unable to hear him. She was similarly unable to hear the voices of her children. Like many people with hearing difficulties she was probably able to lip-read, which would have alleviated the problem but not solved it.

Alix, like Diana Princess of Wales, acquired the reputation of being a natural, free spirit. She enjoyed the popular music of her day, as well as dancing and parties. She supported children's charities and enjoyed mixing with people from the arts, finance and business. Marlborough House, where she and Edward lived, came to be associated with wit, culture, wealth and glamour. It was not necessary to be titled, let alone royal, to be invited to a gathering there. In this milieu Alexandra shone: she was unconventional in that she was at ease with people from all walks of life, unlike other members of the Royal Family, and also in the house she kept and the clothes she wore and was sufficiently decorative to compensate for her inability to engage in profound conversation. She was happy and relaxed, and her warm family background enabled her to socialize naturally. To Edward this was a revelation.

Alexandra was pregnant six times during the first eight years of her marriage. After her final pregnancy, during which she had been neglected by the local doctor who attended her during her confinement, she gave birth to a son who died immediately. She was advised against having any more children. She was twenty-six, the succession was ensured, and now she had more time to devote to her surviving offspring and to the pursuits she had had to set aside during her pregnancies: dancing, skating, the theatre and clothes. Now that she was a mother and had been warned against further pregnancies Edward seems to have turned for physical comfort to other women, invariably married and usually with children. His affairs satisfied his sexual needs, enabling him to find the mother who had rejected him and at the same time punish the father whom he would inevitably have seen as his rival. His attempts at conquest were successful, but he could never make a true commitment because the original one with his mother was flawed. These patterns were to be compulsively repeated.

It was not until his last child was born that he became openly attracted to French night life and the company of the women whose expensive tastes drew them to heavy spenders like himself. Most were professional courtesans, and at least one was a blackmailer from whom Edward had to buy back his indiscreet letters in order to prevent her selling his correspondence to the highest bidder.

As time passed his sexual interests ran over into affairs with many of the married women in his circle of friends. They were usually sufficiently flattered by his attentions to pass the *cinq à sept* with him while their husbands were at their clubs. Out of all his many liaisons, only one illegitimate child has been acknowledged, although others were claimed, probably falsely in the hope of financial gain. Given the uncertainties of birth control in the nineteenth century, it would seem that Edward's preferred sexual techniques excluded penetrative sex. It was as if he had had enough of procreational sexual activity with his wife, both to secure the succession and also in his search for a 'mother'. Recreational sex was not only safer but more rewarding for a man who throughout his childhood had known very little of the give and take of love and affection.

Throughout this time the monarchy became increasingly threatened by almost daily disclosures of scandal. But as many of

Edward's mistresses were popular public figures and Edward's lifestyle became entertainingly grand, the public ceased to condemn him. Towards the end of his life Edward became increasingly admired as a kindly and jovial man. Actresses featured among his partners. Lillie Langtry and Sarah Bernhardt, for example, were, like him, looking for approval and admiration. Another long-standing mistress, Alice Keppel, was so genuinely distraught by his last illness that Alexandra encouraged her to be at his bedside in 1910 when he was dying. History has hallowed Alexandra as a forgiving wife and a selfless mother, but she had little choice other than to tolerate her husband's indiscretions. She could hardly have packed her bags and gone home to Mother. But she behaved with dignity and appeared to see no evil – just as she heard none – in the circulating gossip. A woman with few inner resources, no intellectual interests and an increasingly critical mother-in-law, she concentrated her energies on her children – and on unconsciously avenging herself on her husband. One of the ways in which she did this was with her notorious unpunctuality. She exasperated him by keeping him waiting for dinner or making him late for the opera, particularly cruel since his mother had never had time for him. Alexandra would either ignore what he said to her or would misunderstand because of her poor hearing. By such means she was able to exert a semblance of control within a marriage rooted in duty and compromise, as well as affection.

Her greatest area of influence was the nursery. Although her children came to see her as the personification of love and care, it was *they* who had to please their mother by obedience and good behaviour. Even when they were adults she liked them to address her as 'dearest little Motherdear' and was addicted to the love she had demanded from them when they were children. She could no longer command the unqualified love that Edward had offered her upon their marriage, and as long as Victoria lived he would look to his mother, rather than his wife, for approval. As a man of fifty he still sometimes needed to compose himself behind a pillar before confronting his mother's disapproval for lateness at dinner. Later, he named one of his racehorses Diamond Jubilee in an almost certainly unsuccessful attempt to please her.

The people of Britain, though, took Alexandra to their hearts. They applauded her frequent public appearances, in sharp contrast to the seclusion of the Queen, and seemed to feel that the splendid lifestyle of the Marlborough House set was proof that the state allowance of the royal couple was being well spent. Periodic complaints were made then, as now, about civil-list payments, with the Queen sometimes being accused of hoarding hers, but that Edward and Alexandra's extravagance was tolerantly regarded by so many was, in some measure, due to Alexandra's personal popularity as well as to the proverbial English willingness to 'love a lord'.

Princess Alexandra, isolated though she was by her deafness, suffering as she did from her husband's infidelities and never achieving the approval that she sought from her mother-in-law, retained a keen sense of humour coupled with a steely resolve. At the party held to celebrate her silver wedding anniversary she pinned an orange in her hair (in parody of the orange blossom she had worn as a bride and symbolic of the ripe fruit that the fragile blossom had now become). Few other women of forty-two would have been able to carry off such a gesture.

Her strengths were increasingly demonstrated after her husband's death. She was unwilling to accept that once her daughter-in-law had become Queen her own status had diminished and expressed this reluctance by long refusing to move out of Buckingham Palace and back to Marlborough House. She would not return the small crown she had come to regard as her personal property and finally upstaged Queen Mary at state occasions by demanding – and being granted – precedence over her. The pliable front presented by Alexandra was as artificial as the curls she wore on her forehead. On the face of it, 'Darling Motherdear' was warm and nurturing towards her children, but her smothering affection was demanded back with interest as she attempted to compensate for the love and attention she had been denied by her husband. The power play in keeping her husband waiting – even if she could not keep him faithful – was not enough for her. Nor was the popular adulation she received. With the passing of the years she stayed with relatives outside Britain for increasingly long periods. It might have been assumed that she accepted her circumstances, made the best of them and pleased herself in so far as her position allowed, but 'Motherdear' was a frustrated, troubled and embittered woman who had five cards in her hand and was determined to play them for all they were worth.

Her first son, the Duke of Clarence, was always called 'Eddy' even though, or probably because, he had been christened Albert Victor to please Queen Victoria. He was born prematurely, only hours after Alexandra had been skating at Sandringham. Eddy inherited his mother's large, bulbous eyes, narrow face and sloping chin, and, although he never came to show promise of any kind, his mother was devoted to him. His younger brother George, born a year later in 1865, was more fortunate. He was a better-looking version of his father, with a wide, open face, fair hair and a strong jaw. The boys were treated as if they were twins in the nursery and the schoolroom and like little delinquents by their father, who seemed determined that his sons would not enjoy their childhoods any more than he had enjoyed his. They turned to their comparatively kind and affectionate mother for warmth and compensation. Although she was possessive of her sons, possibly contributing to Eddy's homosexuality and George's difficulty in relating intimately to his wife except through letters, their three sisters Louise, Victoria and Maud (born between 1867 and 1869) seemed to be of less interest to her. Victoria, however, was not encouraged to marry because Alexandra was anxious to keep one child at home with her; 'Toria' was later described as 'little better than an unpaid companion' as she grew older, unmarriageable, spinsterly, embittered and increasingly disliked by other members of the family. That Alexandra remained radiant and adored throughout her widowhood was, to a greater or lesser degree, at the expense of the happiness of her second daughter.

Alexandra's compulsion to make her children meet her emotional needs may be understood if not forgiven. Her husband had neglected her – never more so than during her final pregnancy when she contracted rheumatic fever and lost her third son. Edward was unsympathetic both about the child's death and the illness that from then on disabled Alexandra. He displayed a truculent jealousy, as if, even in her pain and grief, Alexandra should make *him* her priority at the expense of her feelings towards their children either dead or alive. Alexandra's concern for them was a constant, bitter reminder of his own mother's neglect. He envied them their mother's affection and disregarding Alexandra's anguish – and being unnecessarily harsh – punished them accordingly. At the time of their son's death reproving remarks were heard that during her pregnancy Alexandra had spent too much time at her husband's side in society to limit temptations from other women. At Victoria's request he was chided about this by the Dean of Windsor, but, with some indignation and possibly thinly veiled reproof for the professional widow, Edward wrote to his mother, 'I think it is in one's duty not to nurse one's sorrow . . . I shall also be glad when Alix resumes her social duties (with, of course, due care for her health).'

Alexandra also had to cope with Victoria's political truce with Prussia, whose territorial gaze was still fixed on the nearby Danish dependencies, Schleswig and Holstein. Victoria wrote of Alix to Vicky, 'good as she is – she is not worth the price we have paid for her – in having such a family connection'. In November 1863 Alix's father succeeded Frederick VII and became Christian IX, whereupon he was immediately threatened with invasion of the disputed territories by both Prussia and Austria. In Britain Parliament insisted that a neutral stance be adopted, but Victoria assured her daughter Vicky that her sympathies were all with Prussia. She was not pleased when Edward openly supported his wife's differing point of view, and the wedge of friction between the Queen and her daughter-in-law always remained, long after Schleswig was seized by Prussia and Holstein by Austria.

Victoria's behaviour towards Alexandra was unpredictable. Acid remarks in the Queen's diaries allude to late levées, irresponsible entertaining and evening gadding. Later, however, she would remark how dear Alix was and how fond she was of this favourite daughter-in-law. When her Golden Jubilee was celebrated, it was in the unenviable role of favourite that Alix was deputed to persuade the Queen to appear in public in robes of state. She was not successful. Elizabeth Longford tells us that Alix said, 'I was never so snubbed', when the Queen insisted on being driven to Westminster Abbey wearing not a crown but a bonnet.

Edward, meanwhile, continued to try to win his mother's approval, although Victoria's letters to Vicky suggested that he would never do so. In 1864 when Edward attended a reception to honour Garibaldi after his dashing and successful campaign to unify Italy she wrote to Vicky of 'the incredible folly and imprudence of your eldest brother going to see him without my knowledge!' His mother seemed quite unable to understand that for as long as she denied her son and heir access to state papers and red boxes he would have difficulty in understanding the political minefields through which he obliviously trod. She thought him unworthy of such privileged information, yet was ready to criticize him when, as she saw it, he stumbled and blundered. The more she continued to deny him access and influence, the more he sought to compensate through eating, drinking, gambling and sex. Some of his anger could have been sublimated in his favourite pastime, shooting game, at which he excelled.

Victoria had turned her emotionally neglected child into an adult addicted to the very activities that reinforced her view that he was unready and unfit to assume regal responsibilities. The double-binding games, at which she was a skilled player, inevitably left Edward the loser. None the less Victoria imagined that on her death Edward would be able to assume his duties effortlessly, while at the same time wanting him to fail, for his failure would underline her own considerable successes in diplomacy.

Once he became King, Edward had to overcome many obstacles, not the least of which was his mother's neglect, resentment and, finally, revenge in handing over reins she had not trained him to grasp. Edward, however, was brighter than his mother imagined. During his indolent travels as Prince of Wales he had come to know not only courtesans and actresses but heads of state, high-ranking Army officials and royal cousins. He realized, as astute businessmen do today, that as much could be achieved in a box at the opera, salmon-fishing in Scotland or over a good lunch, as in formal circumstances, and that if his guests at the races, at Sandringham or sailing off Cowes were indebted to him for their enjoyment they were less likely to challenge British trade or imperial interests. His type of diplomacy was barely understood, though, and even less valued while his mother was alive, dismissed as further proof of his profligacy, rather than acknowledged as a political skill.

Edward spent several decades hoping for rather more than peripheral involvement in the stewardship of his country, but his hands were tied. He functioned as best he could, running between Paris, Baden-Baden, Biarritz and Cannes, from discussions with heads of state to choosing a favourite cloth for his suits (ever afterwards to be known as 'Prince of Wales check'), popularizing the Homburg hat and training his little dog Caesar. By his common pursuits he reminded the people of Britain that their monarchy existed and showed an endearing fallibility in his well-publicized, often successful gambling at Ascot and on the tables at Monte Carlo. That his sensual appetites might be attributed to the emotional poverty of his childhood did not concern the British people, who saw an expansive man who appeared to share the same pleasures and vices they did. They would have seen him, in the affectionately approving phrase of the time, as 'a bit of a dog'.

Despite the skill, tolerance, discretion, humour, patience and understanding Edward was able to display as a diplomat, he was not a good father to his children and inflicted considerable unhappiness upon his wife. While he did not subject his children to physical cruelty or deprivation beyond what was considered the norm at the time, he did neglect them, through his frequent absences, with his concern for his own pleasures and the freedom he now had to indulge in appetites until then suppressed. While he worked intelligently to avoid political confrontations, his family life was a battleground in which the erstwhile victim became the persecutor. Inheriting a legacy of unhappiness and a miserable notion of what parenthood should be, his own childhood losses were set in a now familiar pattern, passed on largely unaltered to his children.

4

PRINCE GEORGE AND HIS BROTHER THE DUKE OF CLARENCE

'If it moves, shoot it . . .'

King George V reigned over millions in territories that covered a quarter of the world's surface. He was constitutional Head of State to dominions far too numerous and distant for him to visit. He was blessed with better looks than many of his relatives, had a large family and a supportive wife. His wealth was prodigious and – like his father King Edward VII – he was immensely popular.

Although George was a man of limited intellectual powers, Violet Markham's post-mortem opinion of him that 'In the end it is character not cleverness that counts; goodness and simplicity, not analytical subtlety and the power to spin verbal webs' might well have been endorsed by his subjects. As far as his children were concerned, however, Hermann Hesse's comment in *A Child's Heart* is probably nearer the mark: 'Would not God find a way out, some superior deception such as the grown-ups and the powerful always contrived, producing one more trump card at the last moment, shaming me after all, not taking me seriously, humiliating me under the damnable mask of kindness?' Both George's sons were to suffer in the name of kindness just as Edward VII had been made to suffer by Queen Victoria and Prince Albert 'for his own good'.

George was born in 1865, the second son of Edward and Alexandra. He was not their favourite child. He became heir to the throne following the untimely death of his elder brother Albert Victor (Eddy), having married May of Teck to whom Eddy had earlier been betrothed. As the younger brother he had been groomed for naval command, to which he was both educationally and temperamentally suited, rather than for the responsibilities of the Crown.

When he succeeded, it was to wear the crown that had been destined for his brother, just as his bride had been. When he and Mary, as she was now known, moved into their first home, York Cottage in the grounds of Sandringham, George filled it with reproduction furniture from Maples furniture store in Tottenham Court Road, a seemingly bizarre choice for one who could have availed himself of the finest originals. By surrounding himself with fakes, as well as with copies of famous portraits, he lived with a constant reminder that he himself was not authentic either as husband or King.

There was little more than a year between the two brothers who were brought up and educated together – like so many other siblings in the British Royal Family – as if they were twins. They were very close. Eddy grew tall and lanky with elongated arms and neck (which he disguised off duty with high-collared, deep-cuffed shirts), almost entirely lacking face and body hair, and with a frailty suggestive of the genetic disorder Klinefelter's syndrome, often associated with impotence but always with infertility. He had inherited the haemophilia that ran through the female royal genes from Queen Victoria, was partially deaf from birth – which would have resulted in learning difficulties even had he been of normal intelligence – and his speech was affected by a lisp. Although his limited intellect offended Victoria and his father, his mother, who was far from bookish, loved him.

Unlike Eddy, George attained a height of only 5 feet 7 inches, but by contrast he was physically strong and athletic. He became a shy, diffident and self-conscious man who hid himself behind a copious beard and moustache – the 'dark glasses' of the day. George was devastated when Eddy died. His grief was genuine although it is likely to have been accompanied by feelings of guilt: as the second son, with little chance of accession to the throne, George might have envied his elder brother and at times wished him out of the way.

As children, both Eddy and George, together with their sisters Louise, Victoria and Maud, had had to cope with a remote father who had been brought up to equate discipline with strength and a mother who, with her stifling embraces and her possessiveness, was capable of inflicting a similar degree of psychological damage. In the days before effective hearing aids had been introduced a child who had to shout at his mother to make himself heard might conclude that she was not listening to him. When Alexandra talked to her children it was in such a loud voice and with such a heavy Danish accent that verbal communication between them was difficult. None of this, however, could shake George's devotion to, akin to idolization of, to his mother. 'I was brought up in an age of beautiful women, and the two most beautiful of all were Empress Elisabeth of Austria and my own mother.' Like her mother-in-law and later her son, Alexandra found it easier to express herself on paper, and her letters were full of references to 'her dearest, darling little Georgie'.

Neither Alexandra nor Edward VII had been well educated, and their sons were to be brought up similarly impoverished. 'The melancholy thing is that neither he nor the darling Princess ever care to open a book,' wrote Lady Frederick Cavendish of her sovereign and his wife. Prince George, however, was open to instruction on more prosaic matters: his grandmother had given him a watch in 1873 and expressed the hope that it would remind him 'to be very punctual in everything and very exact in all your duties . . . I hope you will be a good, obedient, truthful boy, kind to all, humble-minded, dutiful and always trying to be of use to others!' Most of the Queen's exhortations were taken to heart. George's intellectual powers may have been limited, but they were greater than Eddy's, and both boys were educated at Eddy's slow pace, which undoubtedly held George back. Yet George looked up to his brother, both literally and figuratively, and turned to him for guidance when their father was absent on affairs of state, woman-izing, gambling or engaged in other self-gratificatory activity.

At the ages of fifteen and fourteen respectively the boys were sent to spend three years in the Navy as cadets and were exposed to the traditions described later by Winston Churchill as principally 'rum, buggery and the lash'. While George enjoyed his duties as a sailor, their chaperone the Reverend John Dalton was 'sorry to report that Eddy had become increasingly dissolute, drinking and associating with ruffians in disreputable places'. Despite his best ministrations, the Queen was displeased by the boys' behaviour and wrote in 1872, 'They are such ill-bred, ill-trained children, I can't fancy them at all', which might have been as much a veiled criticism of her eldest son and daughter-in-law as of the two young Princes.

The efforts of Dalton, a classicist, to open the minds of his charges were largely unsuccessful. Loyally and optimistically, he reported scholarly progress, but Eddy was not interested in learning, and George showed enthusiasm only for the Navy, which he had assumed to be his destiny. Even his duties as a seaman had their drawbacks: as an elderly man he told his librarian Sir Owen Morshead, 'It never did me any good to be a Prince, I can tell you, and many was the time I wished I hadn't been . . . so far from making any allowances for our disadvantages, the other boys made a point of taking it out of us on the grounds that they'd never be able to do it later on.' Only a few years later, however, George sent his own unwilling sons to Osborne and Dartmouth for naval training in the belief that 'the Navy is all the education they will ever need', perpetuating his own unhappy experiences as a cadet.

Like their father, Eddy and George acquired a number of tattoos commemorating their various ports of call. It was not customary for the aristocracy, and certainly not for royalty, to be tattooed during service in the Royal Navy; that both Eddy and George chose to identify with their shipmates in this respect says more for their need to be accepted by them than for a desire to have a permanent record of their travels engraved on their bodies. Dalton was only taken to task about their tattoos when it was reported back to London that they had had their noses tattooed in Barbados. He was able to reassure the Prince and Princess of Wales that the boys had been 'sniffing lilies in the botanical gardens there' and that they had neglected to wipe the pollen off their noses. (Some time later, when he had become King, George had his tattoos amended and improved by an eminent British tattooist at the suggestion of Queen Mary.)

Upon their return home from their tour of duty the brothers were sent to Switzerland for six months in an unsuccessful attempt to improve their French and German. It was only after this that they were separated, as George continued his naval career and Eddy began his studies at Cambridge. 'My dear George. So we are at last to be separated for the first time and I can't tell you how strange it seems to be without you and how much I miss you in everything all day long,' he wrote. Although one of his tutors remarked that he did not think he derived 'much benefit from attending lectures. He hardly knows the meaning of the words to read', Eddy was awarded an honorary doctorate of law. Prime Minister William Gladstone asked permission to publish the Prince's reply to his subsequent letter of congratulation. He was forced to alter it himself to introduce structure and grammar and received permission from the Prince of Wales to publish it in its improved form. While at Cambridge Eddy came to rely heavily upon his tutor James Stephen and they corresponded intimately after Eddy left to join the 10th Hussars (a regiment which at the time had a reputation for dissipation and excess and where Eddy's homosexual inclinations went largely unremarked). Stephen's attachment to his pupil became so intense that when they were parted he gave up academic life and was eventually admitted to a mental hospital. He went on hunger strike the day that Eddy's pneumonia was made public and died just before his Prince.

Eddy had apparently been in love with at least two women before his engagement to Princess May of Teck. His behaviour, however, was so reprehensible, and the places he was rumoured to frequent – especially the Hundred Guineas in Cleveland Street, the most notorious homosexual club in London and a male brothel that became closely associated with the Whitechapel murders of Jack the Ripper – of such dubious repute, that doubts about the company he kept, and also his sexual orientation, became a matter not only for public concern but exercised both his family and Parliament. Further doubts about his suitability for kingship were raised. So many scandalous stories about him were circulated (including the fanciful one that he was himself the 'Ripper') that it was agreed between the government and the King that Eddy must either marry or be sent away to govern one of the more distant colonies. Despite his probable same-sex preferences, Eddy had expressed interest in marrying Hélène of Orléans, daughter of the president of the French Republic and a Roman Catholic. Since he was not regarded as being sufficiently able to govern even the smallest or farthest-flung of colonies, suitable princesses were rare and attractive ones rarer still, Queen Victoria had given her permission for this, but the religious impediment was so great that the marriage was not approved in Parliament.

Eddy had been born prematurely before adequate preparations had been made for his birth. Alexandra fed him until a wet nurse was found, at which point his mother's breast was denied him. Maternal comfort had been offered then withdrawn, possibly sowing the seeds of ambivalence in Eddy's later attitudes to women.

He had been created Duke of Clarence and Avondale in 1890. The following year his father described his remaining in the Army as a 'waste of time', and his future, Edward told the Queen, was 'a matter of some considerable anxiety to us'. Edward's concerns were soon resolved most dramatically: on 9 January 1892, the day after his twenty-eighth birthday, Eddy died from a lung infection. Had he lived and married, his likely genetic disorder would have precluded him from producing an heir. His potential for kingship had been often in doubt, and many were relieved when his younger brother became heir apparent. After his death the Royal Family closed ranks, as if he had never existed, and the title Duke of Clarence was dropped from usage.

Prince George craved the attention he had lacked earlier, and perhaps reacted with resentment at the ambivalent way in which he had been treated by his mother: she had not only lavished mother-love on him but had also used him to prop up her low self-esteem, reinforced by her husband's neglect. His seductive and flirtatious attitude towards her contrasts with the usual forms of address used to a parent: 'Dear, sweet, loving, beloved little Motherdear' might have been his attempt to comfort Alexandra for the neglect shown her by his father. He continued to depend on her heavily.

Alexandra, equally dependent upon her children, was a past mistress at making them feel guilty even about things beyond their control. On his fourteenth birthday, in a letter to George, she chastised him about his stature. 'So old and so small!!! Oh my! You will have to make haste to grow, or I shall have the sad disgrace of being the mother of a dwarf!!!'

After his education – such as it was – had been completed, George spent the next few years as a serving naval officer, a life that he would have continued had circumstances permitted. Despite his apparent independence, however, he was capable of lamenting his inability to attend a family celebration by writing to his mother from HMS *Dreadnought* at the age of twenty-one, 'How I wish I was going to be there too, it almost makes me cry when I think of it. I wonder who will have that sweet little room of mine, you must go and see it sometimes and imagine that your little Georgie dear is living in it.' Still, at heart, he was a mother's boy.

Princess May of Teck, young, unmarried, educated and living with her family in grace-and-favour accommodation in London, had become engaged to Eddy in late 1891. The betrothal was made with resignation rather than passion, although Princess May was not displeased at the prospect of improvement in her personal and family fortunes. By royal standards her family was impoverished, and she had not been the immediate choice of a suitable bride for Eddy. Queen Victoria deplored the extravagances of her mother Princess Mary Adelaide and was irritated by her popularity.[1] She was therefore surprised when she auditioned May, who was tall and handsome rather than beautiful, on Eddy's behalf at Balmoral. Victoria found a calm, intelligent, serious young woman with taste, quiet confidence, beautiful manners and exactly the kind of steadying presence it was believed that Eddy needed.

May had acquired an extraordinary respect for and knowledge of the British Royal Family and its constitution and was proud to be part of it – if only, at that time, on the periphery. To be asked to marry the heir to the throne was an honour – to consent almost a duty – that far outweighed any reservations she may have harboured about her future husband. She accepted his proposal in December, and preparations began for a spring wedding in 1892. Early in the New Year, when Eddy contracted his fatal illness and died, May made all the correct noises but possibly grieved more for the loss of the figurehead she revered than for the man she knew so little. 'It is so difficult to begin one's old life again after such a shock,' wrote May to a friend. 'Even reading, of which I am so fond, is a trouble to me & I cannot settle down to anything . . .' After she recovered from the initial shock of Eddy's death, nothing suggests that she suffered further. She could not mourn a man she hardly knew. Her expectations, however, like those of her mother, had been raised. Who could blame her for dreading a return to 'poor relation' and to life dependent on charity when she had seen her future as Queen of England? In any event she was probably less distraught than her ambitious mother who had gained considerable status as 'mother of the bride' and who saw Eddy's death as the disintegration of a dream and forerunner of financial ruin.

The two abortive love affairs that preceded George's 'second-best' marriage to May are well documented. As a young man he was first in love with Julia Stonor, granddaughter of Sir Robert Peel, one of his mother's ladies-in-waiting – but a Roman Catholic as well as a commoner. Alexandra would have blessed the match had it been constitutionally possible. 'I only wish you could marry and be happy but, alas, I fear this cannot be,' she wrote. Later he became attached to and hoped to marry his cousin Princess Marie of Edinburgh, but she chose King Ferdinand of Romania instead. George's options were limited, and, as his father's heir, he was now under pressure to marry, have children and secure the succession.

When the time came, George, with his keen sense of duty, bowed to the inevitable. Weakened by a bout of typhoid fever from which he had only just recovered, and unable to marry the woman he loved, he was heartbroken when Eddy died. A few months later, when George and some of his family were staying on the French Riviera, Mary Adelaide took a house near by. George and May were thrown into each other's company. Mary Adelaide, not the most subtle of women, thought that a marriage between her daughter and the Prince would make perfect sense: May was no less suited to being a royal bride now than when she had been vetted by Victoria for Eddy the previous year. A decorous courtship ensued – both were still in mourning – and in May 1893 their engagement was announced. They were married in July.

Lady Geraldine Somerset, lady-in-waiting to Queen Alexandra, wrote acidly in her journal, 'It is clear there is not even a pretence at lovemaking. May is radiant at her *position* but placid and cold as always.' Lady Geraldine was not to know, however, that, stiff and formal as their public behaviour might be, May (now known as Mary) and George could show affection, indeed devotion, on paper. By expressing himself through *billets doux* – much as tongue-tied lovers of today are able to spend intimate hours on the telephone – George was repeating the distanced and non-verbal communication patterns of his childhood. Although his bride had been handed down to him through the ghost of his beloved brother, and his prize gained by default, the popular press of the day hinted that it was George whom Mary had loved all along and that their marriage was made in heaven. Mary, anxious to deflect any suggestion that she was either a gold-digger or an afterthought, did not demur.

George's unhealthy childhood relationship with his mother affected his marriage. Mary liked her mother-in-law no better than Alexandra had liked hers. Alexandra's possessive attitude towards George was reflected in her wedding gift of York Cottage on the Sandringham estate. Its proximity enabled her to visit the newly-weds frequently and unannounced, making a tacit statement that she retained rights in the property and also in the man. York Cottage had originally been built to accommodate extra male guests shooting on the Sandringham estate. It was neither beautiful nor practical and certainly had not been designed for family life. It resembled a large suburban villa, ivy-clad and gabled, with a network of small dark rooms linked by draughty passages and inconvenient staircases.

George decorated and furnished it according to his own taste, without reference to his bride. One of Mary's later idiosyncrasies, after she had become Queen, was the removal of the ivy that clung to the walls of her much grander houses. Was she metaphorically stripping her mother-in-law of her stranglehold on George? Any wife would have quailed in the face of a mother-in-law who had the temerity to write about her son's marriage that 'There is a bond of love between us, that of mother and child, which nobody can ever diminish or render less binding – and nobody can, or ever shall, come between me and my darling Georgie boy.'

If Alexandra did not always give George and Mary as much privacy as they wished, it was perhaps because she was lonely for male company. Her husband had turned away from her, her first-born son had died, and she had lost her last child, John, shortly after his birth in 1871. The affection of her three daughters had never been important to her, and she looked to her surviving son to compensate for her losses. He was the only man in her life, and she was reluctant to let him go. So possessive was she, so demanding, and so exploitative, that George never fully broke away from her to form a complete emotional bond with another woman. Alexandra, increasingly deaf and with her children growing up, now inhabited a contracting world in which her status would be usurped by her daughter-in-law. Eventually there were grandchildren to lighten and brighten her life, but at the time of her son's marriage – when she was forty-nine and probably going through the menopause – she could, understandably, have felt that her useful life was over.

Throughout his childhood George would have had grounds to fear that his parents would reject him – unless he gave them the unqualified love, obedience and compliance they demanded. His father had never had time for him, and when he became King he tried to compensate for this (as well as for his fear of being kept waiting) by keeping the clocks at Sandringham five minutes fast. Like his father before him George had a passion for punctuality.

George's legacy of low self-esteem was never to leave him, even after his marriage. He felt as inauthentic as his paintings, as much of a replica as the Maples furniture. Only the solitary pastime of playing with his vast collection of British Empire stamps, each of which bore his image, fulfilled his narcissistic needs and reassured him of his existence.

The 'Marlborough House Set' and the flamboyant circles in which his parents had moved did not appeal to George. His low self-confidence prevented him from feeling at home with 'smart' people; he had no wish to follow the pattern set down by the old King and did not feel at home with the intelligentsia. Although Mary might have wished to socialize more, she deferred, as in everything, to her husband who was to exemplify family solidarity, a virtue received with as much enthusiasm in the 1920s and 1930s as his father's profligacy had been earlier.

The George who was typecast as a harmless and fundamentally decent man was, however, by no means the whole man. Shutting his eyes to the reality behind his assertion that 'it never did me any harm', and with the collusion of his wife, he humiliated and tortured, albeit 'for their own good', his children much as he had been humiliated and neglected, making them feel as fundamentally unworthy as he himself had been made to feel. Despite this punitive treatment, he expected to receive love from them, just as his mother had expected to receive love from him, and had no idea that loyalty, affection and trust are the spontaneous response to a mutual loving interchange – which, in George's case, was never initiated – and that respect must be earned.

Birds, animals and children – defenceless victims – became targets for the anger George had never been able to express at the appropriate time or in the appropriate place. Gun in hand, like his father before him, he followed his favourite outdoor pastime of what Tolstoy described as 'evil legitimized', the pursuit of game. George revelled in dominating and rejoiced in destroying birds and wild animals.

At his coronation in 1911 George was faced with a dilemma: his mother demanded precedence in Westminster Abbey over his wife. George collapsed under his mother's pressure, yet again, just as he had allowed her to keep the little crown and to stay on at Buckingham Palace. By clinging to her former status Alexandra proved once again to her daughter-in-law that she was still able to manipulate her son.

George V's dullness and lack of intellect may have helped him to become a popular king. Britain's growing middle classes felt at home with a monarch who seemed comfortable in the field or on the quarterdeck and who instigated the tradition of the BBC Christmas broadcast to the Empire. Few people were privy to the darker side of his nature. Had they known more about his epileptic son John (seldom included in family portraits), who had been banished to live with a nurse and to die unremarked, had they known that his son David, the immensely popular Prince of Wales, was so frightened of his father that at the age of eighteen he fainted in anticipation of a reprimand, they might have revised their ideas about a gruff but kindly King whose 'heart was in the right place'.

George's 'sense of humour' and his liking for practical jokes was another manifestation of his aggression. He was renowned for his habit in the Navy of making apple-pie beds for his fellow cadets. His patent delight in the discomfort of others, remarked upon by his tutor John Dalton, probably reflected a desire to hurt others as he himself had once been hurt.

As a consequence of his relationship with Alexandra, when his own wife became a mother he saw to it that he was not required to 'share' her. His sons in particular were not allowed to take up any more of Mary's time than was essential. As always, she colluded with his wishes – he thought this no more than his due – and gave her children minimal attention. She knew to whom she owed the status which gave her such pleasure and which had restored her sense of self-worth. George, with his tattooed arms and his heavy smoking – Mary, too, enjoyed the occasional Woodbine – was, in many respects, a contradiction to the sedate persona perceived by his subjects. Society and the intelligentsia rather despised the couple, as illustrated in a few lines from a Max Beerbohm poem:

> I found him with a rural dean
> Talking of District Visiting . . .
> The King is duller than the Queen . . .
>
> At any rate he doesn't sew;
> You don't see him embellishing
> Yard after yard of calico . . .
> The Queen is duller than the King

Nevertheless the truth is probably far more complicated. Their habit of committing their most affectionate and intimate feelings to paper continued throughout their married life, often prefaced by an apology about being unable to express themselves face to face. Several years after their wedding George wrote to Mary that he had not been much in love with her at the time of their engagement or marriage but that he had come to love her very much. Her reply, typically, would have expressed agreement and relief.

They seem to have been a well-matched pair. Both were lonely, damaged and insecure people who disguised their inadequacies – perhaps even to each other – with an outward display of hauteur and pride.

George was fond of and respected his father but deplored the way that his mother had been treated. Grief-stricken though he was when Edward died, he expressed oblique disapproval afterwards. 'We've seen enough of the intrigue and meddling of certain ladies. I'm not interested in any wife except my own.'

George was well served by his lack of imagination. This, probably more than anything else, enabled him apparently to overcome the difficulties experienced in his childhood. It did not, however, prevent him from inflicting similar pain on his own children. Having witnessed few examples of constructive parental love and guidance, it was impossible for him to extend this to others. Narcissistic needs and child neglect were once again rearing their ugly heads.

5

KING GEORGE V, QUEEN MARY AND THEIR CHILDREN

'Her price is far above rubies . . .' – *Proverbs*

Princess May of Teck became a senior member of the British Royal Family when, by default, she married Prince George, Duke of York, the second son of Edward, Prince of Wales, in July 1892.

She was born at Kensington Palace in May 1867, the eldest of four children. As the first-born, May received some early attention from her mother – herself a deprived child – but was quickly displaced by the birth of her three brothers. Her father, the Duke of Teck, had been prevented by his father's morganatic marriage from inheriting family titles and money and had to manage on his Army pay. He came from Germany to England with his wife Princess Mary Adelaide, a first cousin of Queen Victoria, and settled in a grace-and-favour apartment given to them by the Queen who took pity on the impoverished Tecks. Between 1883 and 1885, however, the Tecks' financial circumstances were so straitened that they were obliged to live in Italy where the cost of living was lower. May grew up, therefore, with both the expectation of luxury and a fear of the consequences of over-indulgence. With relatively low royal status and with little political importance, she was not expected to make an especially brilliant marriage, but she was, none the less, a royal Princess and could not entertain thoughts of marriage to anyone of lesser rank than herself. This dilemma could well have made an old maid of her, for, by her early twenties, she had developed a stiff, aloof, rather spinsterly bearing. She also had a horror of 'vulgarity' and explained her disinclination to laugh by saying that she thought she sounded vulgar when she did so.

The Tecks' financial troubles had been caused partly by the profligacy of Princess Mary Adelaide. She weighed seventeen stone and became affectionately known by the British people as 'Fat Mary'. She was as flamboyant as Queen Victoria was reclusive and had a passion for expensive jewellery and clothing, inherited by her daughter who, despite being left with only 'two little rings' after Eddy died, did not have long to wait for a more substantial collection. On her marriage Mary received personal gifts of jewellery valued at over £1 million.

Princess Mary Adelaide's craving for food and possessions, as well as her denial of the family's financial situation, suggests that she had unfulfilled dependent needs. Having had very little love in her own childhood, she was unable to provide much for her daughter who yearned for status and respect just as Mary Adelaide yearned for affection and food and who grew up with similar dependent needs. Although May was greedy for the trappings of wealth, she did not take kindly to later criticism by her mother for her enjoyment of them.

Mary Adelaide had enjoyed few luxuries when she was young and had not married until her early thirties, long after she was perceived as being marriageable. She later displayed an understandable enthusiasm to make up for lost time and to enjoy vicariously her daughter's prominence. It was her wish to see May placed as highly as possible, partly so that she herself might be able to afford her own indulgences. In this May colluded, and she accepted as her 'right' all the trappings of senior royalty.

Mary Adelaide, who was not only a voracious eater but voraciously demanding in other respects, had never found it easy to be emotionally generous. Rather, it was May who was supposed to supply her mother, ultimately, with the means to support her lifestyle. When May was born, Mary Adelaide saw an opportunity to gain the love she craved. Her daughter was expected to be pleasing and dutiful, and May conformed to these expectations. In learning from that experience how to become a pleasing and dutiful wife she learned also how to please herself. As a result of her low self-esteem, she developed an insatiable need to be valued and found a way to compensate for her feelings of 'little worth' by adorning herself with the extravagant jewellery to which she was attracted. She saw these prized trinkets as representing love – her birthright and her entitlement. As Queen, she became known as a country-house kleptomaniac. She either pocketed valuables that took her fancy or admired them so vociferously that her hostesses had little choice but to give them to her. They learned quickly to put away their most cherished ornaments whenever Queen Mary – who did not understand that helping herself to 'symbols of love' from other people's homes was wrong – came to visit.

Her passion for adornment was legendary. Never since Elizabeth I was a Queen so bejewelled: pearl and diamond chokers sometimes fifteen strands deep, ropes of pearls hanging to her waist, diamond stomachers, bracelets on both wrists, several brooches and orders pinned across her bodice and rings and a tiara would all be worn at the same time. Jewels in the past have often been the symbol of a woman's captivity or possession by a man; in Mary's case, where many of the gems she wore were the property of the state, they proclaimed her primary allegiance to the Crown. Through self-adornment, and by dressing in magnificent robes, Mary glittered and dazzled as she thought befitted someone of her status. Pomp and ceremony outshone maternity as far as she was concerned, leading her to resent the pregnancies that precluded her from taking centre stage on state occasions. 'Of course it is a great bore for me & requires a great deal of patience to bear it, but this alas is the penalty of being a woman!' she wrote to her husband in 1905. She left her elder children as infants for lengthy tours as Princess of Wales and her entire family on other occasions as Queen. Although Princess May had been embarrassed by what she saw as attention-seeking behaviour in her mother, as Queen Mary she failed to recognize the same characteristics in herself.

The two little rings that May allowed the world to think were the only souvenirs of her first engagement were not long to be her only precious adornments. She and Prince George became engaged in May 1893 and married the following July. They saw little of each other during their engagement and were barely ever alone. It is clear from their letters that they were not yet at ease with each other: in June May wrote to her fiancé, 'I am very sorry that I am still so shy with you. I tried not to be the other day but alas failed, I was angry with myself! It is so stupid to be so stiff together and there is nothing I would not tell you except that I love you more than anyone else in the world.' George replied, 'Thank God we understand each other, and I think it really unnecessary for me to tell you how deep my love for you my darling is.'

It is likely that Mary, whose early life experiences had been cold and distant, would have found difficulty in expressing sexual feelings and would have sought gratification in the acquisition of possessions. Perhaps she regretted that she was not given the opportunity by her husband to furnish their first home, York Cottage, but she had her say in subsequent residences, and only her passion for clothes and jewellery exceeded her zeal for accumulating *objets* with which to adorn her homes. Impoverished and empty within, she allowed her narcissism to exclude those around her, except when they were called upon to satisfy her greed. It was hardly surprising that, surrounded by the glamour and fantasy of the world in which she lived, she appeared cold and selfish. A music-hall joke of the time had Mary asking George on the morning after their wedding night if the common people do 'that'. Her husband replied that yes, he believed they did. 'Well, it shouldn't be allowed. It's too good for them' was Mary's apocryphal reply.

Within a year of marriage Mary had proved her worth by producing a male heir. Four more sons followed over the next eight years. David, the eldest, later became the maverick Edward VIII, Albert (later George VI) had greatness thrust upon him, was a heavy smoker with lung cancer and died suddenly from coronary artery disease, Henry (later Duke of Gloucester) died in 1977, their fourth son, George (later Duke of Kent) was killed in an air crash in Scotland in 1942, and the youngest, John, died at the age of fourteen. Their only daughter, Mary, was born in 1897 and was married – not, it was thought, happily – to Henry, Viscount Lascelles.

The Princess of Wales saw her fecundity as serving her husband and future King but took little interest or pleasure in her children, who were brought up by others and saw their parents as distant and cold. George and Mary may have brought up their family with all the love, interest, patience and understanding of which they were capable, but the results of their poor parenting were manifest in the psychologically disturbed lives of their children. Lord Derby reported that George said, 'My father was frightened of his mother: I was frightened of my father, and I'm damn well going to see to it that my children are frightened of me.' However, one of his biographers, Kenneth Rose, disputes the authenticity of this.

George did, however, possess a measure of kindness and the ability to express pride in and affection for his children when they were very young. In 1894 he wrote to his wife of the pleasure he derived from looking at her photograph and that of 'darling Baby' when he was away from them. 'I like looking at my Tootsums little

wife and my sweet child, it makes me happy when they are far away.'
Mary, however, remained unemotional about motherhood. 'What
a curious child he is,' she wrote wonderingly, after her baby son had
been 'jumpy' in the morning but calmer after being taken out. Of her
two-year-old son David she wrote in 1896, 'I really believe he begins
to like me at last. He is most civil to me.' It is significant that Mary
equated civility and politeness with love and that the onus was on
her son to love and be civil to his mother, rather than the other way
round. 'Members of the House of Hanover, like ducks, produce bad
parents. They trample on their young,' Owen Morshead, the royal
librarian, told Harold Nicolson, George V's official biographer.
Another commentator, Alec Hardinge, a private secretary, remarked
how strange it was that George V who was 'such a kind man was
such a brute to his children'.

Prince Edward Albert Christian George Andrew Patrick David
was born to Princess May in June 1894 at White Lodge, Richmond.
The 75-year-old Queen Victoria was once again displeased that the
new heir had not been given Albert as his first name. As a
compromise – which at the same time honoured the people of
Wales, whose Prince he was –the boy was always called David.

His mother was keen to resume public duties and had regained
her regal (if corseted) figure within three months of his birth. His
father left for Russia a few weeks later to attend the funeral of Tsar
Alexander III, and – shortly afterwards – the marriage of the new
Tsar, Nicholas II, to Alexandra of Hesse. Mary saw her baby briefly
only once or twice a day and engaged a nurse, Mary Peters, to care
for him. Less than eighteen months after his arrival Albert Frederick
Arthur George made his appearance, and he, too, was handed over
to the care of Mary Peters.

Although the psychological damage suffered by the boys was
caused primarily by the neglect and cruelty of their parents, Mary
Peters was also in part responsible. She was so besotted with
Edward that she would pinch him until he cried before his evening
rendezvous with his mother, so that Mary would demand he be
taken away and returned to his nurse. When Albert was born
Peters resented having to look after him as well as Edward. She
showed far less concern for him than for his older brother and has
been accused of neglecting his diet (which medical opinion later
thought may have contributed to his later stomach problems). Her

ministrations might also have contributed to Edward VIII's association of love with pain and some of the problems experienced by George VI in adulthood. Her influence in the nursery at York Cottage continued for three years.

Mary Peters was dismissed when her behaviour was brought to Princess Mary's attention indirectly by Charlotte 'Lala' Bill, the under-nanny. That she had got away with her curiously expressed and damaging affection for Edward and her indifference to Albert for so long says much about the Princess's lack of interest in her children's welfare. It seems extraordinary that in a smallish house, however uninterested or self-absorbed she may have been, she was unaware of what was taking place in the nursery.

With the dismissal of Mary Peters, Lala Bill, who was later to care for Prince John after his banishment, took her place. Lala was a London woman to whom the children became attached. She was cheerful, kind and loving, as was their grandmother Queen Alexandra, and the two women did their best to provide the children with what they lacked in maternal love. Grandparents often find it easier to express loving feelings to their grandchildren than to their own children. They can leave discipline to parents and enjoy the pleasures of indulgence obliquely demonstrating to their own children that *they* were good parents, especially when they knew they were not.

Princess Mary, George and Mary's only daughter, resembled her mother and was the child to whom the Duke of York was able to relate most easily. He felt a deep sense of loss when she married in 1921. 'I went up to Mary's room and took leave of her and quite broke down . . . Felt very low and depressed,' he wrote at the time. George and Mary both looked to their daughter for love to compensate for the absence of satisfactory loving from their own mothers.

Henry, their third son, was born in 1900 and was probably sufficiently insensitive to avoid some of the traumas experienced by his older brothers. He later became Duke of Gloucester, married late and had two sons.

George, the youngest son to survive into adulthood, was born in 1902. He was the tallest and most personable of all the brothers and theatrically handsome. When, as Duke of Kent, he married Princess Marina of Greece they were known as 'that dazzling couple'. George was brighter than his brothers and being so far removed from the succession was probably brought up with less pressure. Like his mother, he was interested in books, history, architecture and pictures, and Mary gave him more affection and attention than she did her other sons. George and his elder brother the Prince of Wales grew up to enjoy the company of commoners and of those working in the arts. He was just one of many royal males to have had only a questionable interest in women. Before his fatal flying accident in 1942 George was rumoured to have had homosexual relationships, as well as to have experimented with then fashionable drugs. He was fortunate in that he chose as a wife a woman acknowledged to feel comfortable with homosexual males among whom were Danny Kaye (rumoured to have had a sexual relationship with Sir Laurence Olivier) and Noël Coward. It seems likely that she would not have made sexual demands on George to which he was unable to respond.

Prince John, George and Mary's last child, died in 1919. He had lived for years apart from the family in the care of Lala Bill. After his removal the Princess, possibly glad to be relieved of this reminder of failure and physical imperfection, wrote to her son but never visited him although he lived only a few miles from York Cottage. His brother Albert, playing a mother's role, had always shown him kindness and love and was saddened by his absence, but gradually the memory of his youngest brother faded. Prince John did not see his mother again. When he died Mary wrote in her diaries of her grief, but there is nothing to suggest that she was truly distressed at his death. He had been his grandmother's favourite grandchild, however, and it was Queen Alexandra who lingered at his graveside and wept.

Pressure was placed early on George and Mary's two eldest sons. Their parents failed to recognize the boys' different abilities and were determined that they should conform to their expectations of them. Their father insisted that they should study hard – not to discover pleasure in learning and acquire breadth of thought but to enable them to pass their entrance examinations to Osborne where they were to become unwilling naval cadets.

Their mother was equally concerned that the boys should be cultured: in the few minutes that she spared them every evening, she read to them from the classics, not always in English, and set them long passages to learn and then recite on the following evening. Far from teaching them to enjoy and appreciate great writers, she made this a chore and in doing so probably ensured that neither would have the slightest adult interest in either literature or art. Many years later, Philip Ziegler tells us, Tommy Lascelles, then Edward, Prince of Wales's private secretary, remembered him returning from a house party. 'Look at this extraordinary little book which Lady Desborough says I ought to read. Have you ever heard of it?' asked the Prince. The book was *Jane Eyre*. Another time he revealed in conversation to Thomas Hardy that he was sure some other fellow had written a book entitled *Tess of the D'Urbervilles*. While their mother read to them, the boys were encouraged to sew, embroider or crochet as she deplored idle hands. At that time boys were often taught needlework but seldom required to take their sewing kits (as Edward did) to the front during the First World War. It seems likely that Mary, famed for her tapestries, was once again displaying the egotism that enabled her to believe that if she, the future Queen, could see some noble point in the pastime so should her sons.

George and Mary went on several tours abroad during the boys' early years. Two of these lasted some months. During their absences the children were cared for by Edward VII and Alexandra. Albert developed a stutter, for which he was reprimanded, and was left-handed which, in accordance with the thinking of the times, was frowned on and 'corrected'. In the care of his grandparents, David was less often reminded of his future destiny, and the boys' lessons would finish early if either the King or Queen decided that it was time to play.

The two older boys had strict instructions to correspond with their parents while they were away: each was required to write a letter on alternate weeks. Not surprisingly the system failed occasionally, and they were duly rebuked for the confusion. Neither George nor Mary understood the importance of spontaneous communication or that their children might wish to address their parents when they needed to do so. They appeared not to miss their children – and could not comprehend that their children might miss and need them. But like battered wives who stand by their men and tormented dogs who remain faithful to their masters, such children retained a pathetic faith in the parents who had so neglected their duties towards them. Instead of affectionately responding to her children's dutiful letters, Princess Mary replied with just a few lines. Not even when children and parents were separated on birthdays or at Christmas did the boys receive loving messages. 'Darling Harry,' wrote Princess Mary, on a postcard from India in reply to one of her son's two Christmas letters, 'Papa and I thank you for your 2 long letters which were very nicely written, also for the little snowdrops you and Georgie sent. There are no flowers like this in this country. Love from Mama.'

Mama was too distracted by the durbars and ceremonies, the many opportunities to wear the Koh-i-Noor diamond, the adulation she was receiving in India, to listen to her children's cries for attention and reassurance. On one occasion, when his parents returned from a long tour, Henry failed to recognize his mother. As adults both Edward and Albert said that they had never been alone with their mother: a servant or lady-in-waiting was always present when they had their meetings with her each evening. A boy who has been deprived of a one-to-one relationship with his mother may find it difficult to establish intimacy with any woman when he is older.

Prince George was anxious to ensure that his two elder sons were intellectually equipped to join the Navy. Despite rigorous tutoring from Henry Hansell, however, Edward's marks were among the lowest in the Osborne examinations and it seems likely that, had he not been the heir to the throne, he would not have been accepted. Small in stature, intellectually limited and teased by his contemporaries (who called him 'Sardine', a laboured diminutive of 'Whales'), he was unhappy there. He felt as lonely and inadequate as his great-nephew Prince Edward was to feel when in 1986 he was given no choice by his father Prince Philip other than to join the Marines.

Things improved a little for Edward when he was joined at Osborne a year later by Albert, who cried when he was separated from Lala Bill and who had fared even worse in the entrance examinations. He looked forward to seeing his brother, but the two were kept apart, and each was subjected to the strict regimes of the system. They saw each other when they could, but opportunities were limited. Albert made some friends and came to impress his teachers with his grit and persistence, but the Princes were at the bottom of their year's intake and neither passed out of Osborne with any distinction. The cadet training, which their father had hoped would form their characters, was academically a dismal failure.

At the end of term Albert, at least, was beside himself with excitement at the prospect of seeing his family, on whom he was still heavily dependent. (Paradoxically, the more time a child spends with his parents the more independent and therefore self-assured he will become.) It says much about the Osborne regime and the dismal report he would bring home that even the semblance of family life was preferable to the disciplines of naval college. Both boys were pleased to leave, even if it was only to continue their naval education at Dartmouth.

Just when Edward and Albert reached an age at which an adult relationship with their father might have been possible, however, their grandfather died and George became King. He was to remain an authority figure whose paternalism, ever tyrannical, restricted their hopes and dampened their aspirations.

6

KING EDWARD VIII

'. . . and thou beside me singing in the wilderness . . .'
– *The Rubaiyat of Omar Khayyam*

Uncrowned, dishonoured, and scarcely mourned, Edward VIII has been the subject of more speculation, investigation and discussion than any other recent monarch. From the moment of his birth on 23 June 1894, through his extraordinary adulthood, to his death in 1972 his story, from bright beginning to inglorious end, has attracted widespread comment.

When Edward Albert Christian George Andrew Patrick David was christened, one prophetic voice was heard in the wilderness of public acclamation. Keir Hardie, Britain's first socialist member of Parliament, announced in the House of Commons that 'From his childhood onward this boy will be surrounded by sycophants and flatterers by the score . . . A line will be drawn between him and the people he is to be called upon some day to reign over. In due course . . . he will be sent on a tour round the world, and probably rumours of a morganatic alliance will follow, and the end of it will be that the country will be called upon to pay the bill.'

When Edward was born, his great-grandmother Queen Victoria was still on the throne. Her son Edward, an ageing Prince of Wales, waited to take the reins, and her grandson Prince George was expected to succeed his father. Although, as was triumphantly pointed out by *The Times*, there were already two heirs in direct line of inheritance, another Prince had now been born to take the Royal Family far into the next century. It went on, 'The young Prince is heir to a noble inheritance, not only to a station of unequalled dignity but more than all to the affection of a loyal people, which it will be his office to keep and to make his own. Our heartfelt prayer is that he may prove worthy of so great a trust.' Most readers of *The Times* would have endorsed these sentiments, and it is ironic that Edward, welcomed as the future protector of the realm, was to be the cause of its greatest constitutional crisis.

Although Mary had not enjoyed her pregnancy, she was delighted to have set the seal on her illustrious marriage by producing the heir for which everyone had been waiting, but when her initial satisfaction in having done her duty faded her interest in her son also faded. Her interest in the Empire, conversely, increased.

From the day of his birth Edward was the Empire's favourite son. Unfortunately the same degree of wholehearted approbation was not forthcoming from his parents. His father was strict, inflexible and quick to anger – although he was also capable of kindness – and his mother never had any doubts about where her first duty lay. According to Sir John Wheeler-Bennett, she would 'seldom stand between them [her children] and the sudden gusts of their father's wrath'. Edward, then, could not rely on his mother to speak for him, he was forbidden to speak for himself, and in the face of his father's harsh discipline he stood condemned. Judged by his parents, with advocacy denied him, the foundations were laid for Edward's adult life to be dogged by feelings of rejection and isolation. The repressed child was to grow into an adult who would, of necessity, remain secretive. Only through sexual activity with the woman who finally understood him, and to whom he clung through hell and high water, was he able to re-enact the pain, the humiliation and the anger of his childhood. Edward grew up terrified of his father, betrayed by his mother, with an unfulfilled longing to experience the rightful privileges of childhood and an inborn distaste for his destiny.

Early on his progress was assiduously followed, while later his every utterance was reported and his social proclivities and idiosyncratic style of dress imitated and reproduced in a way that was unprecedented and which would not have been possible had it not been for the development of mass communication. As Edward grew up, Mary managed to summon up a grudging affection for him, as she came to acknowledge his status and prospects. Her aunt by marriage, Princess Vicky (Empress Frederick of Prussia), who as the Prince Consort's favourite child had had some experience of tender parenting, said that Mary was 'very cold, stiff and unmaternal'. Years later, as Prince of Wales, Edward remonstrated tellingly with one of the daughters of his then mistress Freda Dudley Ward. 'You see, you are so much loved you are spoilt. You have no idea of the lives of many children.' He felt at ease with children and could identify with their needs. It brought him, once again, in touch with a mother whom he desperately needed but to whom he could not make a commitment, since no mother had made a commitment to him.

It was Mary Peters who provided Edward with the only structure and security that he knew as a young child. She came with the best of reputations and references from the Duke and Duchess of Newcastle: she was autocratic, stern and even sadistic, but she was also devoted to Edward. The two Marys could not have been more different: his mother's remoteness and Mary Peters's warmth were poles apart, and the effects of this duality remained with him throughout his life, influencing his subsequent relationships with women. As far as Edward was concerned, his mother had rejected him and his nanny had loved him. His mother represented the glory and panoply of the Crown with its inherent metallic coldness; his nanny epitomized physical contact, love, support and availability. Later, when he had to decide between the Crown and Wallis Simpson, his choice was determined by his indifferent mother having earlier directed him into the open arms of his nanny. That Wallis Simpson instinctively responded to the Prince of Wales's 'nursery' needs, and that he could act them out with her, ensured that his brother would come to the throne in his place. At the age of forty-four Edward, asserting himself at last, insisted – in the face of opposition from Ministers of the Crown – that from now on he would accept responsibility for himself. In Mrs Simpson, who caused him to suffer and then consoled him, he rediscovered Mary Peters – his first and only true love; it was inevitable that he would marry her.

Edward's ambivalence towards women stemmed possibly from the mixed messages he received from Mary Peters, her habit of making him cry before his nightly audience with his mother, then holding him to her to comfort him. Later, as a confused adult, he came to associate love with suffering and sacrificed his royal future for a sado-masochistic one with his wife.

Lala Bill's kindness to Edward and his siblings is widely acknowledged. It was to her that Edward owed the faint Cockney accent that marked his speech. Her affection for him, however, emphasized the remoteness between the heir and his mother and led him ever after, as an adult, to re-enact the happy, physical contacts of his childhood with women who were caring, authoritative, controlling and never of his class. Even Lala Bill, though, who loved Edward unconditionally, let him down from time to time when her duties with his younger siblings, especially Albert, prevented her from giving him her sole attention. Mary was always formal with her son. Her letters are more suggestive of a pen-friend than a mother. When Edward was a child of thirteen she missed the first two weeks of his holidays from Osborne. 'I hope that we will have great fun together when we do meet' is an expression of neither warmth nor affection.

Although Edward's physical contact with his mother was restricted, the presence of his nannies predicated that in later life there would always be 'another' woman to care for him. He replicated this need for two carers by never terminating one relationship before he had set up the next. This pattern continued until he met Wallis Simpson who, fortunately for both of them, encapsulated all his needs.

Edward was an attractive child, but in photographs his face is invariably sad. Although as an adult he retained his boyish good looks, the melancholy expression remained. He was unusually short, which was possibly genetic, but growth hormone secretion could have been inhibited by stress in his childhood. In Edward's case, the neglect of one care-giver and the possessiveness of another may have been a contributory factor.

His mother worked for years on vast tapestries and taught Edward to sew, an activity he continued, unusually, in adulthood. His lack of height and his customary inferior position – on a stool at his mother's knee – ensured that he was obliged to look up to women, not necessarily with affection.

While Edward was neglected by his mother, his father involved himself with his son, but mainly as a disciplinarian whose excessive and humiliating demands crushed the boy's emotional growth and self-confidence. Prince George's certainty that where his sons were concerned he knew best led him to ignore the well-meaning advice of Edward's tutor, Henry Hansell. An honourable man, Hansell had placed his own position in jeopardy by suggesting to Prince George that Edward and his younger brother would benefit from going to school with other boys. Hansell's concern for Edward may have contributed to the boy's insecurity, as his recommendations might have sounded as if even his tutor wanted to be rid of him.

In deferring to her husband's notions of what would constitute
the best education for her sons, Mary once again demonstrated
her priorities. That neither Edward nor Albert cared much for the
sports and games on which Mr Hansell placed great emphasis
concerned her very little. In 1907 she wrote to her aunt Augusta
of Mecklenburg-Strelitz, 'We have taken no end of trouble with
their education . . . one feels all is being done to help them.'
Perhaps she felt that her own efforts to interest her children in
history, literature and the arts were sufficient. Mary's own
introduction to culture came late, and, according to James Pope-
Hennessy, the Queen saw *Hamlet* performed for the first time
when she was seventy-five and discovered the great Russian
novelists when she was in her eighties.

Any attempt to encourage Edward's intellectual development
failed: years later, even when he spent some months at Oxford, he
admitted that he preferred picture books to written texts despite –
or because of – his mother's earlier insistence on his memorizing
and reciting pieces from the classics. When he went to Osborne, and
later Dartmouth as a naval cadet, greater emphasis was placed on
mathematics and the sciences, but he had no great aptitude for
either. The more general benefits of the schoolroom – the inbibing
of a sense of fair play, self-confidence, tolerance, generosity of spirit
and humility – were no easier for him to acquire. None of these
attributes could be imbibed by rote.

As part of their normal development, all infants have negative
behaviour patterns that demanding, controlling, disciplining parents
will attempt to eradicate by employing the weapon of 'parental
disapproval', in the face of which a child is helpless. All children
depend on their parents for love and acceptance, withdrawal of
which will ensure complete but temporary suppression of negative
behaviour – including selfishness, rage, jealousy and greed, the
'deadly sins' of adult life. Parents, naturally, wish their children to
grow into fair-minded, generous and well-adjusted adults, and this
they are more likely to do if they are allowed to express themselves
freely in the nursery. Greed in an infant is normal: he or she has no
mechanism for controlling hunger. Tolerance and the ability to wait
may be learned only with a mother whose availability is never in
doubt. To 'love oneself' must precede the ability to love another. It
is not easy to give love unless one has received it, either in tangible

form as toys or food or in the abstract, as a sense of security and self-confidence. No child can ever love anyone else until he or she has been loved. No child can be selfless until he or she has been selfish. Although Edward's parents must have been familiar with the Christian imperative 'Love thy neighbour as thyself', he grew up with all his 'negatives' – which were to surface at a time when he and the nation least needed them – unsuccessfully suppressed.

By the time he was sixteen and his grandfather Edward VII died, Edward would have been aware of the friendship the King had maintained for twelve years with Alice Keppel, a frequent guest at Sandringham. This perplexing relationship may well have had a profound effect on the sensitive boy. While he associated his grandparents with love and affection, he observed that his grandmother tolerated the presence of his grandfather's mistress in the house. His parents, however, who had always seemed devoted to each other but who were unable to express positive feelings for their children, disapproved of 'Mrs K', as they referred to her. Edward was to grow up with the idea that some happily married women (Mrs Keppel's family were devoted to her) could be sources of pleasure, while others (his mother) were not.

As Duke of Windsor Edward wrote that he could remember only one parental embrace from his childhood and that had been after they had been away for eight months, and as he never saw his mother without a servant or a lady-in-waiting in attendance whatever anger and frustration he experienced could hardly have been expressed. He was destined therefore to carry these feelings with him into adulthood. His fear as a young man of his father, the tears and fainting, were the reactions of a helpless victim whose tears are of rage, rather than of sadness, and ensured that as an adult he would understand and empathize with persecutors. His brief flirtation with Nazi philosophy seems to confirm this. Edward's slight deafness in one ear caused George to shout at him, and he associated even conversation with his father as discordant and harsh.

Unable to articulate his feelings, insecure – his fears of the dark persisted into adult life – and emotionally impoverished, Edward's few efforts at assertive behaviour were doomed to failure. He had been denied his essential needs, and he felt cheated. His final rebellion brought him the love and affection he had craved all his life but cost him what he valued least, his birthright.

During his brief kingship Edward sought to compensate himself for earlier deprivations by demanding almost divine rights. Crown property – from Balmoral to the jewellery he bestowed on Wallis Simpson – was treated as if it were his own. He underestimated his personal wealth by a factor of twelve so that he might receive a larger state allowance after he abdicated, and he fought to keep as much as possible of what he saw as his 'inheritance'. Having been given little but an uneasy sense of destiny, he was unwilling to forfeit its trappings. Although he abdicated kingship possibly as compensation for childhood losses and with what therefore seemed to him good reason, it was carried out without grace and with avarice, which was as understandable as it was inevitable.

Edward was supportive and protective of his brothers and sister, although he could not resist using them as scapegoats for his long-suppressed hostility to his parents. Like his father he was keen on practical jokes, which were invariably cutting and unkind: even as an adult he victimized house-guests by making them apple-pie beds, but he would not tolerate any retaliation. It amused him to see the discomfort of others, but, aware of his status, he balked at being a target himself.

Because he was self-conscious, and unwilling to confront the responsibilities of his destiny, Edward was quick to turn the page of any magazine that carried a picture of him or made reference to him as future sovereign. He threw a tantrum prior to his investiture as Prince of Wales in Caernarvon in 1911 because he feared his fellow cadets at Dartmouth would mock him for the purple velvet robes and white satin breeches he had to wear. Edward was content to enjoy, however, the ease, privilege and wealth that came with his status.

George V, like his grandmother Queen Victoria, was suspicious of friendship, which possibly accounted for his refusal to allow his elder sons to go to public school, although he had been advised that this would benefit them. Edward's initial disadvantages were compounded: as the eldest child of six children, he had been the leader in nursery games; as heir to the throne, while he was constantly made aware of his destiny and importance, he was constantly belittled by his father yet denied the rough-and-tumble of the classroom and playing field. Football with the deferential village lads near Sandringham was no substitute for the levelling of

Eton or Harrow, and Edward grew up without the qualities – a sense of fair play, responsibility, confidence, courage, enterprise and enquiry – such schools aim to instil.

His parents were so concerned at his lack of the qualities which they believed an heir to the throne should possess that they called in a leading phrenologist to examine his cranium (just as Victoria and Albert had the heir's head examined). Many unqualified practitioners then worked as phrenologists, and their opinions were treated as seriously as those of a psychologist would be today. The findings were not revealing. They smacked of sycophancy and an eagerness to please: the shape of Edward's skull was declared to reveal only 'outstanding qualities'.

Further similarities existed between the young Prince of Wales and his grandfather. He should 'learn to govern', his mother decreed, yet, like his grandfather, Edward was not given access to the information, papers and people that might have stimulated an interest in the affairs his parents wanted the heir to address. He was sent instead, as his father's representative, to ceremonies and memorials. Edward described these activities as 'princing'. Some men, he wrote in his memoirs, may be chained to their desks; 'I was chained to the banqueting table.'

The writer Compton Mackenzie noticed a strong physical resemblance between Edward and his grandfather Edward VII. 'If there had been anyone left alive . . . with long enough memories of the likeness between the young Prince of Wales and his grandfather when he was a young Prince of Wales it could not have failed to strike them. They would have recognized the same shyness, the same hint of sadness.' In fact, as the Prince grew older he came more to resemble the actor Buster Keaton, his near contemporary, having the same sad, intense gaze but lacking Keaton's grace.

Some time in his late adolescence it was decided that Edward should learn not about 'love', on which he had missed out in his childhood, but about 'sex'. *In loco parentis*, a Doctor of Divinity (the Reverend Mr Wright), proffered some instruction, which was more likely to have been biological rather than erotic in nature. Shortly afterwards, in a letter to a friend, Edward claimed that he had never been troubled by 'sexual hunger'.

During his time at the front in the First World War Edward was taken by his equerries (who rotated their duties) to a brothel in

Calais where he found the sight of the prostitutes 'perfectly filthy and revolting'. Given the ambivalence towards women with which his upbringing had left him, this is not surprising. Also Edward might not have seen a naked woman before, and the sight of a working-class French prostitute could well have unnerved him. However, he had his first sexual experience in Amiens and thereafter seemed to find such activity agreeable. Following a relationship with a courtesan in Paris, and probably unaware of his grandfather's similar experience, he was unwise enough to write compromising letters to her. A brief blackmail scare followed when the woman threatened to make the letters public, but she was 'dissuaded' and the panic died down.

In London once more, where he was courting Lady Sybil Cadogan, Edward fell in love with the already married Lady Marian Coke, wife of the heir to the Earl of Leicester and twelve years older than the Prince. She might have intuited that a man who is involved with two women at once may be displaying hostility to both of them. Other dalliances followed, none serious, and Edward was advised by his mother not to rush into marriage. He remained a bachelor sufficiently long for her to worry that he had taken her remark too literally. He was content to have numerous 'encounters' with married women, to tour the Empire and to hold court at Fort Belvedere, the architectural eccentricity in Windsor Great Park he had persuaded his father to give him and where he entertained his mistresses and friends. Satisfying his need to be seen as a man in his own right, he also bought a ranch in Canada which he believed wrongly to lie on oil-rich land.

According to her maid Else, Edward's sister Mary, who had a better relationship with their parents than he, found it difficult to understand why Edward did not love her parents as much as she did or why he had grown up to be so bitter and resentful. Mary was her father's favourite child: she was not exposed to the same verbal and written admonishments as Edward and did not suffer the same confusion as the boys, whose letters from their father were often couched in terms of affection before launching into criticism and threat. 'My Dearest Bertie,' wrote the Prince, 'I'm sorry to have to say that the last reports from Mr Watt [at Osborne] are not at all satisfactory. He says you don't seem to take your work at all seriously, nor do you appear to be very keen about it. My dear boy, this will not do.' And later, when Edward was at the front and evidently oblivious to the potential dangers to life in France, his father wrote to him about a breach of diplomatic protocol. 'Ld Cavan has written to Digge about your wearing the ribbon of the Legion of Honour. It is very silly of you not doing what I told you at Easter time.' Queen Mary's lady-in-waiting Mabell Airlie was well placed to observe the tension between father and son. In her memoirs *Thatched With Gold*, she wrote that 'The King was proud of his sons but he was often harsh with them simply because he could not bridge the gulf between their generation and his . . . As the heir to the throne grew older the stream of paternal criticism increased, but the Prince's behaviour, when his father hauled him over the coals for being "the worst-dressed man in London" and laid traps for him with orders and decorations, showed the utmost forbearance.' George V was putting his son in a double-bind by honouring him and then complaining when the medals were not positioned exactly according to protocol. His criticisms might have been justified, but linking chastisement with endearment perhaps rendered loving expression meaningless to Edward, particularly since physical demonstrations of love were non-existent. Having not been given love but only status – about which he seemed to display mixed feelings – Edward, as might have been expected, clung to its benefits when he released himself from its responsibilities.

Edward's indolence showed itself in 1928 when he was on safari in Kenya. He was handed a telegram with the news that the King was seriously ill. Edward had difficulty in confronting the possibility that the responsibilities of kingship were imminent and complained at having to cut short his holiday. He managed to find time, however, before leaving for England to comfort himself by seducing the wife of a government official.

On this occasion the King rallied, but his health went into decline. When he died in 1936 Edward's overt grief is more likely to have been connected to the new realities of his situation than with the loss of his father. His bereavement was the end of his long 'reign' of privilege without responsibility and he could not identify with the grief of other members of his family. On his arrival at Sandringham he immediately readjusted the clocks and began to institute economies at Buckingham Palace in order to augment his own income. King George might have set the clocks fast to make up for the lack of time given to him as a child, but his son's instinct was to minimize the time he would have to give to his duties. In dismantling so soon some of his late father's idiosyncrasies Edward was flexing his muscles and at the same time denying those who grieved some minor but potent memories of the dead King.

As Prince of Wales Edward had been credited with being Britain's greatest salesman as he toured the world ostensibly promoting international friendship and British manufacture. Opinions as to his effectiveness, however, differed. In Argentina in 1931 the American ambassador said that 'his cordial, carefree democratic manner wins even those who would go out of their way to criticize him'. The same year, though, the National Archives in Washington record that in Uruguay the Prince 'appeared to be deeply tired, rather uninterested, and to have unfortunately lost a great deal of the personal charm which was so long the most engaging of his many delightful qualities'.

He was unable to cope with public speaking, and apart from long tours of the Empire, which were virtually prolonged holidays, he fulfilled few public duties and did not associate himself with worthy causes or charities. Edward, whose remark about the plight of miners in South Wales that 'Something must be done' was long remembered, did little but enjoy himself to compensate for the carefree childhood that had been denied him.

It has been said of Edward VIII that he cared only about three things: golf, money and his wife. A concern with finance is only to be expected in one whose sense of self-worth is so low. During the abdication crisis, having been told, to his surprise, that he did not own Balmoral and Sandringham, Edward was allowed to 'lease' a lifetime interest in both from the Crown. He had been left no share of his father's £3 million worth of personal wealth, as George V had assumed that his eldest son would inherit a kingdom and a civil list allowance and was aware that Edward had, in addition, a substantial income from the Duchy of Cornwall. (After the abdication a generous financial arrangement was reached recognizing his interest in Balmoral and Sandringham. By today's standards his annual income would have exceeded £1 million.) Edward's most serious grievance, however, was that, although he would continue to be styled a Royal Highness, his wife's title was that of a non-royal duchess.

Before his liaison with Wallis Simpson Edward had been heavily involved with Freda Dudley Ward. She was several years his senior, a popular society figure, the divorced wife of an MP and mother of two daughters; yet she was regarded as 'very good for him' because she encouraged him to be more responsible. Her sexual interest in Edward diminished after a few years, but she remained his friend, confidante, companion and a smokescreen for his activities. Freda Dudley Ward was petite, sensible, generally well liked and bore a passing resemblance to the Duchess of York. She was well enough placed in London society to move in the same circles as the Prince of Wales and to understand and observe the same rules of discretion that surrounded his grandfather's illicit affairs but not so well placed – or sufficiently emotionally involved – to cause a scandal. In her Edward found a loving 'mother', someone who could show and verbalize affection, and he remained devoted to her for fourteen years.

His well-known affair with Thelma, Lady Furness, might have come as a relief to Freda, although she and her daughters continued to value Edward's friendship. It was Thelma, a ravishingly attractive American whose twin sister had married a Vanderbilt, who introduced Edward to Wallis Simpson early in 1931, unwittingly bringing to an end her own liaison with him.

The most eligible bachelor in the world showed no inclination whatever to marry any of the many suitable young women at his disposal. It was not as if he was required to restrict himself to royal princesses, since his father had made it clear that he could marry a commoner if he so wished. His younger brother Albert had already married Lady Elizabeth Bowes-Lyon, the daughter of the Scottish Earl of Strathmore and Kinghorne, but although King George and Queen Mary were delighted by this match they were perhaps a little disappointed that Elizabeth had chosen to accept Albert's proposal after she had been approved as a potential bride for the Prince of Wales.

Edward enjoyed the company of his two nieces Princesses Elizabeth and Margaret Rose, just as he liked to visit Freda Dudley Ward's daughters, even in the absence of their mother. Yet while he liked to be part of a close-knit group he showed no inclination to create a family of his own. Edward discovered the childhood he had missed after his father became King when he found other 'children'

– bachelor friends – to play with and a series of married women to 'mother' him; he revelled in the attention of his public both on official business, at home or in the Dominions and on holiday. The charismatic Prince was fêted in North America, where the song 'I've Danced with a Man Who Danced with a Girl Who Danced with the Prince of Wales', which he inspired, was pure popular hero-worship. He felt loved at last. Realizing that marriage to a 'suitable' bride would rob him of his independence and dilute the adulation his presence aroused, Edward would have liked to remain in this enchanted and enchanting state. Marriage would have rendered difficult the pattern described by Tommy Lascelles as 'one shattering and absorbing love affair after another' and forced him to consider – from time to time – someone other than himself. His delusions were maintained and supported by the popular press: Edward as the 'caring, sharing' Prince, the man of the people, was as illusory as the image of his great-nephew Prince Andrew when placed in the role of hero after his brief but much publicized participation in the Falklands conflict of 1982. In both instances the press acknowledged the longing of readers for a 'handsome prince'. Edward symbolized the charisma of monarchy, while Andrew's macho image showed today's Royal Family to be in tune with the times.

Edward showed no real concern, however, for people less fortunate than himself; given the lack of emotional input from his parents it would have been virtually impossible for him to be either caring or sharing. Much of his time was spent indulging his own interests, on the beach, in nightclubs, at the casino, in the beds of married women or discussing the cut of a suit with his tailor. His interest in his appearance reflected that of his grandfather Edward VII, who gave his name to the 'Prince of Wales check', while his grandson popularized the 'Windsor knot' (winding the tie twice round the knot at the throat) and the Argyle pattern for sweaters and socks. He wore plus-fours on the golf course, adopted the working-man's flat cap and sunbathed without his shirt. His contribution to fashion also satisfied his need for approval and admiration.

Whereas Edward's desire to appear attractive reflected his inner conviction that he was not, his sexual behaviour reflected his belief that a 'mother' would never love him and that seductive behaviour was an essential prerequisite in making a conquest. An infant's need for a mother's love is so compulsive that if it is not satisfied in a one-to-one relationship during childhood the urge to make up the deficiency will persist throughout life. To make a 'conquest', with its implications of battle and the overcoming of resistance, is in itself a hostile act.

Edward fought for love because he could not believe that it would otherwise be available to him. When he succeeded in acquiring it he could not be convinced for long that he was worth loving, and the process had to be constantly repeated. The compulsion to repeat the patterns of early life led him to be attracted to married women with children since, like his grandfather Edward VII whose childhood was similar, it was a mother's love for which he searched. When the 'mother' was captivated, or rather 'captured' by him, he would have vanquished a 'father' – her husband – his original rival in the Oedipal contest for his mother's love.

Edward first met Ernest and Wallis Simpson in 1931 at the home of Thelma, Lady Furness. Wallis had married her second husband in 1928. This elegantly dressed but almost mannish woman seemed to make little impression on the Prince at the time, but a year later he was the Simpsons' dinner guest. Following that, he fell in love with Wallis. The relationship developed rapidly into the persecutor–victim pattern of Edward's childhood: Wallis humiliated him in front of his friends by nagging and rudeness and more than once reduced him to tears. John Aird, the Prince's equerry, wrote in 1934 that Edward had 'lost all confidence in himself and follows W around like a dog'. Most people at the time believed that she did not love him, yet Edward was infatuated with her, and it was not long before he dropped Lady Furness and Freda Dudley Ward, much to their bafflement and dismay. By 1935 George V had accused his son of keeping Wallis as a mistress, which Edward indignantly denied, but it became clear that he had lied to his father when servants at Fort Belvedere claimed they had seen the couple in bed together. Edward's denial, however, could be interpreted as the truth if he did not have penetrative sex with Wallis. It might be that, in re-enacting the humiliations of his childhood with a woman who enjoyed hurting him, adult sexuality was set aside in favour of passive nursery gratification.

Nevertheless his family became increasingly disapproving, particularly since Edward was known to be giving Wallis not only large amounts of money but also jewellery left to him by his grandmother Queen Alexandra, in particular a collection of emeralds thought to have been entrusted to him for his own Queen. It was at this point, too, that his brother the Duke of York began to lose patience with him. (This became even more apparent when he refused to cooperate with Edward's wishes after the abdication and during the weeks leading up to his exile.) Later, as King, George VI's disapproval was reinforced by Edward's interest in the Nazis, which was shared by Wallis to the extent that it was rumoured she was a German spy whose task was to encourage Edward's infatuation with Hitler. The couple visited Hitler in October 1937 when Edward, as Duke of Windsor, expressed an admiration for the social reforms in Germany that was, in fact, shared by many of his former subjects. But the very idea that Edward could again plunge the nation into turmoil and division in being championed by Germany – with the support of like-minded Englishmen – as a puppet King-in-waiting was politically disastrous for him.

By 1936 it had become clear that Edward intended to marry Wallis Simpson and that 'the fabric [of the monarchy] . . . could crumble under the shock and strain of it all!' – a view expressed by the Duke of York to the King's assistant private secretary but shared by many.

When Edward fell in love with Wallis Simpson he chose a woman a little older than he, who would, like her predecessors, replicate the love he had not received from his mother. If he married her he would also receive the bonus of being relieved of the responsibilities of a crown of which he had been made to feel unworthy and which he had never wished to wear. In Wallis he recognized what he had been seeking all his life: a dominant woman who, he believed, loved him for himself and who would in some way force him towards the choice he was happy to make. He continued to make use of charm, manipulation and seductiveness – the tools of the unloved child – in his behaviour towards her. During his pursuit of Wallis, especially when he was away from her and anxious lest her interest diminish in his absence, the Prince of Wales wrote letters to her couched in the language of the nursery. Long after they were married and living in Paris he would dutifully defer to her as to a much-loved nanny. Diana Hood, who worked for them in Paris, remembers, 'The Duke behaved on occasion with almost childlike impulsiveness . . . One afternoon he called [out of the window] to his valet on the pavement outside. The Duchess, happening to come into the room, simply said, as to a wayward child, "David!" He turned quickly from the window to explain, "It's the dogs, darling. They might have been run over."'

The phenomenon of identification with a persecutor is a defence against the loneliness and isolation felt by a victim in a situation where helplessness is so frightening that the only escape from it is to become at one with the persecutor. The persecutor in Edward's life was his autocratic father, who had denied both his elder sons their democratic rights. Edward was to unload his sense of victimization on to anyone who could even remotely be seen to accommodate it. Women, second-class citizens in the 1920s and 1930s, were suitable candidates.

His brother George VI's feelings of persecution took a different route. Having acceded to the throne just before the Second World War, he saw himself as being at one with his people who found themselves the victims of another tyrant, Adolf Hitler. King George's children were fortunate in that they were both girls. Had he produced a son the repetition compulsion, which exists in the unconscious and over which one has no control unless one is aware of it, would have caused him to use the boy as scapegoat, as he had been a scapegoat for his father's anger.

Alan 'Tommy' Lascelles joined the Prince of Wales's staff as assistant private secretary in 1920. At the time his mixed feelings about Edward were biased towards admiration, and he found him attractive and charming. When he resigned eight years later he said, 'For some hereditary or physiological reason his mental and spiritual growth stopped dead in his adolescence.' In this he was in agreement with Stanley Baldwin, who was even more terse: 'He is an abnormal being, half child, half genius . . . it is almost as if two or three cells in his brain had remained entirely undeveloped.' Lascelles remained on the Prince's staff as long as he could stand the self-indulgence and mercurial moods of his employer. After the abdication he took some glee in analysing the Prince's character over lunch with Harold Nicolson who reported Lascelles as saying, 'He says the King was like the child in the fairy stories who has been given every gift except a soul. He said there was nothing in him which understood the intellectual or artistic sides of life and that all art, poetry, music, etc., were dead to him. Even nature meant nothing to him . . . and his gardening at the Fort meant nothing beyond a form of exercise . . . He had no friends in this country, nobody whom he would ever wish to see again . . . He hated his country since he had no soul and did not like being reminded of his duties.' Lascelles's description of his character suggests that he had a personality disorder. Edward's faults and prejudices, like those of any psychopath, can be explained but not condoned.

Edward did not support women's suffrage, and he was racially prejudiced: in 1925 *en route* for South Africa he noted that it was 'too much' to expect him to dance with black women in Sierra Leone and that he had refused to. Years later, in 1940 during his governorship of the Bahamas, he was able to write of Étienne Dupuch, editor of the *Nassau Daily Tribune*, 'Dupuch is more than half Negro, and due to the peculiar mentality of this Race, they seem unable to rise to prominence without losing their equilibrium.' Such opinions may merely be seen to reflect the commonly held sentiments of the day about 'natives', but the Duke was not a common man: he was custodian of a part of an Empire and Commonwealth that paid more than lip service to notions of democracy, equality and essential human rights. He needed to be reassured that there were other victims in the world, and he played 'role-reversal' games to the extent, as we have seen, that he showed admiration for Hitler. All victims, such as hostages, those who have been violently abused or simply deprived by their circumstances, tend to switch from victim to identification with the persecutor. Latter-day political hostages, when released, have often been only too ready to express views that support those of their captors, on the basis that if you cannot beat them you join them. Edward's deprivations caused him to empathize with persecutors. With hindsight many people came to feel that it was a blessing that such a man had not been entrusted with the guardianship of a kingdom and an Empire let alone a family of his own. With Edward's abdication, as with the Duke of Clarence's death, the people were spared a man whose upbringing and subsequent behaviour had rerouted him into one of history's culs-de-sac.

7

KING GEORGE VI AND
ELIZABETH BOWES-LYON

'. . . and some have greatness thrust upon them.'
–William Shakespeare, *Twelfth Night*

King George VI, the second son of George V and Queen Mary, was a modest, self-effacing man who, after his elder brother's abdication had kingship thrust upon him. He rose to the challenge admirably, and while he was ill-equipped and untrained for the role he was obliged to play he had a strong sense of duty and was later to impress the country with his leadership qualities. Although he had an anxious personality and was in reality an angry and frustrated man, his outer calm and concerned manner endeared him to his people during the stresses and hardship of the Second World War.

George VI was not an able public speaker – Winston Churchill's wartime demagoguery more than made up for this – but his quiet dignity, the example he set as paterfamilias and his assiduous guardianship of the people and what was left of the Empire compounded his popularity. His renowned temper, like that of his father and grandfather, was a reaction to neglectful mothering and his nanny Mary Peters's preference for his elder brother. He was later robbed of Lala Bill's affection when she was taken away from him and placed in sole charge of the ailing Prince John.

'Now that you are five years old,' wrote George V to his second son in a birthday message, 'I hope you will always try and be obedient and do at once what you are told, as you will find it will come much easier to you the sooner you begin.' The threatening tone of this greeting illustrates the 'conditional' love to which George's and Mary's children tended to be exposed. Approval was forthcoming if they were good and complied with parental expectations.

Mabell, Lady Airlie, one of Princess Mary's ladies-in-waiting, wrote of the shy but affectionate Albert in 1902, 'He presented me with an Easter card. It was his own work and very well done for a child of six – a design of spring flowers and chicks . . . He was so anxious for me to receive it in time for Easter that he decided to deliver it in person. He waylaid me one morning when I came out of his mother's boudoir, but at the last moment his courage failed him, and thrusting the card into my hand without a word he darted away.' The loving and generous instincts of the child were coupled with a fear of rejection, and it is significant that the card was made not for his mother but for a woman who seemed, to Albert, to be warmer and more approachable. Albert suffered both from his parents' humiliating disregard for his feelings and the mental and physical demands they made upon him that he was incapable of fulfilling. He and his brother Edward, joint victims of persecutory parenting, accepted their parents' treatment of them as normal but were to develop behavioural problems which in Edward's case had national repercussions and in Albert's personal ones. Family life was essentially an autocracy. Power was in the hands of George V and his wife, whose authority was absolute. Democratic values did not exist, issues were not debated, and no child had rights. Repressive orders from above were executed by minions on innocent victims with no right of appeal.

George and Mary, who spoke with one voice so that neither could act as an advocate for the accused, had no idea of the damage they were inflicting on their children. This was in keeping with the times. They were simply carrying on a tradition handed down to them by their own parents, who had been similarly treated. This does not excuse their behaviour, nor did it provide any compensation for their children. If they thought about it at all, their actions were justified by the paternalistic belief, accepted by parents for at least another generation after theirs, that what they were doing was for the children's good. In reality, they were merely pleasing themselves.

Like many children Bertie was untidy, which caused constant friction between him and his father who was obsessionally concerned with order and neatness, an attribute seen by him as a *sine qua non* for a future naval cadet. Albert was not academic and, like his brother Edward, unlikely to have gained a place at Dartmouth had it not been for his rank. Despite coaching and parental exhortation he remained at the bottom of the class in all his assessments. At first the officers were concerned about his speech defect, with its inherent risk that as a naval officer he would be unable to issue a command during a crisis. Later, however, they became impressed by his firmness of purpose. His father, obviously, had not been. When Bertie was approaching his twelfth birthday the King wrote to him, in his usual reproving terms, 'You must . . . remember now you are nearly 12 years old and ought no longer to behave like a little child of six.' He appeared to have no sense of a child's natural progress and continually interfered in an attempt to control his son's development.

Albert eventually did reasonably well at Dartmouth, winning the respect of his peers and tutors, both for his courage and his aptitude for games and sports. He played tennis, squash, football and cricket and, unlike his elder brother, was accepted by his fellow cadets. As a result of this he later promoted a national movement for the development of municipal playing fields, which would encourage the fraternization of boys from public schools with those from less advantaged backgrounds. In the society of young men Bertie had found a comfort and acceptance he had not previously experienced. Although a few years later he was to make a popular and nationally celebrated marriage and become the devoted father of two daughters, he was never more at ease than when he was addressing groups of young people from backgrounds less privileged than his own.

Although Bertie and Edward had always been close to, and supportive of, one another, Bertie's examination results at Dartmouth, his personal appearance and his public utterances would never receive the same press coverage as those of his brother, and he would always, as he thought, be number two. This had its advantages in that it afforded him more freedom than his brother and allowed him to express his anger more overtly than Edward. During the war, in 1916, as a senior midshipman on HMS *Collingwood* during naval manoeuvres, Bertie was usually far removed from the centre stage of the battle, but in May that year he saw action at the Battle of Jutland. He was able to rid himself of some of the frustration arising from years of having to play second fiddle to his brother who was not allowed to be anywhere remotely dangerous while he was in France.

'When I was on top of the turret,' Albert wrote to the Prince of Wales, 'I never felt any fear of shells or anything else. It seems curious, but all sense of danger and everything else goes except the one longing of dealing death in every possible way to the enemy.'

At last he had a real-life enemy and was able to act out all the suppressed rage generated by boyhood neglect, his resentment of his family and even jealousy of his older brother, towards the person of the Kaiser – his second cousin – for whom he could express legitimate hatred without fear of reprisal.

As a young adult Bertie began to show signs of addictive behaviour. The dangers of smoking had not yet been recognized, and the number of cigarettes he smoked each day was probably responsible for the arterial disease and the lung cancer that caused his death in 1952. Smoking was then considered a sign of sophistication and virility, a sad irony since it may have caused George VI to become impotent. He suffered from Buerger's disease, in which circulatory obstruction occurs in the arterial supply to the legs and almost certainly results in reduction in the blood supply to the penis, leading to erectile impotence.

In 1916 a duodenal ulcer was diagnosed. His feelings of anger, resentment and jealousy, as well as the cruelty and pain to which he was subjected during his years of childhood neglect, were manifested in a physical illness that legitimized, by making publicly acceptable, his mental anguish. The legacy of Mary Peters who, as some historians suggest, provided an unsuitable and damaging diet, was proving to be something of a time bomb, and the combination of poor diet and the stressful atmosphere of Bertie's childhood made the development of his ulcer inevitable. (Later he became attracted to a young woman sympathetic to men who had 'suffered'.) Bertie also drank and came to depend upon alcohol to some degree. He needed his whisky every day to relieve stress and reduce anxiety.

Albert thrived during the First World War, first in the Royal Navy until his gastric problems necessitated hospitalization and later in the newly formed RAF until he was discharged from active service on grounds of ill health. King George V was very conscious of the need to reduce criticism of the Royal Family's role during the war. He discouraged any quick return to civilian life for his two sons and insisted that they did not leave the services until the spring of 1919. There had been some rumblings in the trade-union movement vaguely reminiscent, to the sensitive, of the violent anti-monarchism in Russia in 1917 – after which the fate of George's cousin Tsar Nicholas II, his wife Alexandra and their children had sent shock waves through the British Royal Family. Moreover malicious rumours had been circulating concerning Albert's frequent and often prolonged periods of sick leave while on war service.

The 'losses' of Albert's childhood – his mother, his nurse, his parents' long and frequent absences, his 'banishment' to Dartmouth – did not augur well for adult life. He made a friend at Dartmouth, Surgeon Lieutenant Louis Greig, who was his tennis and squash partner and who eventually became his equerry, but it was hard for Albert to establish strong bonds of friendship because of his shyness and the difficulties that he had in communicating with others on account of his stammer.

When the time came for Bertie to marry, it was inevitable that he would gravitate towards a woman who had grown up with similar parental attitudes and who consequently had similar views on performance-related approbation. The young girl who had learned much about cheering up, entertaining and nursing the wounded would not have found it difficult to adapt to caring for Bertie's psychological wounds. In tending these she was simultaneously rewarded by a husband's unflagging devotion, massive public attention and approval and the wholehearted embrace of the Royal Family. Her childhood had not been marked by cruelty or significant unhappiness, but it had been characterized by unintentional neglect. She and Albert saw much of themselves in each other.

He finally won his mother's approval – if not her love – when he became King and Queen Mary deferentially kissed his hand as her monarch. The experience of being second son and second best had been compounded in early adulthood when Albert began to deputize for Edward at official engagements. With his brother's abdication he achieved a status which he may have unconsciously wanted since he first realized that he was less important than the heir. Although he may have resented the role that was forced upon him by events, he finally had his mother's approval and no longer needed to please his father.

Following Edward VIII's abdication, a coldness developed between the two brothers who had previously been so close. When Edward made requests for money and status in exile, George VI was much less obliging than might have been anticipated. He vehemently opposed his brother's petition for his wife to be known as Her Royal Highness and turned down his application for property and access to it in England, as well as for the governorship of

Australia. The most he was prepared to concede was governorship of the Bahamas, a sinecure that might have seemed appropriate for a man who liked to work on his tan but one with which Edward soon became bored and frustrated and which he resented.

The First World War was a watershed for Prince Albert since it established him as an adult whose status was acknowledged for the first time, but the Second World War established his reputation as a wartime leader which may perhaps be explained partly as his identification with the free world in its battle against autocratic tyranny but also by the success of his wife who was the making of his ultimate popularity.

'A perfect little duck,' said Admiral Beatty.

'The perfect neighbour for a bungalow,' remarked Wallis Simpson.

'The most dangerous woman in Europe,' declared Adolf Hitler. Elizabeth Bowes-Lyon has been patronized and suburbanized, yet Adolf Hitler recognized her power, although he might also have over-estimated it.

Elizabeth Bowes-Lyon, born in 1900, was the ninth and second youngest child of the Earl and Countess of Strathmore and Kinghorne. She was referred to as a commoner upon her marriage – as was Lady Diana Spencer – but although she was not royal she was well born. Her popularity with the press and the British people has been attributed to what was falsely regarded as her 'Cinderella' status.

Elizabeth spent an untroubled childhood in the family homes at Glamis in Scotland, Hertfordshire and Mayfair. Glamis is a fine example of Gothic Scottish baronial architecture, complete with turrets, high and narrow stained-glass windows and fortified stonework. A story persists that at the end of some long, dank passage is a room in which lives the so-called Monster of Glamis, a hairy, egg-shaped creature with spindly legs that has survived, generation after generation, cared for but incarcerated and from time to time clanking its chains. The legend has the same veracity as that of the Loch Ness monster, but although it was never discussed above stairs it might have been the subject of staff gossip, rumour and speculation during Elizabeth's childhood.

Elizabeth and her younger brother David had a bolt-hole they called the Flea House in which they hid forbidden chocolate and Woodbines, addictions formed very early in their lives. Because of her childhood at Glamis, Elizabeth was to feel at home when she married into a family that harboured secrets. Most children enjoy the frisson of 'safe' fright – imagined ghosts and the fantasy demons of fairy-tale and theatre. Elizabeth was particularly attracted to the theatre and to dressing-up. She became a consummate role-player, the body language expressed in her gracious hand waves appearing to dismiss the flawed reality of her past.

Elizabeth, like Queen Victoria and her own daughters Elizabeth and Margaret Rose, participated in family charades and Christmas pantomimes. She had been an extrovert child and enjoyed the limelight, which did not often come her way. By the 1920s it had become acceptable for well-bred young women to work in the theatre, and, had circumstances been different, she might have elected to go on the stage. As it was, she made an outstanding success of her central role in the Royal Family's public performances.

Elizabeth's parents, like those of her husband's grandmother Alexandra, attached little importance to her education. She went to school for one brief period of a few months and was otherwise taught by governesses. She learned the social graces, a little French but not much else and attended lessons with her younger brother David, with whom she had a close, loving relationship. She rarely read a book, developing instead a liking for outdoor pursuits such as riding and walking.

Photographs taken when Elizabeth was young show her to have been a pretty child with thick dark hair, large eyes and a sweet smile. She remained small and prone to putting on weight. From an early age Elizabeth Bowes-Lyon had used food to fulfil her needs. As a daughter, wife and mother she craved attention. Her hats were chosen to display, rather than to shade, her face, which she explained by saying that people who make the effort to watch her public duties had a right to get a decent view. Even in later years she almost always wore high heels, no matter how inappropriate the occasion, nor how unfashionable they might appear. High heels make any woman seem taller; in Elizabeth's case, albeit unconsciously, she might have donned them to achieve the social stature she had earlier been denied. Her constant seeking of admiration – even in old age – may have reflected her desire, as one of the youngest children in a large family, to be acknowledged.

Her parents were kindly but remote. As the second youngest child Elizabeth was often solitary, lacking playmates, particularly after her brother David went away to school. The skeleton in *her* cupboard was not the legendary monster but her lonely childhood and a mother who was probably depressed. One of Elizabeth's idolized elder brothers, Alexander, died when she was eleven and her mother forty-nine. A second brother, Fergus, was killed at the Battle of Loos when Elizabeth was fourteen, her mother fifty-three and perhaps suffering from the consequences of the menopause. Bereavement after the death of a child is probably more intensely felt than any other grief, so unnatural is it for a parent to survive a child.

During the First World War, when Glamis was converted to a nursing home for wounded officers, Elizabeth was little more than a child. With her limited education now abandoned and her mother in a melancholy decline (which lasted until 1938 when Lady Strathmore died aged seventy-six), she took upon her shoulders the responsibilities of the house. Over thirty wounded officers could convalesce at one time at Glamis. Like most young girls Elizabeth enjoyed being given responsibility and particularly welcomed the attention bestowed upon her by her 'heroic' and 'glamorous' young men. She was now able to express her talents and abilities to the full and, while identifying with the sufferers, proved herself to be kind and caring. She was able to absorb her grief at the death of her brothers by helping others to be restored to health.

According to Penelope Mortimer, Elizabeth once took twelve-year-old David, dressed as a girl, round the ward and introduced him to the patients as her 'cousin'. Perhaps an unconscious wish to defend him from the fate of her elder brothers caused her to represent him as a girl. Using her brother as her *alter ego*, she was employing him to please grown-ups. Elizabeth is reported to have enjoyed her hospital duties and, with great charm, to have diverted the recuperating soldiers, who were grateful for her attention.

By her mid-teens she was attracted to men, many of them dependent like the wounded at Glamis. They brought out her sense of compassion and furnished her with the attention she had sought but which had not previously been forthcoming. Having a captive audience of bedridden and wounded men with whom physical contact was not merely legitimized but essential, she experienced a form of intimacy that was missing from her relationship with her father. It was also a form of contact that placed her in a position of power and superiority. The end of hostilities was as much an anticlimax for Elizabeth as it was for Prince Albert and others who had thrived on the stimulation and excitement of the war.

Although Elizabeth Bowes-Lyon had few material deprivations while she was growing up, she had been denied the full attention of her parents, the company of children her own age, an education, ongoing nursery care (maids and governesses were constantly changing), the company of her two deceased brothers and her right to remain a child and to develop at her own pace. Most important of all, she was denied her mother, whom she lost when her brothers died, which resulted in her employing charm with increasing frequency to gain the attention which, as a child, should have been hers as of right.

After the war she was involved in the traditional débutante round of dances, balls, parties and attendances at the Season's fixtures, such as Henley and Ascot. Although Elizabeth may not have been aware of it, Queen Mary was observing the attractive and confident young woman and considering her as a potential candidate for marriage to Edward, her eldest son. Her approval was sealed when she invited Elizabeth to be a bridesmaid at the marriage of her daughter Mary, the Princess Royal, to Viscount Lascelles. (Elizabeth, however, might have been irked to find that when the official portrait of the wedding group was completed she had not been painted in.) Whether or not it concerned her that the Prince of Wales showed none of the interest in her for which his mother had hoped is not known. What is known, however, is that during the abdication crisis in the mid 1930s the Duchess of York, as by then she had become, was hostile towards him in the manner of a 'woman scorned'.

By the early 1920s Elizabeth had become used to the attention of men, had experienced their gratitude (as she ministered to them in their sick-beds) and had read enough newspaper accounts extolling her charm and beauty to turn any girl's head. During the war Chips Channon had written, 'Everything at Glamis was beautiful, perfect. Being there was like living in a Van Dyck picture . . . I fell madly in love. They all did.' Except for the Prince of Wales.

Realizing that such a suitable bride was worth holding on to, just as she herself had been retained, Queen Mary made Elizabeth aware of her second son, Albert, and encouraged his courtship of her. Elizabeth was prepared to consider him, but she needed repeated proof of Bertie's love and did not make things easy for him. In making him work so hard to win her hand she possibly revealed her low self-esteem. Perhaps, too, she was unsure that she wanted to marry him. In any event, she needed to reassure herself that her future husband was committed to her, and she made him jump through a series of hoops before she accepted him. Albert proposed to Elizabeth on three separate occasions. On the first two he was turned down. Although disappointed, he did not consider looking elsewhere, and his persistence was ultimately rewarded – but only after Elizabeth had made absolutely sure of his devotion to her. Robert Lacey writes of Elizabeth's exacting standards: 'one immensely attractive man, the son of a neighbour, kept on trying. But he also had flirtations in between, and she wouldn't have that . . . More than any of her friends she knew what she wanted and that was absolute purity' – that is, absolute and unadulterated love.

What Elizabeth wanted was the unconditional love that a daughter has the right to expect from a father. She needed to be certain that she would receive this from her husband. No suitor who was the least bit shop-soiled would do for her. Previous interest in a woman meant immediate disqualification. She had to be 'number one', to take top billing and to be totally accepted.

At the time of Albert's proposals Elizabeth had a great many admirers, notably the Honourable James Stuart, a friend of Prince Albert, who was given an overseas posting when the Prince decided that he wanted to marry her. Albert needed all the persistence for which he had been praised at Dartmouth, before she accepted him, just over two years after their first meeting as adults. Elizabeth's distanced relationship with her father and the losses of her adolescence had led her to doubt the permanence of male affection. Originally, too, she had had doubts concerning the demands and pressures that being a member of the Royal Family might bring. Eventually, however, she told him, partly in jest, that if he was going to pursue her indefinitely she might as well say yes. A delighted Albert, who had informed his parents of his intentions *vis-à-vis* Elizabeth and who knew that for once his enterprise had their full support sent them a tersely worded triumphant telegram stating, 'All right. Bertie.'

Elizabeth so charmed the frequently testy George V that he looked tolerantly even on her habitual unpunctuality and conceded to his son that he was lucky to have won her. She entered married life with the approval of her in-laws in addition to the devotion of her husband. Whatever reservations she may have had about her gauche, stammering and emotionally disabled Prince, Elizabeth was sure at least that she was treasured and cherished by him. She was also immediately embraced by the British people. They welcomed the panoply of her wedding in the post-war period of gloom and austerity, just as they were to welcome the marriage of her daughter Elizabeth to Prince Philip shortly after the end of the Second World War in 1947. Elizabeth's ongoing love affair with the public, who regarded her as 'one of them', contributed to the popularity that, as Queen Elizabeth the Queen Mother, she continued to enjoy until her death in 2002 at the age of 101.

In marrying Elizabeth Bertie had at last done the right thing and done it before his elder brother. When the wedding celebrations were over, however, Elizabeth might have felt that her life was undergoing another anticlimax. She had a series of 'minor illnesses', not the least of which was the pneumonia that blighted her honeymoon in Scotland, after which, it is said, on most mornings she stayed in bed until eleven. Her behaviour seems to have been that of a woman who was depressed, and although the birth of her two daughters increased her popularity and that of her husband her life seemed a see-saw of excitement and boredom during the early years of her marriage.

The popularity of the Duke and Duchess of York was enhanced by three seminal events. They were the births of Elizabeth and Margaret Rose, the abdication crisis – from which the Duke emerged as a reluctant but selfless hero – and the Second World War.

No one was more surprised than the plump little 'Queen' of Glamis – wife of the untrained tortoise who overtook the hare – when she became Queen of England. Like Lady Macbeth, however, she rose magnificently to the challenge. By her resolve she strengthened the purpose of her stuttering, self-conscious husband and made him an effective wartime leader and King.

When the Duke and Duchess of York were married in 1923 neither had reason to suppose that Albert would accede to the throne. The Prince of Wales was still young, and it was supposed that he would marry and have children. The Yorks' wedding – in the light of the Prince of Wales's seeming disinclination to find a bride – proved a popular and welcome diversion. When Princess Elizabeth was born in 1926 and when Princess Margaret Rose was born in 1930 the Duke and his wife might have hoped for a son, but the 'happy family' that they and their daughters represented provided a reassuring example to the nation. Through the increasing number of illustrated periodicals and newsreels their lives were followed with interest. The activities of the Yorks became an industry, and when their faces were reproduced on everything from mugs to the covers of magazines sales soared.

At last Elizabeth was receiving the adulation she had always craved. Her husband doted on her, and her father-in-law – mellowing in late middle age – expressed affection for her that previously he had been able to give only to his daughter Mary. The British people, enchanted by the Duchess and her daughters, provided her with even more fondness and trust.

Elizabeth, the actress, took to the limelight and public acclamation and revelled in it. She might have kept her husband waiting before she accepted his proposal, but by giving birth to their daughters she enhanced his public image and his sense of self-esteem. Recognizing in Albert her source of love she grappled him to her soul with hoops of steel.

After their marriage and until the outbreak of the Second World War, the Yorks had few official duties and led undemanding lives. The Duchess followed the example of her mother-in-law and accompanied her husband on visits around the Empire, leaving her daughters at home with their grandparents and nurses. This provided her with the necessary stimulation to counter any depression and gave her opportunities to shine. Like Queen Mary Elizabeth needed the 'fix' of public approbation. She no longer needed to seduce her husband, but, like all seductive people, her need for approval and reassurance might have been stronger than that for sexual satisfaction. In danger of slipping into apathy after the early years of marriage, Elizabeth chose to neglect her children in pursuit of the gratification of public esteem. It was perhaps as a result of this that after he became King George VI formed an unusually close relationship with their elder daughter, Elizabeth.

Until the abdication of Edward VIII, the young Princess was not considered to have particular constitutional importance. Her father had, however, always lavished more affection and attention on her than had previous royal fathers on their children. King George V, when he was elderly and unwell, was similarly captivated by the Princess and had requested her presence during the long period of recuperation after one of his recent illnesses. Princess Elizabeth's significance for her father echoed that of Princess Mary to George V and of 'Pussy' to Prince Albert. To a lesser extent it was the forerunner of Prince Philip's relationship with Princess Anne. The Duke of York's daughter, apparently with no future constitutional role to play, was able to be loved and indulged, rather than disciplined and trained, as she might have been had a crystal ball been available.

Later the King showed his reluctance to accept that Elizabeth was independent of him. He resisted her wish to participate in the war effort as a uniformed member of the Auxiliary Territorial Service. He obstructed her engagement to Prince Philip, then insisted on a long and painful separation, while she accompanied the family to South Africa for several months following the Second World War. On her marriage he wrote a touching letter that exposes a father's sorrow at losing his much-loved daughter to another man. 'I have watched you grow up all these years with pride under the skilful direction of Mummy, who as you know is the most marvellous person in the world in my eyes, & I can, I know, always count on you and now Philip, to help us in our work . . . I can see that you are sublimely happy with Philip which is right but don't forget us is the wish of your ever loving and devoted Papa.'

Queen Elizabeth II had every reason to be confident in her father's love.

8

QUEEN ELIZABETH II AND PRINCE PHILIP

'We are blessed in the change' –
William Shakespeare, *King Henry V*

Queen Elizabeth II had a stable childhood and enjoyed a warm, loving relationship with at least one of her parents. The chain of psychological damage inherited from her ancestors, however, appears to have remained unbroken and is reflected in the breakdown of her children's marriages and the apparent inability of her youngest son to form any relationship at all for some time and then only after downgrading his status.

Although neither blame nor responsibility for the Charles-and-Diana crisis in the Royal Family can be laid directly at Elizabeth's door, it seems remarkable that until Charles married Camilla after his divorce from Diana not one of her sons nor her daughter had been able to leave behind their dysfunctional legacies to produce integrated families of their own.

When Elizabeth Alexandra Mary was born on 21 April 1926, at the home of her parents the Duke and Duchess of York, in Bruton Street off Piccadilly in London, she was third in line to the throne. Both her parents and her grandparents were delighted, Queen Mary overcoming her displeasure that the baby had not been born in Buckingham Palace. The British people took Princess Elizabeth to their hearts, and they have continued to admire and remain loyal to her ever since.

The excitement generated by Elizabeth's birth continued throughout her childhood as the public clamoured for news and photographs of her. She was pretty and photogenic. Her style of dress was widely copied as were many of her activities, in particular her much publicized membership of the Girl Guides. She led a healthy outdoor existence, and her family life seemed happy. All this assumed great public importance during the late 1920s and 1930s when the press coverage of the life of the Royal Family provided a welcome antidote to the social and economic problems of the time.

The First World War had left Britain exhausted and drab. Although it had been instrumental in raising the status of women, resulting eventually in an emancipation from which they have never looked back, the population was depressed and resentful that victory had not provided the improvement in their lives they had been led to believe would take place – life was, if anything, harder. The 'all pull together' spirit had evaporated, there was no longer a legitimate enemy as a focus of negative feelings, and wartime excuses for severe shortages and hardship no longer applied. The continued existence of a wealthy and privileged nucleus of socialites did little to comfort the embittered majority.

The Royal Family, however, the embodiment of both the glorious past and the recent victory, escaped this contumely and remained popular. The hunger, unemployment and poverty of Britons waiting patiently for a sight of the green and pleasant land promised them seemed more endurable in the dazzling light cast by the monarchy. But with millions out of work, inadequate social services and very little to lighten the gloom the Royal Family could provide only a modicum of relief.

The birth of Princess Elizabeth was seen as a symbol of a bright future, a promise of better times, a hope that the post-war period was drawing to a close and that prosperity was on the horizon. Yet with the 1926 General Strike and the Jarrow Hunger March still to come, the bleak years were far from over. Public attention was temporarily diverted by interest in the little Princess. The charming self-assurance with which she came to deal with their adulation was to ensure the enduring devotion of her subjects.

Princess Elizabeth, however, with her gravitas and dignity, was more than an attractive royal 'starlet'. (Both she and her near contemporary Shirley Temple captivated their audiences in childhood and were later to become 'ambassadors' of their people.) Winston Churchill met the Princess at Balmoral and wrote to his wife, 'There is no one here at all except the family, the household and P. Elizabeth age 2. The latter is a character. She has an air of authority and reflectiveness astonishing in an infant.'

Elizabeth had the attention of her parents when time permitted and the unqualified affection of her paternal grandparents – by whom she was referred to as 'the bambino' [sic]. Her grandfather George V asked for her to be with him while he was recovering from his penultimate illness at Bognor, and he said that the child was a tonic for him. He would allow her to tug his beard and would go down on all fours so that Elizabeth could pretend he was her pony while she rode on his back. No adult had played like this with him when he was a child, and neither had he frolicked with his own children. Now, however, he found himself able to take an interest in his grandchildren and discovered that he *was* able to give love and affection to a child, just as Edward and Alexandra had with their grandchildren. Princess Elizabeth appreciated this attention from a father figure who was both available and loving. Her own father was loving but was only intermittently available.

During the 1930s the monarchy was fortunate – or astute – in the timing of its pageants. In 1934 the stage-managed marriage of George, Duke of Kent, to Princess Marina of Greece had been warmly received. In 1935, with the economy still depressed, the Silver Jubilee of King George V provided a welcome distraction from the struggle for survival. Both events were outdone by the coronation of King George VI and Queen Elizabeth in 1937.

For Princess Elizabeth sadness at the death of the old King in 1936 and the trauma of his funeral procession (with the lying in state at Westminster Abbey) was shortly followed by the abdication crisis. Now briefly transcending fears of another war in Europe came the ultimate in spectacle in Westminster Abbey, an event that was broadcast. A new, respected young king, his popular wife and their two pretty daughters reflected once again hope for stability and security.

Princess Elizabeth held centre stage for four years before her sister Margaret Rose was born in 1930. Charles Higham, one of her biographers, suggests that Elizabeth was in danger of being slightly spoilt and had a tendency towards imperiousness. Bored, as her mother chatted to a female visitor, the three-year-old Princess rang for a footman and said, 'Kindly ring for a taxi. Our guest is leaving!' Charles Higham asserts that this imperiousness prevailed after Elizabeth succeeded to the throne, enquiring of slouching courtiers if they were unwell and, upon being reassured that they were not, reproving them for failing to maintain the bearing expected by a sovereign.

As a child Princess Elizabeth preferred to play with soldiers rather than dolls, which might have reflected her parents' disappointment that she had not turned out to be a son. Although she enjoyed outdoor pursuits, Elizabeth was by no means a tomboy and was – possibly influenced by her mother – both feminine and fashion-conscious. She even became – far more than any subsequent royal child – a trendsetter. For decades after her early girlhood generations of children of both sexes were dressed in fitted double-breasted overcoats, often made of bluish-grey herringbone tweed and almost always featuring velvet revers. Her full-skirted dresses with puffed sleeves, little lace collars and a sash at the waist remained the basic model for the frocks of small girls until well into the 1960s when fashions for children began subtly to change in parallel with a burgeoning youth cult. The Queen Mother had seldom been associated with fashion, but, like Queen Mary, she enjoyed wearing ceremonial robes, had a taste for 'Winterhalter-style' ballgowns and a passion for jewellery. On a brief visit to Paris in 1938 she took with her fifty trunks of clothes and £7 million worth of jewels. Her daughter Elizabeth was subsequently to establish a close connection with her mother's favourite dressmaker, Norman Hartnell.

When Princess Elizabeth was eight months old she was left in the care of her nurse for five months while her parents visited Australia. Such neglect would justifiably attract criticism today, but in the 1920s it was considered unremarkable among the higher echelons of society, as it is to a lesser extent now.

Elizabeth's parental care may indeed have been intermittent, but it was genuinely affectionate, and she had, too, the constant support and devotion of surrogates. Her nurse Alla, Clara Knight, cared for her throughout her babyhood and was assisted by Margaret 'Bobo' MacDonald, at first the nursery maid and later her confidante, who until her death at her home in Buckingham Palace in 1993 at the age of eighty-nine was the Queen's dresser. Both women overlapped with Marion Crawford – 'Crawfie' – who came into the household when Elizabeth was five and her sister still a baby.

Miss Crawford's first encounter with the Princess was in the night nursery. The child had tied her dressing-gown cord to her bedposts and was holding the ends as if they were the reins of a carriage-horse. She solemnly informed her future governess that she usually took her horses for a drive round the garden before going to sleep. Crawfie stayed with the family, as teacher, friend and adviser, until Margaret was eighteen. In 1950 she published *The Little Princesses*, which, unlike *Diana: Her True Story* published forty-two

A representation of Queen Victoria and Prince Albert in 1846 with five of their children by Franz Winterhalter

Queen Victoria, March 1863, in mourning for Prince Albert who had died fifteen months earlier. With her eyes on the bust of Albert she seems barely aware that her heir Edward, Prince of Wales, had married eighteen-year-old Princess Alexandra of Denmark hours earlier.

Edward, Prince of Wales, demonstrates his skill at hunting, c. 1879. His victim is one of the wild white bulls at Chillingham Castle in Northumberland.

King Edward VII with his son and grandchildren in Highland dress, the traditional Scottish uniform of the British Kings. Conformity has been highly valued by the Royal Family.

King Edward VII on the royal yacht at Cowes about four months before his death in 1910. Queen Alexandra is at his side in spite of his well-publicized infidelities.

There is no doubting the determination on the face of Princess May of Teck aged three. Forty years later she would become Queen.

Above: Princess May was betrothed to Eddy, Duke of Clarence (*left*), heir to King Edward VII. Despite his premature death in 1892 she fulfilled her destiny by marrying his brother Prince George (*right*) a year later.

Left: Queen Mary (formerly Princess May), resplendent at the wedding of her only daughter Princess Mary to Henry, Viscount Lascelles in 1922

The Duke of York with Lady Elizabeth Bowes-Lyon (*centre*) shortly after she consented to marry him in January 1923, having turned him down on two previous occasions.

The Duke and Dutchess of Windsor photographed in in 1937 in Nazi Germany with Dr Robert Ley (*centre*), leader of Hitler's Labour Front. Dr Ley was indicted as a war criminal on 20 October 1945 and hanged himself in his cell four days later.

A teenage Princess Elizabeth with her younger sister Princess Margaret Rose gardening at Royal Lodge, Windsor, in 1940.

Queen Elizabeth pictured with Princess Elizabeth and Princess Margaret Rose during a pantomime at Windsor Castle in 1941. Margaret played Cinderella.

An unusually relaxed and cheerful Prince Philip at his stag party in November 1947

Princess Margaret admires an umbrella at the British Industries Fair in London in 1953. But the true object of her affection Group Captain Peter Townsend, the man she was forbidden to marry, remains in the background.

In 1954 Prince Charles, remarkably self-sufficient at the age of six, acknowledges his subjects from his chauffeur-driven limousine.

As a teenager Prince Charles fails to live up to his father's expectations on the polo field at Windsor Great Park in 1965.

Princess Anne at one with her horse at the Windsor Horse Trials in 1975

Queen Elizabeth II poses for her official portrait to commemorate her Silver Jubilee in 1977. Her ubiquitous handbag is once more in evidence.

A happy but apprehensive Diana Spencer
appears to be under arrest on the day of her
engagement to Charles in February 1981.

A less than wholehearted embrace
as Prince Charles leaves his fiancée
Diana for the first time for a five-
week tour abroad in 1981

The acceptable face of public grief.
The Queen's horse loses in the 1985
Epsom Derby.

An inadvertent early revelation by Diana
in 1981. More devastating ones were to
come later.

Princess Margaret seems indifferent to her fate as she smokes a cigarette shortly after major lung surgery in 1985.

Princess Diana has sat on the bonnet of her husband's sports car, severely denting his ego.

Princess Beatrice is born to the Duke and Duchess of York in 1988. Sarah has eyes only for her new baby.

An evidently unhappy Queen Elizabeth the day after Windsor Castle was damaged by fire in November 1992. A few weeks later she was shaken by the breakdown of her son's marriage to the Princess of Wales.

Prince William (*centre*), his girlfriend Kate Middleton and brother Prince Harry watch rugby at Twickenham Stadium in London, 10 February 2007. In April newspapers reported that William and Kate had ended their relationship. It was said that the split was caused by huge pressures on the couple and because of William's career in the Army.

William and Kate leave St Mary's Hospital, London, with their newborn son George on 23 July 2013

Left to Right: Prince Andrew, Sophie, Countess of Wessex, Camilla, Duchess of Cornwall, Prince Charles, Duke of Cornwall, Prince Edward, Queen Elizabeth, Princess Anne, Prince Philip, Duke of Edinburgh, Lady Louise Windsor, Catherine, Duchess of Cambridge, Prince William, Duke of Cambridge, Princess Eugenie, Prince Harry and Princess Beatrice watching a Royal Air Force fly-past with their family from the balcony of Buckingham Palace after the Trooping the Colour at the Horse Guards Parade in London years later, was regarded as little less than treason, breaching as it did the Palace's code of 'discretion', then more moral than official, and resulted in her disgrace.

When Crawfie first met Elizabeth she immediately assumed responsibility for her. Margaret Rose was still a baby in the care of Alla, and Crawfie was able to establish a strong bond with Elizabeth before her sister joined them in the schoolroom. Marion Crawford always showed a preference for the elder sister. She said, 'Elizabeth was the better scholar, the sweeter-natured, the more natural swimmer and rider, had a better figure.' Margaret Rose, she conceded, could be bright, charming, disarming and quick-witted, but in her book all the more dignified virtues are ascribed to Elizabeth. Her account of life in the royal household has the Princesses invariably laughing and playing in their parents' rooms for an hour or so each morning before lessons began. As indicated, some historians have noted that Queen Elizabeth seldom rose before eleven. It is possible that the girls received less attention from their mother than was suggested by Crawfie, who maintained that, on the rare occasions when both parents were at home, the family had lunch and tea together. The Princesses certainly saw a great deal more of their parents than was customary in the Royal Family, but the portrait Miss Crawford painted was the one she thought the public wanted, rather than a true account. Such wholesome depictions were commonly used in the advertising of the time to promote family products such as Ovaltine and Hovis: a cosy hearth before which Father reads and Mother sews, while at their feet the children complete jigsaw puzzles and listen to the wireless. The Royal Family and their life at home clearly inspired such images.

The Duke and Duchess of York had decided that their daughters were to be brought up and educated in an ordinary way. The Princesses' childhood, though, was only ordinary in so far as it was devoid of the abuse suffered by their father and included only those aspects of their mother's childhood she considered sound and healthy. Lessons usually finished at lunchtime, and outdoor activities were encouraged as well as work in the schoolroom.

As an adult, Elizabeth felt happiest with her dogs and her horses. Dorothy Laird wrote in 1959 that Elizabeth had once said that when she grew up she would like to be 'a lady living in the country with lots of horses and dogs'. Her sister was different. Margaret Rose's enthusiasms – ballet, opera and theatre – took place indoors and usually in the dark. The only outdoor pursuit which she was known to have enjoyed was sunbathing in the West Indies. As many biographers have noted, Elizabeth was always neat and tidy, apparently conforming to the structured upbringing in which she felt secure. Since the Duke and Duchess of York did not accede to the throne until she was ten years old Elizabeth had their love and much of their attention at the most critical times in her development. She was adored by her grandparents and her nannies, but George VI and his Queen were themselves the victims of loveless childhoods, and repercussions were inevitably felt by their daughters.

'No one ever had employers who interfered so little,' wrote Marion Crawford. 'I had the feeling that the Duke and Duchess, most happy in their own married life, were not over-concerned with the higher education of their daughters.' Crawfie was writing with gratitude for the free hand she was given in matters of the girls' education, but what seemed to her to be a commendable lack of 'interference' could also be interpreted as a lack of interest, especially in the case of Margaret Rose who was not, unlike her sister, required to take lessons in constitutional history with the Vice-Provost of Eton, Sir Henry Marton. Elizabeth's strong sense of duty and destiny was instilled in her by her father and her grandmother. It was Queen Mary who saw to it that she learned to appreciate art and culture. Margaret Rose did not receive the same intensive tuition.

As they grew up Elizabeth wore stockings while Margaret was still in socks, and in the more formal portraits Elizabeth had two rows of pearls to Margaret's one. Princess Elizabeth not only had new clothes, while her sister often wore her cast-offs, but was treated preferentially in every way. She grew up with greater self-confidence, greater self-esteem and more assurance than her sister. Even Betty Vacani, their dancing teacher, reported that while Margaret was 'quicksilver' Elizabeth was 'pure gold'. She was always to outshine her sister.

Of course vigorous sibling rivalry will exist in any healthy family, and it was only normal and logical that a four-year age difference between sisters would lead to different routines, bedtimes, clothes, lessons and privileges. Realistically, the six-year-old Margaret Rose could not have been treated in exactly the same way as the ten-year-old Elizabeth. However, when it suited their parents – for the purposes of portraiture or public appearance – the sisters were presented as if they were twins. This habit of treating the two eldest siblings near identically had been perpetuated within the Royal Family since Victoria and Albert robbed their heir and Prince Alfred of separate identities by ensuring that their upbringings were parallel for many years. In retrospect Margaret would doubtless have agreed that her elder sister should have received small recognitions of her superior age, but at the time – and having often been presented as half of a pair – the younger Princess would probably have felt puzzled and deprived while Elizabeth's confidence and sense of self-importance would have become more firmly established.

Queen Elizabeth II's style of dress has remained more or less static since her coronation in 1953. Her hairstyle, clothes and general appearance, adopted in early adult life when she believed she was loved for herself, have altered little. After the stress of the coronation, the upheavals of marriage and motherhood, the loss of her father and grandparents and the social problems of her children, she seems to have put change behind her.

Margaret's fashion-conscious appearance, by contrast, reflected both the times and the expectations of others, and she relied on external factors to compensate for the imbalance of a childhood that resulted in her sister's self-confidence and her own lack of self-esteem. Both girls enjoyed dressing up, and Margaret's interest in theatre persisted into adulthood. The Queen, however, while dutifully attending premières and galas, has never seemed seriously interested in the performing arts. She is, however, the custodian of a magnificent private art collection.

At the time of the abdication crisis Elizabeth was still a child. Her secure upbringing had prepared her psychologically for her forthcoming role. She was by nature a serious, rather shy girl who had, none the less, acquired a strong sense of her own importance: she had been allowed at the age of nine to say goodbye to the dying George V. She was about to move from a childhood that had been dominated by adult companionship into an adolescence and early adulthood spanning both the abdication crisis and the Second World War.

Elizabeth emerged as a young woman primed for her destiny. The circumstances of this, extraordinary by any standards, meant that the mothering of her four children might not have been entirely successful. Like her forebears Elizabeth II has put duty to her country before attention to her children. Queen Mary was probably right when she said of her granddaughter, 'There's something very steadfast and determined in her.' These qualities, however, suggest inflexibility, not a trait likely to enhance the nurturing of one's children.

Between 1937 and 1940 Elizabeth's life underwent rapid change. Apart from the onset of her adolescence, her uncle David had been exiled, her father was now King and she was expected to curtsy to him whenever he entered the room. King George VI was as fond of his elder daughter as he ever had been, but he now had other things to think about. The family moved into Buckingham Palace (where it took five minutes to walk from the nursery quarters to the garden) from their comfortable home at 145 Piccadilly. The King began to educate Elizabeth in affairs of state and instruct her in her future responsibilities. In later 1939 for the first months of the Second World War the Princesses were separated from their parents. They stayed in Scotland with Crawfie and then moved to Windsor, where they were visited by the King and Queen whenever possible at weekends. Despite this splitting up of the Royal Family, its public image – guarding hearth and home and refusing to compromise the values for which the nation was fighting – was a powerful and inspiring one. If the popularity of the monarchy had been dealt a blow by the abdication crisis it recovered public esteem during the war.

Elizabeth blossomed under her father's care and tuition, which increased throughout the war years. Having been taught to drive when she was seventeen, she joined the Auxiliary Territorial Service, taking a driving and vehicle maintenance training course at Aldershot. She qualified as a driver in April 1945 and was promoted to junior commander in July. She visited factories, broadcast to the children of Britain, and was colonel-in-chief of the Grenadier Guards. Margaret, once again, was relegated to second place.

At the end of the war George VI commented that the 'poor darlings' had not had any fun yet. While it is true that the excitement of a Season, parties, balls and frivolities were denied to Elizabeth during the war, she had had the heady substitute of involvement in the national drama. Margaret, accustomed to sharing activities with her sister, had not. And by the time the war was over Elizabeth had fallen in love.

Aged thirteen, she had first met Prince Philip in 1939 when he was eighteen and a cadet at Dartmouth. Marion Crawford records that she was immediately impressed by the handsome, fair-haired distant cousin. When the Royal Yacht sailed away from Dartmouth, accompanied by a flotilla of small boats, one cadet followed its progress far out into the open sea. The oarsman was said to have been Philip of Greece, and the Princess is reported to have stood at the stern of the yacht with her binoculars trained on him. Prince Philip has said that the story is exaggerated, but that this was the occasion on which the couple first met is not disputed.

Despite his nickname 'Phil the Greek', Philip's ancestors are Danish and German, and he has no Greek blood. His family survived the turmoil of nineteenth- and early twentieth-century Greece when, having rid themselves of their own monarchy, the Greeks offered the throne to princes from elsewhere in Europe. Their first choice was Alfred, Queen Victoria's second son, but he declined. Eventually Prince William of Denmark, encouraged by his parents, accepted the throne, and became King George of the Hellenes. He and his Russian wife Olga had seven children; their second youngest son, Andrew, was Philip's father.

Prince Andrew had been imprisoned and then exiled when his brother the King was deposed in 1922. He was told that he was lucky his life had been spared and that only the intervention of his cousin King George V had saved him. The Greek dictator General Pangalos had personally driven him to the quayside where he embarked on the naval cruiser HMS *Calypso* which had been sent by Britain's Foreign Secretary Lord Curzon to rescue him and his family. They sailed to Corfu, then a British protectorate, where the year-old Philip, his mother, born Princess Alice of Battenberg, four elder sisters and their entirely female staff lived in a small house named Mon Repos. Philip is said to have been carried on to the ship in an orange-box, and, leaving most of their possessions behind, the family went to Brindisi in Italy. They took the train to Paris where Prince Andrew, tiring now of his increasingly deaf wife with whom he was unable to share much conversation, rapidly found distracting companionship. He spent much of his time on the French Riviera, in particular in Monaco where he was usually to be found in the casino.

Like George V and his siblings Philip suffered the disadvantage of his mother being unable to hear him. He learned to communicate with her in sign language, which was less likely to encourage intimacy. Parental input was minimal since his father was feckless and largely absent. All of Philip's sisters were much older than he, the youngest being seven years his senior, and all eventually married German princelings. When the possibility of his marriage to Princess Elizabeth was under discussion, soon after the end of the Second World War, the German connection caused some embarrassment. Stateless exiles, Philip and his family had settled in Paris, with other wealthy dispossessed relatives from the fragmented royal families of Europe, although they also spent long periods in Switzerland, Bucharest and Bavaria and on the French Riviera. After a brief stay near the Bois de Boulogne, they went to live at Saint-Cloud, outside Paris, in the lodge of a mansion owned by Prince Andrew's brother George who was married to a glamorous and rich psychoanalyst, Princess Marie Bonaparte, a disciple of Sigmund Freud. This aunt-by-marriage, together with the American Ambassador to Paris, accompanied Freud to London when in 1938 he was forced to leave Vienna by the Nazis. She was kind and generous to Philip and his family, but she could have conveyed a confusing messages to the child since she represented stability, security and comfort at the same time as an alluring bohemianism.

Nurse Roose, Philip's nanny, was English but had been baptized in the Greek Orthodox Church. It was she who made sure that he could communicate with his mother. He could speak English, German and French but no Greek. Nurse Roose as much as anyone wanted to ensure that he grew up to understand the ways of an English gentleman. The support of the Milford Haven family, the English branch of the Mountbattens, ensured that this would take place. Roose had prepared Philip for integration with his relatives and for probable education in Britain. Philip's family depended heavily on the goodwill of relatives, including the Milford Havens who passed their clothes down to Philip's sisters. The family was also supported by royal relatives in Romania. Philip formed friendships with his Uncle George's two daughters, and the company he kept was almost exclusively female. The Milford Havens were, by most standards, an unconventional aristocratic family. Uncle George, the Marquis of Milford Haven, was married to an exotic beauty, Nada, who was widely believed to be a lesbian and the lover of her sister-in-law, Lady Louis Mountbatten. Uncle George was a collector of erotica which he kept in the library at Lynden Manor.

By normal standards Philip's extended family was far from poor, and the children were educated privately. Philip attended the Elms, an infant school founded mainly for American children in Saint-Cloud. It cannot have been pleasant, however, for the family to live on charity, and this must have been a confusing time for Philip. He had a mother who was unable to listen to him, displaced if dazzling princesses around him and a father who was increasingly absent. According to Tim Heald's biography, however, Philip denied that he felt disorientated and dismissed any idea that the upheavals of his childhood could possibly have affected him.

By the time Philip was eight, it was decided – partly because of the absence of male role models in his life – that he should be sent to school in England. He went to Cheam, and during the holidays he often stayed at the home of George Milford Haven. When Philip was ten the family home at Saint-Cloud broke up. His sisters had all married within a year, between 1931 and 1932, and his mother entered a sanatorium before returning to Athens to engage in charitable work.

Philip's homes became the German castles of his married sisters. His sister Theodora, the wife of Berthold, Margrave of Baden, made him especially welcome, and it seemed natural that Philip should continue his education in Salem, close to Baden.

The school had been founded by the revolutionary educationalist-philosopher Kurt Hahn and aimed to bring out the best in boys by inspiring self-confidence and moral strength through physical training. A strong body would, in theory, generate a healthy mental attitude to life, *mens sana in corpore sano*. Physical fearlessness would lead to intellectual bravery. Hahn was a Jew and vehemently opposed to Nazism, although his German upbringing encouraged parallels between his own aims and the Nazi motto 'Strength through Joy'. He was forced to leave Salem and in 1934 founded a similar school, Gordonstoun, in Morayshire, Scotland, where Philip was one of its first pupils.

He thrived at Gordonstoun, excelling in sailing, climbing, cricket and athletics and took part in school dramas. By the time he left at the age of eighteen he was Guardian or head boy. Throughout these years George Milford Haven and other relatives ensured that Philip was cared for during the school holidays when he was unable to get back to Germany. Whether he became acquainted with Milford Haven's collection of pornographic books – *Raped on the Railway, A Tale of the Birch* and *Lady Gay: Sparkling Tales of Fun and Flagellation* – is not known.

Lord Louis Mountbatten was to influence his nephew's life profoundly. As Philip entered his late teens Mountbatten seemed to assume the parental role previously taken by his brother George. Both Philip's childhood and early adulthood were shaped by brothers who had no sons of their own and who might have seen him as representative of the continuation of their dynasty and have planned accordingly. Mountbatten had supported Edward VIII during the abdication crisis, but with his charm and extraordinary good looks he and his wife Edwina had retained their popularity with the rest of the Royal Family. A distinguished naval career before and during the Second World War also helped. George VI, however, was reluctant to support Mountbatten's plans for a match between Princess Elizabeth and his nephew, first put forward in 1944 but possibly conceived some years earlier. Certainly it was Mountbatten who enabled Philip to enter Dartmouth Naval College at the age of eighteen, although few pupils were admitted if they had not begun their training at Osborne at the age of eleven, and Philip's German connections were not in his favour. Later, when the war was over and Philip had relinquished any claim to the throne of Greece and adopted the anglicized version of his mother's name – Mountbatten – his engagement to Elizabeth was announced. It was remarkable that this was achieved in spite of the existence of his close German relatives.[1]

In any case it had been Mountbatten who arranged that Philip, the eighteen-year-old cadet, should entertain the Princesses Elizabeth and Margaret on the occasion that their parents visited Dartmouth in 1939. From that day her future with Philip was sealed.

Princess Elizabeth and Prince Philip met again at a Christmas party in 1943. Afterwards the seventeen-year-old Princess kept a photograph of the dazzlingly handsome Prince – with full naval beard and moustache – in her room. The two corresponded, and after the war Philip began to visit Elizabeth at Buckingham Palace.

He came frequently to have supper with her, invariably joined by Margaret. Occasionally the three of them would go out together.

In autumn 1946 King George and Queen Elizabeth invited Philip to join their party at Balmoral. The visit lasted about a month, but no engagement announcement was forthcoming. The King, in particular, was anxious that because of the sheltered life Elizabeth had led she should make the right choice of marriage partner. Both parents were concerned lest she fall too hastily for the first young man to court her.

Elizabeth and Philip were, in fact, allowed to become unofficially engaged, but it was announced, almost at once, that both Princesses were to accompany their parents on a cruise to South Africa early in 1947. This four-month absence would provide the 'cooling off' period it was felt Elizabeth needed. Her parents did not want her to marry before her twenty-first birthday. Elizabeth remained firm in her determination to marry Philip, and their engagement was formally announced in July 1947. They were married on 19 November, and a year later their first son, Charles, was born, followed, less than two years afterwards in August 1950, by Princess Anne.

A newspaper poll undertaken at the time of their engagement showed that 40 per cent of the population was opposed to the match: Philip was foreign, he had German relatives (his sisters were not allowed to attend the wedding), and Britain was involved in acrimonious negotiations with a new government in Greece. Despite his distinguished war record – at twenty-three Philip had been the youngest first lieutenant in the Royal Navy and had his own command – he was not seen as a suitable partner for the Princess. Perhaps it was his negative image, together with a need to prove that he was a man to be taken on his own terms, that decided Philip, once his wife was crowned, to become anything but a deferential consort.

Until the Queen's coronation Philip pursued his career in the Navy with notable success. He was promoted to lieutenant commander at the age of twenty-nine and in 1953 was appointed an admiral of the fleet. Having been so much more than husband and father, the role of consort was not one that would have appealed to him. Although he was soon retired from naval duties he continued to be involved in activities that allowed him to be out of the country for long periods. His opening of the Melbourne Olympic Games in 1956, for instance, incorporated a four-month-long detour to study the wildlife in remote islands that were by no means on a direct sea route from Britain. It was at around this time that rumours began to circulate about Philip's interest in women other than the Queen. A well-known French cabaret singer was said to be his most regular companion. She named her daughter Charlotte. Later there were suggestions that he was involved with a distinguished actress. However, in 1992, when asked about the rumours of his infidelity by Fiammetta Rocca in the *Independent on Sunday*, he said, 'Have you ever stopped to think that for the last 40 years I have never moved anywhere without a policeman accompanying me? So how the *hell* could I get away with anything like that?'

The Duke of Edinburgh, as he had been known since shortly before his marriage, had been able to restore his sense of self-esteem by being in command of a ship. He had become used to travelling – if not drifting – throughout his childhood and adolescence and felt at home on the sea. His private rooms now are as sparsely, neatly and plainly furnished as a ship's cabin, echoing the cold formality of his childhood – in marked contrast to the swags, drapes, pastel colours and clutter preferred by his wife.

His prolonged absences, however, were not compatible with attentive fatherhood: he was absent for six of Prince Charles's first eight birthdays and for several of Princess Anne's earliest ones. Having had little experience of conventional family life himself, and having suppressed the memory of his own traumatic childhood, he was not really in touch with the needs of children.

The Queen, re-enacting *her* childhood, spent long periods away from her children, although she made a point of telephoning them every day. Even so, first as a Princess and later as Queen, she showed little hesitation in leaving her children in the charge of others. Apart from the long and, arguably, essential tours throughout the Commonwealth, Princess Elizabeth toured Northern Ireland when her son was just a few months old, remained in Malta with her husband when Charles had tonsillitis in 1950 – before the availability of appropriate antibiotics this was considered quite a serious condition – and later that year left her two-day-old daughter Anne in London while she attended Princess Margaret's birthday celebrations at Balmoral. She left both children and her sick father the following year when she and Philip took Canada by storm on a highly successful visit. After her coronation the new Queen embarked on yet another tour, this time of six months' duration, when as 'mother' of the peoples of the Commonwealth she was obliged to show herself. Her biological children were the victims of her long absences, and, like her great-great-grandmother Queen Victoria, Queen Elizabeth II was demonstrating that she was at least as good a mother to her subjects as she was to her own flesh and blood. Prince Philip had had a poor role model on which to base his paternal instincts and had been given in his childhood what was thought to have been good for him, including schooling at Gordonstoun. Later he asserted his limited authority by sending his three sons there, against the wishes of the Queen, who had preferred the idea of Eton – sometimes referred to as Windsor's 'local comprehensive'. Philip applauded physical activity but had little understanding of, or interest in, the emotional or intellectual aspects of child-rearing. His daughter, Anne, seemed to get on with him better than anyone because she appeared intuitively to understand this and took up many of his outdoor interests.

Having been brought up surrounded by exotic royal relatives, and unsettled by his earlier experiences, he has tended in adulthood to turn towards the conventional and is suspicious of anyone who strays outside the norm. Prince Philip, hands clasped firmly behind his back, indicates a desire to keep his past behind him as, with his jaw thrust aggressively forward, he faces the future.

Philip's frustration at the disruptions, upheavals and separations of his childhood could account for some of the tactless and irritable comments for which he is renowned. In 1987 he gave offence to the Chinese by warning a group of British students in Beijing that if they stayed much longer they would come back with 'slitty eyes'. He had previously enraged working people in Britain by telling them to 'get their finger out'.

Philip is a man of many parts. He lends his patronage to youth schemes such as the Duke of Edinburgh Awards and Outward Bound, runs a team of polo ponies and keeps carriage horses, activities that are competitive and performance-related. He is also President of the Worldwide Fund for Nature, yet, paradoxically, he shoots. He is an accomplished photographer and a passable painter of wildlife and landscapes. He is said to deride Prince Charles's interest in philosophical and intellectual matters yet admits to reading poetry and sermons. He has been a strict father, possibly as a reaction to his own father's inability to be any sort of father at all. He has shown little interest in life beyond the superficial, as if by digging deeper he might discover things better left undisturbed. When his youngest son Edward decided to abandon his training with the Royal Marines in 1987, expressing a wish to work in the theatre instead of the armed forces, Philip was angry. He felt compelled to encourage his son in conventional military activity and insist on a lifestyle to which Edward was clearly not suited. The pressure of tradition dies hard in him. Dispossessed and displaced as a child, he has made it his business to make a place for himself in Britain. It may have been thought that he would learn tolerance, but he had not acquired it when his children – in particular his sons – most needed it. His attitude to his sons is paradoxical. His own background was insecure, and he could well have been unloading his early conflicts on to them. He has an urge towards creativity acquired with his sisters but typically male defences against it.

Philip displays opposing attitudes towards his three sons and his daughter: it is as if he is in competition with his sons. With Charles he has displayed disappointment mingled with jealousy (Charles will probably be King and Philip never will); from Andrew, who has been able to pursue his naval career, unlike Philip who had to give it up, he withholds approval; and he denigrates Edward's artistic aspirations.

Only towards his daughter does Prince Philip show affection. From the day of Anne's birth her father saw her (as Prince Albert did Vicky and George V his daughter Princess Mary) as a source of love, compensating for the distanced love of his mother. The Princess Royal, who has had her own problems, has, none the less, been spared the ordeal of having to live up to her father. There is between them something that approximates to a 'normal' relationship, underpinned, now that they are both adults, by mutual admiration, affection and approval. It is not unusual for a specific bond to develop between a father and his only daughter, particularly if she aspires to be the 'chip off the old block' her brothers have no ambition to become, realizing from early childhood that this would please him and provoke loving responses that he was only too happy to exchange with her.

Perhaps because he was aware that his own marriage was to some extent arranged, and therefore his choice limited, he refused to support Margaret in her desire to marry Peter Townsend, the man she loved. Philip may have seen Townsend as a member of a privileged clique who had enjoyed the approval of King George VI and who had done everything in his power to blunt Elizabeth's affection for himself.

Philip has expressed his 'otherness' from the royal clan by wearing flannels, rather than the kilt, when he was being 'auditioned' by George VI at Balmoral and by being seen openly drinking, dancing and smoking at nightclubs, after he had taken Princess Elizabeth home at the required hour of 10.30 p.m. Before his marriage he displayed a provocative desire to irritate the powers-that-be, and after it had taken place he strove to retain a separate identity.

King George VI died on 6 February 1952. The following year Elizabeth lost as her adviser Prime Minister Winston Churchill, who had a stroke and on whom she had relied in much the same way as the young Victoria had relied on Lord Melbourne. In March 1953, three months before Elizabeth's coronation, her grandmother Queen Mary also died.

At the coronation the world's attention was focused upon Elizabeth as never before. A series of highly stressful events had marked her life in the previous five or six years, and she appeared tense, gaunt and frightened as she was clothed in her coronation robes by the Archbishop of Canterbury. By the time she walked down the great nave of Westminster Abbey however, anointed and crowned, she radiated dignity, confidence and optimism and displayed a power that was reported by *Time* magazine to represent, express and affect the aspirations of her subjects throughout the world. In demonstrating to the Commonwealth her ability to bear her responsibilities, the Queen found the strength to wear the three-and-a-half-pound symbol of state on her head, the substantial weight of the velvet train behind her and the sceptre and orb in her hands for the long walk down the aisle of Westminster Abbey. Rejoicing in the guardianship of her crown, the new Queen did not immediately remove it on returning to Buckingham Palace.

Sadly for her children – two infants and two as yet unborn – the main thrust of Elizabeth's power and the principal disposition of her strength were to go towards maintenance of the remnants of

Victoria's Empire and the Commonwealth. 'Thank God I was wrong,' wrote Winston Churchill to R.A. Butler in 1953, reflecting on his support of Edward VIII at the time of the Abdication. 'We could not possibly have got a better King.' Churchill was referring to George VI and, by implication, his daughter. But the great surge of royalist euphoria that attended the Queen's coronation lasted only four years, during which Churchill retired, John Osborne wrote in *Look Back in Anger* that the monarchy was 'a gold filling in a mouth full of decay', and rumours of the Duke of Edinburgh's infidelities and Princess Margaret's unseemly passion for a divorcé were circulating.

The Queen was under enormous pressure. In commendable efforts to be progressive she abolished the presentation of débutantes at court, supported the introduction of life peerages, appeared on television for Christmas broadcasts, travelled widely throughout the Commonwealth and endured the criticisms of Lord Altrincham who described her as sounding like a 'priggish schoolgirl' for whom 'it will not be enough to go through the motions: she will have to say things that people will remember and do things on her own initiative which will make people sit up and take notice'. It is evident that this has long since occurred.

In the face of such criticism it is little wonder that the Queen had at times erred on the side of caution, made mistakes, and – although she had good reason to suppose that she would be able to muddle through like any other young mother – been unable to spend more time than she did with her children.

It has been rumoured that before the coronation Elizabeth suffered from stress-related symptoms. Given the adverse life events she had to confront this would have been understandable. Her children must have suffered from her preoccupation with her duties: their mother was not only bereaved but had to cope with the excruciating pressures of her new role. She spent her energy on preserving the institution of the monarchy as well as bringing up her children but left them to join their father – still a serving naval officer – as often as she could.

While she had been raised to believe that nothing was beyond her, and had already proved herself capable, having assumed the Crown at a time when she might reasonably have expected to enjoy several years of relatively normal married life before her accession, nothing in her training had prepared her for her dual role.

A few years into Elizabeth's reign, when some stability might have been anticipated within the family, a new crisis shook the constitution. The Queen was faced with the uncomfortable duty of discouraging Princess Margaret's relationship with Group Captain Peter Townsend, whom she wished to marry.

This public and domestic drama was played out against a backdrop of speculation that problems existed within the Queen's own marriage as her husband's name was linked with those of other women. His long friendship with the French cabaret star was once again scrutinized, and it was suggested that he had a sexual relationship with the actress Pat Kirkwood. (In 1988 Miss Kirkwood told the journalist Terry O'Hanlon that 'I might have developed a crush on him . . . but despite all those rumours we did not have an affair.') The Queen's dignity allowed her to rise above such gossip, however, and by the end of the 1950s harmony seemed to have been restored with the announcement of the Queen's third pregnancy and Princess Margaret's engagement to Antony Armstrong-Jones. Prince Andrew was born in February 1960, three months before Margaret's wedding.

The Queen, despite her unimaginative image, has quietly been much more than the statutory figurehead proclaimed by her detractors. She is said to have opposed Margaret Thatcher over the issue of sanctions against South Africa in 1986, the Prime Minister being opposed to the implementation of such sanctions against the apartheid regime. Rather less significantly, she publicly greeted her daughter-in-law's father Major Ronald Ferguson after his well-publicized visit to a massage parlour. Later she showed a sensitive understanding of the problems occurring in her children's marriages. This displays a tolerance and an independence of spirit that says much for the tolerance and love she experienced as a child. Also, however, it shows that like many other high-principled people she is understanding and forgiving of others' peccadilloes.

The Queen carries her handbag wherever she goes. In a television documentary she even took the bag into breakfast in her own homes. A Jaguar car once owned by the Queen was recently auctioned; the news reports made particular mention of the customized compartment for her handbag. The contents of a woman's handbag – which typically include keys, identity documents, money, driving licence, cheque book, credit cards and makeup – represent both security and independence. A handbag may also represent those aspects of the self that are highly valued, namely integrity, both personal and sexual. The constant presence of the handbag may indicate that the Queen will never relinquish its symbolic contents. Those women unsure of themselves may cling to their handbag through thick and thin and will often feel lost without it. The Queen's handbags, moreover, are unusually large considering that they may need to contain little more than a handkerchief and a lipstick. Compared with the diminutive clutch purses held by Madame Delors or Nancy Reagan at photo calls before state dinners, the Queen's bag seems out of proportion. Perhaps its size indicated the extent of her need for a prop. The Queen's ubiquitous handbag gives the lie to all that we have come to believe about aspects of her security and independence. Of all the royals since Victoria, she alone has received appropriate and at least adequate parental attention. While acknowledging her undoubted strength of purpose and leadership, however, and until recently her command of her mount when she took the salute as colonel-in-chief of the Regiment at the Trooping the Colour ceremony every year, we see that she carries her survival kit with her almost everywhere. Only at Balmoral where she feels most secure, and at sporting events where she is in touch with her true self, has she been seen to abandon it. Even at the races, however, the Queen has a prop – her binoculars. These have a more practical purpose than the almost empty handbag but they are, none the less, a comforting weight at her side and something with which she can screen her face and mask her emotions when she feels free to enjoy herself.

From Balmoral Queen Victoria's 'I will be good' echoes down the generations. Queen Elizabeth has displayed the same sense of duty at the expense of her children as Victoria but has been only as good a mother to them as her commitments have allowed. In a speech in the City of London to mark the fortieth anniversary of her accession to the throne Queen Elizabeth admitted that members of her family, by implication like any other family, were not immune to the consequences of human frailty. She pleaded for more understanding and expressed the hope that history would take a more compassionate view than those of contemporary commentators. The year 1992 had certainly not been a happy one. First Andrew's and then Charles's marriage finally came to an end, and the fire that threatened the destruction of Windsor Castle, if not the House of Windsor itself, seemed an omen from the ashes of which the phoenix of a 'new' monarchy might arise. There is no doubt of the 'quality' love that Queen Elizabeth II has bestowed on Charles, Anne, Andrew and Edward, but 'quantity' love – the continuing availability of one care-giver for as long as it is needed – has not, of necessity, been available to them.

Paradoxically she has also been a good 'father' to her children, just as George VI was a good father to her, since Philip was often emotionally distanced from them. A father serves no biological need in being present during his children's upbringing. By nature he is the provider, the hunter, the protector. In that all the family's wealth is invested in her, Queen Elizabeth, like Queen Victoria, has been 'father' and 'mother' to both her people and her children. Sadly, in the case of both these monarchs, it is the children who, in having to share her so extensively, may have lost out.

9

PRINCESS MARGARET

'Now that Papa is King, I am nothing.'
– Her Royal Highness Princess Margaret

For Princess Margaret Rose, born to parents who were hoping for a boy, life would not be easy. She was the first female member of the Royal Family in recent times to test the boundaries of the rigid formality into which she was born. She blazed a trail that has been enthusiastically followed by the next generation. So convinced were the Duke and Duchess of York that their second child would be a boy that girls' names had not even been considered for the new baby. 'Margaret' and 'Rose' were names quickly chosen to pre-empt her grandmother, Queen Mary, insisting on her preferences.

Margaret Rose, as she was then known, was destined to be neither a favourite child nor a favourite grandchild. Queen Mary, who described Elizabeth as 'enchanting', considered her younger sister 'very ugly'. Physically Margaret Rose was different from her sister. She was small and dark and in appearance unlike other members of the House of Windsor. From the beginning she was compared unfavourably with her sister, which would have made her feel unwanted, unloved and excluded and left her with the impression that she was always to be the odd one out. Queen Mary's tactless remark to her second granddaughter, 'Why are you so small? Why don't you grow up?' would have done nothing for Margaret's already low self-esteem.

'Let Margo burn,' Princess Elizabeth is reported to have said when her sister chose to stay in bed during morning fire drills at Sandringham. This may have been intended to be humorous, but, according to Freud, there is no such thing as a joke, and the remark might have reflected barely concealed animosity.

Although Elizabeth would seem to have been the favoured one, it was she who was displaced when Margaret Rose was born, and it is quite possible that she felt some hostility towards her sister. Given the circumstances of their respective childhoods and the separations from their parents, each might have assumed that the other was receiving the most parental attention.

The two sisters were, for the most part, close to and fond of each other, but this would not preclude Elizabeth's taking advantage of her seniority, leaving Margaret Rose angry and frustrated. However devoted two sisters may be, jealousy will inevitably be felt at times. 'Look after your Empire, and I'll look after my life' is said to have been Margaret's sharp retort as an adult to the Queen after being reprimanded by her sister for her flirtatious behaviour. This remark must surely reflect feelings suppressed in the nursery. Elizabeth and Margaret did, in the event, attend to their respective spheres of influence, and each, in their own way, was moderately successful.

Young Margaret Rose's feelings of jealousy and of her own unimportance were reflected in her childhood complaint to her parents, 'You gave Lilibet three names. Why didn't you give me three instead of only two?' and later, as a girl of sixteen, it is said that she sulked if she was not allowed the same degree of freedom that Lilibet was gradually acquiring.

Her feeling of inferiority, reinforced by her diminutive stature – she was barely five feet two inches tall – was later echoed when she continued to wear platform-heeled shoes and bouffant hairstyles long after both had gone out of fashion in an attempt to elevate both her presence and her stature.

Princess Margaret was, like her father, left-handed, which may have added to her sense of apartness. She took after her mother in height and had a tendency to put on weight. Again mirroring both her parents she suffered from unintentional neglect and discrimination in childhood, which reinforced her compulsive needs.

Margaret Rose was born in 1930 at Glamis, her mother's family home. Here, at least, there was rejoicing at the arrival of the first royal Princess to be born in Scotland, and the announcement of her birth was celebrated by the lighting of beacons across the country. At the time there was no reason to suppose that the Duke and Duchess of York would not eventually produce a male heir; there was therefore no pressure on Margaret Rose to be anything other than a welcome addition to the York family.

Unfortunately, however, she was considered unattractive not only by her grandmother but later by her governess, Marion Crawford, who openly favoured Elizabeth. In her book *The Little*

Princesses she described the two sisters in their bathing costumes before their first swimming lessons. 'Lilibet looked so pretty in hers. She was a long, slender child with beautiful legs. Margaret, everyone owned, looked like a plump navy-blue fish.'

An antipathy existed between Marion Crawford and Clara Knight (Alla), who was in charge of the nursery and who cared for Margaret Rose in the years after Elizabeth had begun lessons.

It is likely that Marion Crawford's greater attachment to Princess Elizabeth came about because when she first came to teach the girls Margaret was still a baby. Crawfie had several years of a one-to-one relationship with Elizabeth before Margaret was old enough to join them for lessons.

Margaret Rose's small stature and her boisterousness contributed to her being thought of as the baby of the family long after she was emotionally mature. Just as Clara Knight was reluctant to see Margaret join Elizabeth in the schoolroom, her father later refused to acknowledge that she was a woman with womanly emotions, which might be associated with her need for 'fatherly' attention. George VI died unaware that Margaret had been in love with a married man since she was sixteen. Perhaps the King, having been obliged to instruct Elizabeth in her future responsibilities as Queen, had wanted to keep Margaret a child as long as he could.

Margaret was not only dressed identically to her sister but often had to wear Elizabeth's hand-me-downs, which gave her what Cecil Beaton described as a 'home-made' look. Their identical frocks may have been a source of irritation to Margaret – who felt unable to express her own personality – but her mother, keen to set an example of domestic thrift and penalizing only Margaret, let it be known that Elizabeth's clothes, sometimes identical to garments Margaret had outgrown, were always saved until the younger sister had grown into them. At their parents' coronation in 1937 Margaret was dismayed to find that her train was shorter than her sister's. Elizabeth was given regular pocket money, while Margaret received the occasional shilling. The bias went deeper than pocket money: Margaret was not allowed to attend the gillies' ball at Balmoral at the age at which Elizabeth first went; she was not encouraged to drive until some time after she was legally allowed to; when the two girls toured South Africa with their parents after the Second World War, and were each given a collection of diamonds, Margaret's were inferior. It is hardly surprising that, having been brought up to think small, when she chose a car for herself in the early 1960s she selected a Mini.

Princess Margaret was clever, had a love of mimicry (like the Prince Consort and her mother) and was cheeky, charming and manipulative. Queen Mary described her as 'so outrageously amusing that one can't help but encourage her'. That from an early age Margaret had to develop a seductive charm and manipulative behaviour to provoke loving responses from indifferent adults is a sad reflection on her parents and governess. Throughout her adult life she was always looking for an alternative to the nurturing she failed to receive in her childhood. The apotheosis of this lay in her doomed relationship with Group Captain Townsend.

Margaret sensed that the role in which she would be most acceptable within the family was that of 'tearaway'. Elizabeth Longford recounts how Margaret was dressed as an angel for a children's fancy-dress party. Her mother remarked, with amusement, that she did not look very angelic. 'That's all right,' replied Margaret. 'I'll be a Holy Terror.'

Royal children are taught to ride as a matter of course, but unlike her sister Margaret never developed a love of horses, dogs or any outdoor activity although she was encouraged to do so by her parents and governess. She certainly never favoured any of the blood sports. Margaret's interests, by and large, removed her from the mainstream of Royal Family life, but since that in itself seems not to have been particularly agreeable to her it is understandable that she should have turned her back on it. Her apparent wish to make night into day, often frequenting night-spots and dark theatres, contrasts sharply with Elizabeth's love of fresh-air pursuits. (During the painful years between her decision not to marry Peter Townsend and her eventual marriage to Antony Armstrong-Jones, she and her friends staged a revue to raise money for a children's charity, for which Margaret not only understudied but played the part of a night-club hostess.) In *The Picnic Papers*, published in 1983, in which social luminaries were asked to describe their favourite picnics, Margaret's was indoors at the Banqueting House of Hampton Court. 'Night' and 'darkness' are reminders of childhood separation from care-givers: a neglected child may never learn to cope with being alone at night. Many children avoid going to bed for as long as possible each evening, because they are afraid that their parents may die while they are asleep, leaving them to fend for themselves. Margaret's need to turn night into day was perhaps a defence against her separation fears.

As a child Margaret came into her own in family charades and pantomimes. Dressing-up and appearing before an appreciative audience provided her with welcome attention. On reaching adulthood she turned to the fantasy world of the theatre and later to the sunshine and warmth of the West Indies to bask in its 'nurturing' sun, an attempt to enjoy a life-enhancer freely available to all. Princess Margaret lived in Kensington Palace but owned no property in Britain. The only place she could call her own was a house in the Caribbean, on the island of Mustique given to her as a wedding present by her eccentric friend the late Colin Tennant. Living on an island satisfied her expectations of being cut off from mainland and mainstream activity.

Like many lonely children Margaret had imaginary friends. She shifted the blame on to 'Cousin Halifax', 'Pinkle Ponkle' and 'Bombax' for her alleged misdemeanours. She learned to gain attention by being disobedient and excused her behaviour by absolving herself of responsibility and displacing it on to her 'friends'. In the garden of the replica house at Frogmore, Y Bythwyn Bach, given to the girls by the people of Wales, Princess Margaret chose to grow potatoes (buried in earth and, like her, seldom to see the light of day) rather than the more obvious fragrant flowers chosen and chosen and grown by her sister Elizabeth. As a young woman, when Margaret sat for one of her first official portraits without her sister in a Hartnell ballgown, she remarked to Cecil Beaton that the elegant embroidery on the dress reminded her of potato peel.

The differences between the two Princesses became even more apparent as Margaret grew older. She smoked, even against medical advice following lung surgery in 1985, and occasionally drank excessively, while Elizabeth both as Princess or Queen did neither – although in 1982 Michael Fagan, an intruder who scaled the walls of Buckingham Palace and found his way into the Queen's bedroom, claimed that Her Majesty had a packet of cigarettes on her bedside table and that he asked if he could have one. (Of course may be an unreliable witness.) Margaret's addictive habits perhaps partially compensated for her lack of maternal attention in childhood:

substitutes for the breast are inevitably oral. Her father, whose childhood was also deprived, drank and smoked to excess, while her mother, who was more or less abandoned by her mother (who was increasingly unavailable after her two sons died), was also known to imbibe small but regular amounts of alcohol.

Unlike Elizabeth, in adulthood Margaret always chose her own friends – uncommon in the Royal Family. While Elizabeth is said to avoid evening engagements whenever possible and when she is at home enjoys a simple meal on a tray, her sister would give dinner parties for her friends at Kensington Palace or would go with them to the opera or to restaurants.

Elizabeth grew up a conformist and Margaret a rebel. In her wish to please both parents the elder daughter followed many of the Queen's mainly outdoor interests but Margaret, finding it difficult to gain the approval she needed, gave up trying and opted instead for opposition. According to Lady Airlie her father referred to her as an '*enfant terrible*'.

Only when her parents were crowned in 1937 could the six-year-old Margaret have begun to realize the way in which her life might develop. Disruption following the Abdication, the family move, first to Buckingham Palace and then to Windsor after the outbreak of war in 1939, must have been both baffling and exciting for her. The 'second-fiddle' Princess must have noticed that her father spent more and more time with her sister than with her, and she was probably envious that Elizabeth was able to join the Auxiliary Territorial Service while she was still at lessons with Crawfie. Her high spirits, at the same time indulged and deplored, were the only way she knew of asserting herself.

In 1947, when Princess Margaret was sixteen, she accompanied her parents and sister on an extended post-war tour of South Africa. It was during this trip that she fell in love with the man she would not be allowed to marry. It was the first time she had been allowed to wear clothes of her own choosing that were neither cast-offs nor copies of her sister's and that she was treated as an adult, particularly during her official engagements. Her father's equerry Group Captain Peter Townsend was deputed to be a companion for the two young Princesses, and four months later, by the time the tour ended, a strong affection had developed between him and Margaret.

The romance was decorous, conducted properly and privately,

and the bond between them became stronger over the next few years. Margaret continued to go to parties, the theatre and night-clubs with her friends, while Townsend quietly divorced his wife, citing her adultery. The furore when the relationship became public did not surface until 1953, after the Queen's coronation.

The likelihood of Margaret's acceding to the throne became more remote with the birth of each of her sister's children. When the Duke of Edinburgh was created Regent upon his wife's coronation, Margaret lost her right of regency and was no longer a Privy Counsellor. While never having voiced a wish to be queen, as far as we know, Margaret must have been aware of her diminishing constitutional importance and, as a consequence, displayed ever less reverence for duty than her sister. Her strongest suit was her personal charisma and popularity, which was followed with interest by the media and which brought about the cataclysm in her life. By the time she was crowned, Elizabeth was a young matron with domestic as well as constitutional responsibilities and Margaret was required to stand in for her sister on many public occasions; her expertise as a deputy, her charm and good looks attracted attention wherever she went. She even inadvertently upstaged her sister at the coronation – with disastrous personal results.

When Margaret casually removed a speck of fluff from Peter Townsend's jacket before the world's cameramen their secret was out. In an unguarded moment, with her unambiguous proprietorial gesture – more shocking at the time than Sarah Ferguson's South of France exposure forty years later – Margaret had as good as announced publicly that Peter Townsend was the man for whom she cared. When she confirmed to her sister that she wanted to marry Townsend, a family and a constitutional crisis simultaneously erupted. The abdication of Edward VIII was too fresh in the public mind and family memory for there to be any question of a member of the Royal Family marrying a divorcé. Margaret's relationship with Group Captain Peter Townsend was discouraged and a judicious separation arranged.

Townsend was posted to Belgium, and Margaret was given to understand that if she waited until she was twenty-five and still wished to marry Townsend she would be permitted to do so on condition that she renounced her right of succession and forfeited all royal privileges including her Civil List income. These sanctions, coupled with pressure from her family and from the Church, led her to make a poignant public statement in which she said she had decided to give up Group Captain Peter Townsend. In the vanguard of those who pressed hardest for her rebuttal of him was her brother-in-law Prince Philip.

It was at about this time that Margaret bought herself a tiara. In the Royal Family, by tradition, it is only married women who wear tiaras; these are family heirlooms usually bestowed at the time of a wedding. Believing that she was never to receive one through marriage Margaret – like any unhappy woman who consoles herself with a new hairstyle or outfit – went shopping for a tiara. Denied her wish to marry the man who loved her, Margaret suffered a blow not only to her self-esteem but to her femininity. Hair symbolizes sexuality and is a woman's 'crowning glory', thus Margaret made a statement about her sexuality, her femininity and her attractiveness by emphasizing hers with a tiara.

In 1956 Margaret accepted a proposal of marriage from an old flame, Billy Wallace, but the engagement, on her side, was as short-lived as it was half-hearted. The Princess was unwilling to compromise and not yet ready to enter into a serious new relationship. It was another three years – probably spent in loneliness and resentment – before she announced her engagement to Antony Armstrong-Jones, whom she married in 1960. Noël Coward wrote that some members of the family disapproved of the match: Marina, Duchess of Kent, and Princess Alexandra 'were not pleased . . . there was a distinct *froideur* when I mentioned it'. Her immediate family, however, was relieved.

For a while Princess Margaret appeared to be happy with her husband, but in 1977, after they had been living amicably apart for some time, they agreed to divorce. In the light of this divorce, and those of other close family members more recently, the Princess had every right to feel bitter that she was prevented by royal protocol from marrying the man she loved.

The aftermath of the break-up of her marriage, civilized as this was, and the media attention that was focused on her a year later during her friendship with Roddy Llewellyn, took its toll. She was believed to have overdosed on sleeping tablets, but she denied this. 'I was so exhausted because of everything that all I wanted to do was sleep . . . and I did, right through to the following afternoon.'

When she was asked whether she would ever marry again, the Princess's reply was 'Remarriage would be a devil of a trouble. And one would not want to be a bind . . . But if one did find someone nice . . .' Through this wistful, yet candid and defiant statement Margaret reveals her sense of humility – coupled, in her use of RAF slang, with an unconscious reminder of Group Captain Townsend.

Princess Margaret lived in a large grace-and-favour apartment in Kensington Palace. After her divorce she had one much-publicized romantic involvement with a younger man, but there has was no suggestion of remarriage. Her children and friends – clever, amusing, artistic and discreet – seemed to sustain her, as did her passion for opera, ballet and the theatre.

Given her sad history and the social expectations of her day, it is not hard to see how Princess Margaret came to be perceived by some as hedonistic and irresponsible. She had, in fact, fulfilled more than her share of royal duties and had graciously bestowed her patronage on numerous worthy causes. The Royal Family give their support to the charities of their own choice, and Margaret had involved herself with the Migraine Trust, perhaps understandably since her life has been such a headache; she became Patron of the National Society for the Prevention of Cruelty to Children, identifying with disadvantaged children – as later the Princess of Wales did with Aids victims – having been disadvantaged in childhood by always seeing herself as the 'number two' Princess. The way in which she brought up her own son and daughter reflects her awareness of the need in all children for loving attention.

As a young mother, however, she left her son shortly after his birth when she went on holiday to the West Indies. In the unenlightened climate of the day, as far as child-rearing was concerned, she was spared the public outcry that ensued when Sarah, Duchess of York, left her baby to join her husband in Australia. Margaret's two children appear to be well adjusted and successful, although her son Viscount Linley has had his share of ups and downs. The custom-built furniture business he established has thrived, but he has collected a string of speeding convictions and demonstrated a degree of public arrogance. Moreover there were unconfirmed reports in 2007 that he was the royal at the centre of a well-publicized gay-sex videotape scandal. He married Serena Petersham in 1993, and they have two children. Her daughter, Sarah, now Lady

Sarah Chatto, is a painter and lives quietly with her husband and children outside of the royal spotlight.

Self-expression is difficult for members of the Royal Family. Princess Margaret never sought to make her views public but managed to achieve a degree of self-fulfilment and gain self-esteem through her many artistic interests and involvement with selected charities. In her heyday she was the 'Princess Diana' of her devoted public, and, like the Princess of Wales, her every move was followed, photographed and commented upon. But unlike Princess Diana she failed to make more than minor changes to the nation's perception of the Royal Family. Greater changes had to wait for the fall-out from the marriage of her nephew Prince Charles to nineteen-year-old Lady Diana Spencer in 1981.

Princess Margaret died in hospital from a stroke at the age of seventy-one in 2002. She had lived quietly during her later years and was a devout Christian, and the faith that helped her through major surgery emphasized her moral strength. She acquired a serenity and dignity more often associated with her sister, and although it has been claimed that she was a difficult woman she was often misunderstood and underestimated. The stories of the 'fairy-tale' childhood that had always been ascribed to her did not take into account the less favourable aspects of her upbringing.

The Princess described herself as being no angel. When she said that she had no ambition or that only her startlingly blue eyes were worth looking at she displayed the same false modesty as that with which the Princess of Wales announced publicly that she has a brain 'the size of a pea'. Both Princesses were 'fishing': they longed to be contradicted and thereby reassured of their value. Many paradoxes surrounded Margaret: having been at the epicentre of a major constitutional crisis she was able to say, 'In our family we do not have rifts. A very occasional row but never a rift.' Having associated herself with the unconventional and theatrical she refused to be photographed with Boy George because of his appearance; having courted the attention of the media with her eyebrow-raising activities she was able to announce, 'I have been misreported and misrepresented since the age of seventeen.' Although somehow she managed to weather her storms, the price was high. Her friend Jocelyn Stevens said, 'I have always regarded her as a bird in a gilded cage. She would have loved to break free but was never able to.'

Had a film been made of the life of Princess Margaret the obvious choice for the role would have been Elizabeth Taylor. The two women were the same age, shared similar physical characteristics and endured and overcame many of the same problems. They had glamour, courage and spirit and surmounted the disadvantage of having been in the public eye since childhood. Both were survivors. The long shadow of her great-great-grandmother fell on Margaret. All her life she tried to be 'good' and 'dutiful', but she had neither Queen Victoria's position nor her power.

Princess Margaret had a large collection of seashells, which she kept in Kensington Palace and tended herself. This collection perhaps symbolizes the inner vulnerability and softness that lay beneath the carapace under which she concealed her vicissitudes. With her ear to an empty shell, if she listened carefully, she might hear the sea on the shore of a tropical island, the distant sounds of a paradise she once glimpsed but lost, never to regain.

10

PRINCE CHARLES

'When the husband walks back from the altar, he has already
swallowed the choicest dainties of his banquet. The beef and pudding
of married life are then in store for him – or perhaps only the bread
and cheese.' – Anthony Trollope, *Framley Parsonage*

By the summer of 1992 the unhappy relationship between the Prince
and Princess of Wales had reached crisis point. Widespread sympathy for Diana was due, in part, to Andrew Morton's *Diana: Her
True Story*, published apparently with the Princess's approval, which
revealed her version of what the marriage had been. When a tape-
recording of what purported to be a conversation between the
Princess and a male friend was made public, many people wanted
to believe that it had been faked, while others thought that it was
indeed the voice of the Princess complaining about her treatment by
her husband. It was generally felt that the media had overstepped
the mark in sensationalism and gone beyond the bounds of decency
in their invasion of privacy.

The 'Diana tape', available for a while to telephone callers and
its contents transcribed and printed in the *Sun*, followed the newspaper publication of photographs of the topless Duchess of York on
holiday in the South of France, embracing her 'financial adviser'
beside a swimming-pool, taken immediately before the Duchess was
said to be returning to Balmoral to patch up her marriage. That the
Duchess's two small daughters Princesses Beatrice and Eugenie and
her detectives were witness to the impropriety seemed inexcusable.
The reputation of the House of Windsor was being destabilized as
much by its members as by the media, and the continuing existence
of the monarchy, in its present form at any rate, seemed seriously in
question.

In the light of these revelations and playing devil's advocate, the
newspapers howled not for the blood of the Royal Family – whose
activities, after all, sold a great many newspapers – but for a curb to
their privileges and, in keeping with the recessionary times, a tax on
the Queen's fabled income. Throughout all the mud-slinging, rivers
of condemnatory newsprint – from salacious tabloids to respected

broadsheets – and the full-frontal attacks that the sexual revelations made on her family, the Queen maintained a dignified silence.

What, if any, conclusions can be drawn from the fact that it was the marriages contracted *outside* the royal circle – Princess Margaret and the Earl of Snowdon, the Princess Royal and Captain Mark Phillips, the Duke and Duchess of York, and the Prince and Princess of Wales – that seemed to have come to grief? Did the old dictum that royalty must marry royalty (however minor) account for the previous apparent stability of the reigning family? Would Charles's union have had a greater chance of success had he married Marie-Astrid of Luxembourg with whom his name had been linked before his marriage to Diana Spencer?

In the light of tabloid intrusion and all forms of electronic social messaging the Royal Family has lost its cherished privacy. Customs and behaviour adhered to over millennia are in danger of dis-integrating – not through marital crises with their ensuing scandals, nor because the prejudiced have become more prejudiced and the judgemental more condemning but because 'Buckingham Palace' has become a soap opera beamed into our homes by television cameras. The Royal Family, hitherto a 'closed' or 'secret' society, has been infiltrated by commoners lacking an overriding sense of duty, untrained by years of conditioning to maintain 'in-house' confidentiality. Demystification, now leading many to see the Royal Family as they see themselves, may gradually rebound upon itself, making the need for them redundant. As a nation we are unhappy with behaviour we feel is conspicuous and ostentatious; as individuals we value self-effacement and modesty. Splitting off the extravagant in ourselves and displacing it on to the Royal Family enables us to disown an aspect of our psyche frowned on by our culture.

The Prince of Wales regards himself as being the end product of centuries of carefully planned breeding. He acknowledges that in his blood and bones reside the aspirations of nations. With his separation from Diana the future of the Royal Family was seriously threatened. How much of the responsibility can be laid at Charles's door? Trained all his life for kingship and, having played fast and loose with his marriage, he appears to have shot himself in the foot. If the so-called 'Camillagate tapes' that emerged in Britain in 1993 are ever proved conclusively genuine there could be the major constitutional problem of a self-confessed adulterer assuming the role of Defender of the Faith and Head of the Church of England when such activity is proscribed by that Church.

Like his great-uncle Edward VIII, a former Prince of Wales, Charles demands the deference and privilege of his rank but simultaneously wants to be seen as a man of the people. Needing the security of limits and boundaries Charles is a stickler for protocol – any informality seems forced and artificial and appears to have been stage-managed. Only his immediate family may call him by his first name, and even his former girlfriends were required to address him as 'sir'. His well-publicized interest in social problems, the environment, architecture and competitive sport reflects a need for structure and acceptance by his peers, since the 'architecture' of his inner world seems uncertain and in peril. His concern with the problems of farmers in the Duchy of Cornwall echoes his great-uncle Edward VIII's hollow remark in the face of the sufferings of miners in South Wales that 'Something must be done'. Might Charles and his predecessor have been asking for something to be done for *them*, to redress unrecognized wrongs within their respective psyches?

Princess Elizabeth and the Duke of Edinburgh might well have supposed when Charles was born in November 1948 – his father was playing squash at the time – that since his grandfather King George VI was only fifty-three and seemed likely to reign for many more years that their son's early childhood could safely resemble as far as possible that of any other young aristocrat. They hoped to create an 'ordinary' environment for him at their homes in Clarence House and at Windsor, although since Charles was second in the line of succession this idea seemed far-fetched. The premature death of George VI in 1952 threw Charles's immediate family into turmoil and put paid to any hopes of 'normality' as far as his upbringing was concerned.

In any event, he was unlikely to have experienced anything other than minimal parental involvement during his infancy. His father was a serving naval officer, and his mother joined her husband abroad whenever she could. Elizabeth was also expected to resume her royal duties towards the end of Charles's first year. He thus spent a great deal of time with his grandparents, and a special bond of affection grew between him and Queen Elizabeth, the Queen Mother, echoing the bonds that had existed between Queen Alexandra and her grandsons, as well as that between George V and Princess Elizabeth. Charles remained Queen Elizabeth's favourite grandchild, and this could be seen to have compensated her for never having had a son herself.

His sister Anne was born twenty-one months after Charles. She was only four months old at Christmas in 1950, when her parents spent several weeks together in Malta leaving the two children at home with the King and Queen. In 1951 they were again left behind, when Elizabeth and the Duke of Edinburgh embarked on the tour of Africa which was cut short in February 1952 by the death of George VI. Although the Princess did her best to communicate with her children on the telephone every day when she was away, it was of necessity a 'long-distance' affection or 'love at arm's length' she was expressing, such as Charles would come to believe was acceptable in his later commitments.

Three women were influential in Charles's early life: his mother, whom he respected but to whom he was not close, and two nannies, Mabel Anderson and Helen Lightbody, with whom he was more intimate and who provided him with constant and ongoing affection. This pattern of a loving 'hands-on' relationship with his nannies and a more formal one with his mother led to a need for two simultaneous partners throughout his life. His wife Diana – at first the untouchable Madonna on a pedestal, looked up to but out of reach – had always to compete with other women, notably Camilla Parker Bowles who reflected the warmth and love of his erstwhile nannies.

Charles was put in the care of several other surrogates during his childhood, leading him to believe that others, usually women, would always be available to him. He was never short either of paid attendants (nannies and teachers), unpaid ones (his grandparents) or other admirers (his watchful and appreciative public). His routine at Buckingham Palace was strict and his time with his mother, when she was at home, was limited. He would be dressed by 7 a.m., spend two hours in the nursery and then visit the Queen at 9 if her schedules permitted. He saw his mother again at teatime, and she would occasionally bathe him, after which he was sometimes dressed again to be presented to distinguished visitors. By the time he was three Charles had learned to bow to his grandmother and to stand in his grandfather's presence unless given permission to sit

PRINCE CHARLES

down. These rituals were perpetuated throughout his early adult life, and it is said that as a young man he would insist that those leaving his presence do so backwards. It is conceivable that he does not feel happy or comfortable when people have their backs to him and sees this as a rejection, having been sensitized to being 'turned away from' by frequently absent parents. In his expectations of deference from all with whom he associates, he is re-enacting, through role-reversal, what was expected of him as a child. Self-aggrandizing rituals may also be seen as a defence against feelings of inadequacy: it is hard for a child to convince himself that there is a valid reason for his parents' absence without his suspecting that he is to blame for it and that he is unworthy of their love. Anthony Holden has described Charles's father as being little more than a 'stranger' who described his first-born son dismissively as a 'plum-pudding' to him during his childhood. The Duke of Edinburgh was probably unaware of the importance of his presence on the occasions of his elder children's rites of passage, since he was absent for six out of Charles's first eight birthdays.

When George VI died at the age of fifty-eight and Charles became heir apparent, his mother had to cope simultaneously with her grief at the death of her beloved father and the burden of her new responsibilities. She became preoccupied with the preparations for and the consequences of her coronation. Family concern with her sister's romance with Group Captain Peter Townsend, and the move to Buckingham Palace from Clarence House caused further tensions. Charles's status within the royal household was immediately changed, and at the age of four he was assigned his own car and driver. Far from being bewildered by this treatment, Charles grew up to accept not only distant parenting but also special privileges as the norm.

By the time he became heir to the throne the paradoxes that were to characterize his life were increasing: he was being encouraged to be independent long before he was ready for it, and therefore his dependent needs were ignored. No child at such an age should be asked to play a role for which he is not ready, while having withheld from him the love, support and attention only a mother can provide. Jealous of the duties and obligations that took his mother away from him, and envious of his siblings whom he would have felt were the recipients of the love he was missing, Charles grew up to be fiercely competitive with all males. In describing his brother Andrew as 'the one with the Robert Redford looks' he was expressing both insecurity about his own appearance (reinforced as a child by being nicknamed 'Fatty' at school and teased about the size and shape of his ears) and his feelings of being short-changed by his parents. His sister Anne established a bond of affection with their father that Charles never achieved. His younger brothers enjoyed childhoods in which their parents were around much more and had possibly ingested some of the wisdom of child-rearing disseminated by, among others, Dr Benjamin Spock whose book on child care had become a household bible.

Charles's resentment of his siblings was displaced on to his relationship with Princess Diana: he was sometimes as dismissive of his children's needs as he felt his parents were of his. He is on record as saying, 'Girls are so much nicer than boys, don't you think?' (a comment he perhaps heard in the nursery) and 'I would love to have a daughter', perhaps reflecting his hope that a loving daughter, like Prince Albert's Vicky or George VI's Lilibet, would make up to him for the disappointments he experienced as a child.

Charles was old enough at the time of his grandfather's death to be aware of his mother's distress and of her increased public obligations, but he learned by imitation that emotions must be controlled and that the self-sufficiency demanded by parental unavailability was essential. Many parents value and reward 'pseudo-independence'; as a result, their children grow up in isolation with an arrogant disregard for the fundamental need to relate to others – which, indeed, was noticed in Queen Victoria as a girl. In adult life Charles's privileges led him to become solitary, over-solemn, to approach friendship with caution and to experience difficulties in integrating with his peers. Charles's behaviour was fashioned by the formality of the Palace, by the constant presence of the adults by whom he was surrounded and by their high expectations of him. He was required to be tidy and neatly groomed at all times since he was frequently 'on show', and his over-concern with appearance has persisted. A preoccupation with the outward façade is often a defence against inner decay, which may be neither recognized nor acknowledged. He is criticized for emphasizing how buildings look rather than how they function, which might well have been the case in his own home with Diana, a home definitely not in good order.

Many had refused to believe the problems that were leaked almost daily to the press. The Royal Family's more loyal subjects tended to believe the monarchy was above reproach. Royalty has a human face, but hitherto few had wanted to see it. Until the arrival of Diana Spencer and, more recently, Kate Middleton, the Royal Family had feared that public disclosure would eat away at its fabric and, if not sympathetically managed, could lead to its demise. Millions throughout the world who depend on the existence of royalty refuse to accept this possibility. The Royal Family acts as blotting paper for our envy and jealousy, pride and inability to express love and devotion. As with the icons of the Russian Orthodox Church, we may see only a two-dimensional image, but it is one that allows us to focus beyond on to a 'Holy Family' through whom we can experience hope and aspiration, rage and violence, love and compassion. The secularization of this fantasy family would leave us having to deal with emotions within ourselves.

When Charles was five his formal education began under the tutelage of a young Scottish woman, Catherine Peebles. The change in his routine coincided with his parents' absence on a six-month tour abroad. He was no longer seeing as much of his nannies as he had done before, and an exaggerated sense of self-sufficiency was forced upon him early. His need for love to help him adapt to the many changes in his usual routine would have been intense. His anger at having parental attention withheld when it was most needed may have encouraged him to seek scapegoats to punish in adult life. Although it was his mother who was responsible for the absences that led to Charles's early 'independence', it was another 'mother' – Diana – who bore the brunt of his suppressed hostility. This was well illustrated when, shortly after their engagement, she caused a sensation by appearing at a charity gala wearing a strapless black taffeta dress. Charles disguised his disapproval by declaring that black was an unsuitable colour for her, but in reality his discomfort was related to the public glimpse of her breasts caught as she was getting out of her limousine, the ultimate source of nurture – and in his case a disappointing one.

As a child Charles did not demonstrate outstanding intellectual ability. He found it difficult to learn because of the absence of other children in the school. As an adult, however, he likes to mix with academics – architects, writers, historians and philosophers.

When he was eight Charles was sent to Hill House School in Knightsbridge, at which point Catherine Peebles left the family's employ – another change associated with the absence of a care-giver. Charles was the first heir to the British throne to go to school: to begin with he attended only in the afternoon, whereas the other children were there full-time; they integrating with one another throughout the day, leaving him isolated and lonely. Some months later another change took place when he was sent to his father's former preparatory school, Cheam, by now located in Hampshire. The Queen asked the headmaster if he would kindly explain to the parents and to the other boys that Charles must be treated as any other pupil. Inevitably he was not. He found it hard to make friends, and, not unlike other children sent to boarding-school, had difficulty in adjusting to sleeping in a dormitory after having his own quarters in Buckingham Palace. He remembers his early days there as being disagreeable and unhappy.

Eventually he learned to mix, but, being aware of his position and suspicious of other boys' motives, he was wary of overtures of friendship. When teased, he learned to retaliate with his fists. His reports were quite promising, but the only subject for which he had any noticeable gift was music. Sport was encouraged, and, doubtless to his father's satisfaction, Charles became captain of both cricket and rugby, but apart from polo, on which his father was keen, Charles displayed no interest in team games after he left Cheam.

Gordonstoun, where his father had been Guardian or head boy, followed. The Queen had wanted Charles to go to Eton, which was close to Windsor and his family, but Philip was adamant that the rigours of Gordonstoun were what were needed to toughen up his son. He also mistakenly believed that its remote location would spare Charles from the public gaze. Charles was less keen than his father on the pursuit of 'rugged individualism', but he lost weight, fished and enjoyed seeing his grandmother whose private home, the Castle of Mey, was near by. He made respectable but not spectacular academic progress.

By the time he was ready to go up to Cambridge in 1967 Britain was undergoing social changes that threatened to make the Prince of Wales an anachronism. A socialist government was in power, and the monarchy was openly criticized. The mid to late 1960s saw the continuing rise of a 'youth cult', and it is hard to imagine a more mature teenager than Prince Charles. His short, neat hair was as unfashionable as his formal clothes and the upper-class vowels of his speech.

At Trinity College, Cambridge, Prince Charles studied history and archaeology, a choice that proved apposite, unconsciously driven, as he was, by an internal, unresolved and almost certainly unrecognized concern with his personal past. The mistakes of the past will be repeated by all those who forget it. Although 'lest we forget' memorials were erected everywhere after the First World War, another generation had clearly forgotten what had gone before and therefore repeated the vicious persecutor–victim cycle. An individual understanding of history cannot affect the course of events, and the archaeologist who digs up our collective past learns nothing about his or her own. The urge to uncover what has gone before is present in all those whose early life remains a mystery. The thinking-out of personal problems to avoid repeating them can be obscured by defences such as acting-out (Trooping the Colour), scapegoating (Charles used his wife for this), role reversal, the unloading of feelings of victimization on to others (his unintentional indifference to his children's needs) or through being camouflaged by an interest in history and archaeology. Charles's concern with these subjects reflects an urge to return to a past whose secrets he had suppressed.

Charles's work with the Prince's Trust, the charity he set up to enable disadvantaged young people fulfil their personal and professional potential, suggests that in his own adolescence he was robbed of opportunities for personal growth. Because he feels disadvantaged he is able to experience satisfaction in encouraging others to make the best of themselves. He identifies with young people, supporting rock concerts and raising money for his Trust. (It was claimed, however, in a television documentary about Britain's monarchy that Charles's attention span in these projects is limited and that he soon loses interest in individual enterprises.) Wearing a double-breasted suit and seldom smiling, he appeared to endure rather than enjoy the music of those who may one day be his subjects. Over the years it has been the lot of journalists to create an image of Charles to suit the times. During the late 1960s, when he made a couple of weak jokes in public and appeared in a Cambridge revue, he was said to have a 'wacky sense of humour'; his friendship with the late comedian Spike Milligan reinforced the idea that

Charles was a frustrated comedian. During a safe and sanitized period in the Forces – he spent some time in the Royal Air Force and the Navy – he was depicted as 'Action Man'. Following his enthusiasm for organic vegetables and plants and having formed a friendship with the South African writer and philosopher Sir Laurens van der Post, he was lampooned by the satirical magazine *Private Eye* and others as an eccentric. Since childhood, when he found it hard to please his father, through early adulthood – when his attempts to seem 'with it' were unnatural and forced – to early middle age, when the job for which he has been trained still eluded him, Charles had seldom been allowed to be himself.

Prince Charles's marriage to Lady Diana Spencer in 1981 could have been arranged by Central Casting: the bride was young, beautiful and virginal, and it was she who would rescue the Prince from sadness and isolation. Before his marriage, Charles had a number of aristocratic girlfriends, many of whom were blonde and often a little older than he. They tended to be sporty, outdoor types, unsullied by scandal. One of them, with whom Charles was said to be smitten, was quickly dropped when it was belatedly learned that she had once lived with another man. By the time he was thirty Charles was under public and family pressure to marry. It has been assumed that any one of the heir's *inamorata* would have been willing to accept a proposal from him, although he had made it clear on several occasions that he could not afford to make a mistake and had to be extremely careful in his choice of future queen and consort. Few women surely, however, would relish being required to address a boyfriend as 'sir' (even, it has been said, in bed), and another – with whom the Prince is said to have been in love – ended her relationship with Charles after a ball at Windsor during which he completely ignored her.

Charles's brief was to find a girl who was well born, although not necessarily English, and untainted by scandal. By the early 1980s this was by no means easy. Diana Spencer had had a distant schoolgirl crush on the Prince when he was dating her sister Sarah. When he and Diana started to see each other she had grown into an attractive, charming nineteen-year-old. She was taller than Charles and, although he might have resented looking up to her, she seemed, in a limited field, to have most of the necessary qualifications for the job. Her background was impeccable, she was congenial company, no skeletons lay in her cupboard, and she was touchingly devoted. She had no interest in horses, was fond of neither sailing, classical music nor Scotland, but at the time of their courtship this seemed not to matter. The Prince of Wales was not free to follow his own heart, and Lady Diana Spencer was a highly acceptable compromise.

When the couple were asked if they were in love, Diana's reply was an unhesitating 'yes', while Charles mumbled – significantly – that he supposed so, 'whatever being in love means'. From the moment of their engagement in February 1981 Diana became the object of the world's adulation, and Charles was judged a lucky man.

The Princess of Wales was allowed to upstage her husband on the memorable day of their wedding. When she continued to do so he was less happy. Marriage to Diana heightened, at the time, Charles's own popularity. She was delightfully open, friendly and like a breath of fresh air in royal circles. Later his quips – 'I'm sorry I've only got one wife, and she's over there on the other side of the street. You'll have to make do with me instead' – betrayed his envy and bitterness.

To establish his precedence over his wife Charles embraced causes that excluded her. It was not that Diana had little interest in intellectual pursuits but that Charles had wanted it presumed that concerns such as the environment or philosophy were his alone. The resentment that he displayed towards his wife underlined his inability to take pride in her successes. When these reflected well upon him, and she appeared to flatter his self-image, he could afford to be generous towards her. Once it became clear that she had made a niche for herself in the public estimation and that she was not merely her husband's satellite he sulked.

His jealousy of what the public thought of as his 'glittering prize' was reinforced during the Gulf War in 1991 when Diana had hoped to visit the troops, but was relegated to meeting only the wives by her husband who wanted all the credit for himself. Charles was also said to have deleted her name from thank-you notes, preferring such gestures to appear to come only from him.

Charles's marriage to Diana gave him an identity as the husband of a beautiful and esteemed wife and the father of two sons, William and Harry. As Diana's confidence and independence grew, however, after she had become a mother, sex with her was taboo. Once again Charles turned for support from a 'nanny' of his childhood, in the persona of his old friend Camilla Parker Bowles. As far as Diana was concerned, Charles expected, unreasonably, that her needs would be satisfied by the adoration of the public and the affection of her children. It became increasingly apparent that the rifts in their marriage, known to their friends to be serious and deep, had been growing more significant for some time. In 1992 the 'authorized' revelations in Andrew Morton's book seemed to confirm publicly what many had suspected. As Diana and Charles went their separate ways the marriage became increasingly threatened, and in December of that year they officially agreed to lead separate private and professional lives.

As early as the first Christmas of their marriage, Diana – according to Morton – had attempted suicide by throwing herself down the stairs at Sandringham. If this was a cry for help Charles did not heed it. Insufficient attention having been paid to him as a child, he found it hard to show concern for others, especially his wife. His 'coldness' is reflected in his concern for the preservation of old buildings rather than for the protection of human beings, and his paintings seldom, if ever, include people.

It has been suggested that the Waleses' happiest period was when Diana was pregnant with Harry. Although Charles's friendship with Camilla Parker Bowles had continued, some of the pressure on the Prince and Princess to be the ideal couple had been removed as the succession was assured. This could have been a time to establish the companionship side of the marriage. The Princess has said, however, that the spiritual side, such as it was, of her marriage died on the day that Prince Harry was born, when her husband, having remarked dismissively on his new son's reddish colouring, left for a polo match, just as his own father had opted for squash when Charles was born. Shortly afterwards, at the christening, Charles insulted Diana's entire family by complaining to his mother-in-law about her grandson's appearance. Although he was a middle-aged man he still experienced the baffled hurt of a neglected small child, and so fierce was his resentment that he felt the need to belittle his baby son during the ceremony marking his baptism into the Church.

While Diana continued to devote her energies to her children and to the welfare of the disadvantaged, Charles concentrated on his own good causes. The royal commentator James Whitaker made a cogent point about the Prince's dedication to public service when he said that Charles's summer engagements were worked around his polo programme. Fifty matches in the season meant that he played nearly every day – while at the same distracting himself with women friends who bolstered his ego. That Diana was so easily able to find out that he was still friendly with Camilla Parker Bowles by checking his telephone calls to her indicates Charles's indifference to his wife's feelings.

Charles's silence following the publication of Andrew Morton's book might have indicated his contempt for it. It might, on the other hand, have suggested a desire to see his wife fall flat on her face after years of public adulation. It was not until January 1993, however, that the real reason for his low-key response became apparent. The so-called 'Camillagate' tape-recording made in 1989 of a telephone conversation allegedly between Charles and Camilla Parker Bowles, published in an Australian newspaper and subsequently in the UK, suggests not only that an ongoing sexual relationship existed between them but that they had been in love for many years. Few questioned Diana's motives in allegedly endorsing a book in which Charles came out so badly, and most readers sympathized with her.

Self-aggrandizement has always characterized Charles's behaviour, but, then, a small child who is given a car, staff and a personal suite as well as a sense of destiny is likely to develop a strong belief in his own importance. His elder son is perhaps already demonstrating his father's tendency to hide behind his rank. He told a fellow pupil at school, 'My daddy is the Prince of Wales and he can beat up your daddy.' It was more likely, though, that Prince William was, as small boys often do, boasting of his pride in his father.

Although throughout his life Charles has been surrounded by sycophants, he was deprived of crucial early nurturing by the one person who really mattered: his mother. Had he received this attention his adult life might have been happier and he would certainly have made a better father. When Prince Philip told his son, shortly after his marriage, that if it was not working well after five years he should look elsewhere, he was revealing his unconscious contempt for women and offering his son a chance, at last, of forming a man-to-man bond with him. Charles was seemingly given *carte blanche* to allow his marriage to fail, and had he not acted upon this advice he would, yet again, have disappointed the father whose approval had always eluded him. It is interesting to note that Camilla Parker Bowles is, in fact, a descendant of Alice Keppel, the last and most beloved of Charles's great-great-grandfather's mistresses.

Throughout his adult life Charles has had a series of male mentors who have supported and advised him in a way that his father failed to do. At Cambridge he relied upon the kindly care of R.A. Butler, Master of his college. Later his equerry Sir John Miller fulfilled this role. Sir Edward Adeane, the Prince's private secretary, was similarly privileged. His two best-known counsellors, however, were his uncle Lord Louis Mountbatten, to whom Charles referred as his 'honorary grandfather', and Sir Laurens van der Post. Mountbatten was as keen to see Charles married to his grand-daughter Amanda Knatchbull as he had been to see his nephew married to Princess Elizabeth, but Charles showed no interest in her. He continued, however, to confide in his uncle and to rely upon his worldly experience. With van der Post Charles was able to express the metaphysical side of his nature as he never could with his father.

Like his grandfather George VI, Charles was regarded as being on a short fuse, particularly during the time when his marriage was coming to an end. He was impatient not only with those who failed to offer him what he perceived to be proper respect but also with servants who were in no position to answer back. He has said with some candour, referring to his sons, that he does not like four-year-olds, which probably reflects his own unhappy memories of being that age. It seemed possible at the time that the pressure of royal duties would prevent him from being no better a father to his sons than Philip had been to him. His wife's devoted mothering of their children compensated them for the absent mothering of her own childhood, and she supplied Princes William and Harry with unconditional love. Since her premature death in 1997, however, there is no evidence that Charles has been anything other than a caring father.

In the early days of his marriage to Diana Charles continued to demand respect and approval; he also insisted on petty economies in the running of his household echoing his feelings of 'inner poverty'. He found great difficulty in giving to others something he never had: a sense of worth acquired from loving, freely available parents.

When at leisure he fishes, gardens and – like his father – depicts in landscape paintings an idealized unpopulated world that he would like to inhabit. His concern with ecology suggests that the world is not to his liking. Possibly by making a belated attempt to protect the interests of Mother Earth, he hopes that she might bestow on him what has always been denied him. He plays the cello, an instrument that has been compared to the female form. On the polo field, at one with his pony, he is able to demonstrate to his father – a fellow polo enthusiast as well as a rival for his mother's love – that he, too, is dominant and powerful. Through risk-taking activities such as parachute jumping, in which he was involved as a young man, he was able to obtain the arousal and stimulation lacking in his infancy. While variety is said to be the spice of life, the life source, namely the mother, should have been able to provide him with the contentment and satisfaction that would have fulfilled his needs. Spice, in the form of variety, would then have been less necessary. Competitive activities carried out compulsively may compensate for poor parenting. Those who are addicted to performance games, such as tennis or squash, play to win and are heavily dependent on the satisfaction gained from spectator approval. A bad loser cannot cope with absence of admiration and will often feel rejected.

Charles had learned to anticipate rejection as a child and made it difficult for his wife to love him. It could be that he will only feel at ease with himself if and when he is seated on the throne of England. Should he decide to stand aside in the interests of Prince William he will have the satisfaction of knowing that he has survived the crises of his younger days and should be remembered now for his concern for the environment and future generations.

11

PRINCESS DIANA

'A girl who danced with the Prince of Wales'
– line from a popular song by Herbert Farjeon, 1927

Lady Diana Spencer was a commoner when she married Prince
Charles, but, like her grandmother-in-law Elizabeth Bowes-Lyon,
she came from among the highest echelons of society.

Her immediate family background was troubled. Her father –
Earl Spencer who died in 1992 – was a genial, friendly man who
was fond of his children. He had three daughters, of whom Diana,
born in 1961, was the youngest, and a son, Charles, born in 1964.
Despite her material advantages Diana was not happy. Shortly after
her brother Charles's birth her mother, the former Frances Roche,
fell in love with Peter Shand Kydd, and when Diana was six the
Spencers divorced. Frances sought to keep her children, but amid
considerable publicity their father was awarded custody. It was he
who brought up Diana, although she continued to see her mother
during school holidays.

Children often blame themselves for the break-up of their
parents' marriage, and Diana was clearly disturbed by the divorce
and the divided life she led afterwards. Until she went to boarding-
school, aged eight, she had experienced the constant care of her
governess Gertrude Allen and had an affectionate relationship with
her siblings for whom she developed a protective concern. When
her brother Charles outgrew his baby clothes Diana dressed her
teddy-bear in them. A cuddly toy, a transitional object, usually acts
as a comforting reminder of the child's former attachment to the
mother. Diana's teddy-bear in this case perhaps became a surrogate
for her brother in her mother's absence. Fortunately for Diana she
had a loving grandmother in Ruth, Lady Fermoy, who showed
kindness and compassion to the sick and socially disadvantaged and
must have recognized intuitively that the emotionally bruised Diana
needed special care.

At an early age Diana dealt with her feelings of being a victim of society by identifying with the helpless and the trapped and caring for a series of small caged animals and other household pets. She was helpful and seldom naughty. This is typical of a child who feels abandoned and grows up heavily dependent on approval that was conditional but which should have been available to her freely and by right. She was neat and tidy, perhaps trying to compensate for the chaos and disorder in her life. The unhappy child who compensated for the absence of her mother by raiding the larder and compulsively consuming the left-overs seemed already set on the course that would lead to later eating problems. No matter how loving her grandparents and other care-givers may have been they would have been unable to compensate her for the feelings of emptiness caused by her mother's absence.

Further painful separations took place when Diana was sent away to school. She lost her governess Gertrude Allen – who left the family – and her cat, whom she adored, died at the same time. These events would have reinforced the grief first experienced when she lost her mother two years earlier. It seems that Diana tended to fantasize. Finding reality intolerable, she invented a world in which she could live more happily. She lost regular contact with her father and brother, and when in school holidays she visited her mother she had to adapt to seeing her with a man who was not her father. It was from around this time that Diana would probably have first become aware of feeling depressed. Although the losses she experienced did not result from the death of a loved one, the more subtle losses of apparently being abandoned, of change and of moving on occurred too early for her to be able to cope with them. Later in life this would lead to inappropriate compensations such as overeating and hopeless attachments. Life's losses are inevitable and necessary – and must be confronted. Most of them, however, occur later in life, together with the realization that 'letting go' is essential for growth, development and emotional well-being.

For years Diana was ferried between her mother and father. She acknowledged Althorp as her home, but even that secure base was disturbed when her father remarried. She did not form a close relationship with her stepmother Raine, the daughter of the novelist Barbara Cartland. Her older sisters mothered her, however, and the girls were supportive of one another. Diana, as the youngest, could not easily articulate her frustration and anger and therefore experienced her father's transference of affection to another woman more acutely than her sisters and her brother. Later she expressed her feelings through food, seeing it at first as compensation for a caring mother, then rejecting it. This unsatisfactory situation was replicated in her marriage. At first she binged on the adulation of an adoring public, the glamour of the Crown and Charles's acceptance of her as a royal Princess. Circumstances soon after obliged her to re-evaluate her role, however. Although there is a well-documented connection between eating disorders in adults and childhood sexual abuse, in Diana's case there was no evidence of this other than her feeling that Charles, in turning away from her sexually after the birth of their children, abused the position of trust that he occupied within their marriage, compromising his role as husband and father. Childhood abuse does not necessarily have to be sexual, and its echo in adult life may take place with another 'father'.

Diana's compulsive urge to eat sweets and nursery food persisted as she grew up. She looked for other compensations such as admiration but would inevitably have been disappointed, as early patterns tend to repeat themselves. The seeds of her need for approval and love were sown in early childhood. After her mother left it seems unlikely that she would have been allowed to verbalize her anger and anyway would have found it difficult to do so for fear of alienating her father on whom she had become heavily dependent. During this time she fell off her pony and broke her arm. This could have been an accident waiting to happen, since anger turned in on itself may be destructive.

A teacher at Diana's first boarding-school says that she was known as 'the Duchess' because she was neat, composed and serious. Her feelings remained over-controlled, unless she broke down when she became unreachable. On one occasion during an art class Diana burst into tears without explanation. Her pictures were usually dedicated to 'Mummy and Daddy', reflecting a wish to see her parents together.

The role of teachers, the surrogate mothers of many, is to care for their charges throughout the day until the children are returned to their real mothers. The teachers *in loco parentis* to Diana could never hand her over to her mother at the end of the day, nor even at the end of term, since Diana's remarried mother spent much of her time in Australia. If Diana believed it was her fault that her mother had left her, two courses of action were available, both of which she exercised. The first was to be as pleasing as possible to authority figures, so that they would love her and stay with her rather than abandoning her. The second was to attempt to relieve her guilt through self-inflicted suffering. She was pleasant and agreeable throughout her childhood, but after marriage and motherhood she came to realize that the approval of others was poor compensation for self-esteem. She could hardly have been expected to like herself. At some level she might have thought that she had been abandoned because she was unworthy or not valued or that it was her bad behaviour which had driven her mother away.

As Diana grew into an adolescent she became increasingly self-conscious. Most adolescents have image problems, are easily embarrassed and sensitive to criticism, but Diana had a real struggle with her appearance since she saw herself as both overweight and unattractive. Like many of her peers in the late 1970s, her role models were tall and slim. She was tall, but in her compulsive need for food she not only found momentary comfort but gained weight. She knew that slimness was valued and preferred, but because she believed herself unlovable she set out to prove it. The chocolate and puddings of her nursery days represented the love on which she had missed out, and her compulsive need to binge could only be managed if weight gain was controlled by inducing vomiting.

At school Diana never spoke of her parents' divorce. Even later, at West Heath School where she is remembered as being good company and gregarious, she never discussed her feelings. She continued to satisfy the expectations of teachers, was a good team player at games, a particularly keen swimmer and kind to younger pupils. She read the romantic asexual novels of her step-grand-mother Barbara Cartland and yearned for maternal affection that would never be hers. She dressed as flamboyantly as possible when not required to be in uniform, and took more baths each week – like many other girls concerned with their appearance – than the regulation three that the school required. 'I knew I was in the wrong shell,' she has said of herself at that period. She was unhappy with her body, but the frequent baths could not wash away her unhappiness.

Later on at school Diana's true feelings began to surface. Not only was she miserable; she became rebellious. Unlike her older sisters she failed to distinguish herself academically and, because of her fear of failure and the disapproval that this would provoke, she decided not to retake her O levels. It is possible that she was 'examphobic', believing that there was no test that she would ever pass sufficiently well to please others. She insisted on being sent to finishing school in Switzerland but returned home after just six weeks. 'Home', however, was no longer home. Since the advent of her stepmother Raine, and in common with her sisters and brother, Diana no longer felt comfortable there.

Diana gravitated towards menial work, perhaps reinforcing her view that she was a person of no importance or intelligence, while her compulsion to care for and serve those who were disadvantaged and helpless was to persist. At school she had been commended for her work, which she had enjoyed, with sick and handicapped people. She was as much a success in these activities outside the classroom as she had felt a failure within it. She gained reassurance from activities that proved to her that she could be useful to others.

Like many other well-connected young women who mark time before marriage by working as waitresses, nannies or barmaids, Diana took a succession of short-lived jobs in London. Comforted by a need to create order out of chaos and by caring for others, Diana, according to her erstwhile flatmates, enjoyed vacuuming and washing-up. At Highgrove, the Waleses' house in Gloucestershire, in the early days of her marriage she was said to do her own ironing to the accompaniment of soap operas such as *Neighbours* or *Eastenders*. This enabled her to identify with the family life of television characters such as she herself had never enjoyed.

Money inherited from her American great-grandmother enabled Diana in 1979 to buy a flat in an exclusive block in Kensington she shared with three friends and a collection of ornamental frogs, including a cushion on which was inscribed 'You have to kiss a lot of frogs before you find your Prince.' She had many friends but no serious male admirers. She shopped, went to parties and enjoyed two years of freedom and anonymity. She drove her Metro car, weekended in the country and played practical jokes with her flatmates. One of their favourite pastimes was targeting others for pranks. These included telephoning people whose names they discovered in the directory and which they found amusing.

Doorbells were rung at dead of night and car locks interfered with: Andrew Morton tells us that, after some minor disagreement with Diana, her friend James Gilbey found his cherished Alfa Romeo covered in a solid 'pastry' of eggs and flour. Diana's pranks could be hurtful, aggressive and, like many practical jokes, sadistic. Her adolescent acting-out, however, excluded sexual activity. It is not easy to give love if it has not been received.

Diana's later interest in AIDS perhaps suggests an unconscious conviction that sexual activity is contaminating and flawed. Diana Spencer had seen how sex had influenced the breakdown of her parents' marriage. Her flatmate Carolyn Bartholomew remarked that Diana was 'surrounded by this golden aura which stopped men going any further'. Diana herself said, with hindsight, 'I knew I had to keep myself tidy for what lay ahead.' Tidy, in her vocabulary, meant good, well behaved but, above all, virginal, an echo of Queen Victoria's 'I will be good' before her marriage to Prince Albert.

Diana entered her relationship with Charles sexually and emotionally naïve, without even one serious relationship or former boyfriend with whom to compare him. Charles, on the other hand, knowing perhaps that the pressure for him to marry could only increase, embarked on his relationship with Diana having had no fewer than three intimate friendships with women in the previous year. Althorp is in Northamptonshire, but the Spencer family has property close to Sandringham, and when Diana was at home during school holidays she was a frequent visitor. She was the same age as Prince Andrew, whom she had known as a child, and had been considered a potential bride for him. She was sixteen when she again met Charles, who was twenty-nine. When he first took an interest in her she was working at the Young England kindergarten in Pimlico. An enterprising press photographer was responsible for the image of her that captured the imagination of the world. A simply dressed, natural-looking Diana was caught on camera with two small children, the sun behind her and with the silhouette of her slim legs clearly visible beneath her skirt. The picture showed everything that the public wanted in a bride for the Prince of Wales: maternity, responsibility, beauty, naïveté and sex appeal.

Diana was nineteen at the time of the announcement of her engagement to Prince Charles in February 1981. The marriage took place in July just after her twentieth birthday. She had lost a considerable amount of weight, partly owing to stress and partly because as the royal dressmaker Elizabeth Emanuel remarked, 'All brides lose weight.'

Most brides need their mother's support while preparing for their weddings. Diana needed her mother but at the same time may have been angry with her for having left her. She would have identified with her mother as a defence against separation – identification in this context means a reluctance to lead a separate life and a wish to remain at one with her. Later, as a mother herself, she was also to leave her husband. This inner conflict contributed later to bulimia being diagnosed. Diana's therapy may have helped her to realize that vomiting symbolizes both a rejection of what the mother could not provide in the first place and the need to retain a slim elegance to encourage the admiration and approval of others. She had visited her mother in Australia while considering Charles's proposal. During her stay, she was perhaps giving her an unconscious non-verbal message that, however worthless and unlovable she had felt as a child, the Prince of Wales wanted to marry her and the entire world would love her. She would also have been reminded of the first commitment of all, the primary love affair between mother and child that had been such a disappointment to her. In that first commitment she had learned that nothing lasts and that the one who claims to love you will ultimately leave you. This was all too painfully borne out in December 1992.

Responsibility for Diana Spencer's confusion during her engagement, however, cannot rest entirely with her ambivalent relationship with her mother. The girl who, as photographs suggest, was pleasant enough to look but no great beauty was now expected by the tabloids and their readers to fulfil the public desire for a 'fairy-tale princess'. She was never an 'ugly duckling', but few slightly overweight girls have achieved sylph-like elegance with such speed. The engagement was publicly celebrated, and basking in this mass approval would have encouraged her to acquire the image the public so ardently desired.

Little can have prepared Diana for her relationship with Charles, even though she had known the Royal Family peripherally all her life. Although she had had no serious boyfriends she knew that none of her contemporaries had to address a boyfriend as 'sir' until an engagement was announced. She might have hoped to hear more often from Charles during his visit to Australia and to be greeted on his return with more than a bouquet of flowers delivered to Clarence House from his office. From the beginning Charles played a distant role, familiar to her in childhood and reminding her of the often unavailable parent of the opposite sex. Diana's early life experiences were beginning to repeat themselves.

It is hard to avoid concluding that Charles was not in love with Diana when he married her. He had not severed his friendship with Camilla Parker Bowles and had, indeed, established that since Diana did not hunt he and Camilla would be able to meet on the field. The child who had depended on two nannies was, as a man, unwilling to enter marriage without another 'nanny' in the background.

Diana described herself as being 'as thick as a plank'. She made such remarks with confidence and humour, which suggests that she knew them not to be true and hoped that she would be told so. Affection surrounded her everywhere: the press, the public and her children supplied her with the unqualified devotion, admiration and acceptance that she needed. She and Prince Charles were attracted to each other because their needs were similar. Charles's mother had 'deserted' him – not permanently as had Diana's but inter-mittently by her comings and goings. Each time she left him she reinforced his sense of being abandoned. Diana's popularity attracted love and attention to them both, while her husband's status gave her the platform upon which she would flourish. But while he continued to seek the flattery and reassurance of other women, she had to make do with a loving but distant admiring world. Charles hoped to find the love he missed out on as a child yet simultaneously penalized Diana who had become the scapegoat for his own mother. Diana came to recognize that her marriage could only disappoint her and that once again she would experience loss. Her despair and anger, previously turned in on itself, would now be directed at her husband.

Up to a point Diana must have expected Charles to be sparing with his affections. Arm's length involvement was, after all, what she had been accustomed to. Feeling neglected and lonely within her new family, she took, as Andrew Morton claims, to the attention-seeking devices of the psychologically desperate, and several episodes of non-fatal deliberate self-harm occurred at this time.

Throwing herself against the glass of a show cabinet or attempting to cut herself with a lemon-juicer may be thought of as attempts to draw attention to herself, but the unhappiness that encouraged such actions cannot be denied. It is unlikely that Diana wished to kill herself: no mother as devoted as she would choose to deprive her sons of the depth of care that she had lacked. Her ongoing affair with the people of Britain and the world and the support of her friends and children would have been her one consolation.

She was known to have received counselling but rejected suggestions that she take antidepressants, perhaps in the belief that this would not resolve her problems. Diana's devotion to her children may have saved her, but it could not save the marriage which she said was over when her second son was born. Since that time she had been neglected by her husband who, now that she had ensured the succession, saw her as far too much of a mother to interest him sexually. Diana was in danger of becoming, like Alexandra of Denmark, too smothering a mother for her sons' good. 'I hug my children to death and get into bed with them at night. I always feed them love and affection. It's so important.'

It would have been be damaging to the young princes if Diana – like Alexandra – came to make demands of her sons that should more properly have been met in the first place by her parents and later by her husband. That Charles chose to go hunting without her during their first New Year at Sandringham as newlyweds, causing Diana to hurl herself down the staircase, indicated his indifference to or unawareness of his wife's needs. Ten years later he was still hunting, leaving Diana to look for emotional input from her sons and from friendships outside the marriage. There was little attempt from either Charles or Diana at reconciliation: like Victoria and Albert, they each sought the opposite-sex parent in the other, but, unlike Victoria and Albert, they acted out their needs elsewhere.

When Diana was a child and was asked what she wanted to be, she is said to have answered that her ambition was to become the Princess of Wales. At that time the Royal Family was an example to Diana of all that was perfect about family life. Her fantasy of participating in a fairy-tale came true at one level, but at another more realistic level she realized that her lifestyle was no different from the one she had experienced in childhood, which had cheated her of unconditional ongoing love from both parents.

Diana had always been preoccupied with her appearance: she wanted to look attractive and therefore lovable and went to a great deal of trouble to achieve this. She had obsessional character traits relating to cleanliness and tidiness and tried to impose order on a life that brought her to the height of happiness as a royal Princess and to the depths of sorrow as a cheated wife. As with her eating problem, she was either 'too full' or 'too empty'. She used washing rituals to wash away the guilt feelings she believed she had caused. She knew she was valued not by her worth as a wife but by the role she played in public life. Her desire to please had led her to become a chameleon. Her self-esteem was so low that she only felt she existed when she took on the colouring of her surroundings, identifying with whatever company she was in. She was a Princess in Kensington Palace, a characteristic Sloane Ranger in Knightsbridge and an Essex girl when listening to pop music in public or chatting to a car dealer.

The Princess of Wales, like her sister-in-law the Duchess of York, was an exhibitionist. She had sought and received massive paparazzi attention and had received the approval of the public for her charity work, which highlighted the differences between her and her husband. While she concerned herself with human suffering she knew that he was concerned with the form and structure of inanimate objects. When their elder son was seriously ill in 1991, after an accidental blow to the head that could have been fatal, Charles did not stay with his wife at the child's bedside. He had an engagement. The hours which Diana described as being among 'the worst of her life' were dismissed by the Prince in the interests of duty. He had an engagement, just as his parents had had many engagements that prevented them from being with him when he needed them. Charles was scapegoating another mother for the parental neglect that had left his problems unattended.

Friends of the Princess told Andrew Morton that any recent show of support or solidarity from Charles 'is simply a PR exercise to improve his increasingly threatened public image'. It was he, they asserted, who insisted that he flew home from Switzerland with Diana against her wishes after the death of her father, and Charles who left her alone with her grief once they arrived in England. The photographers were shown the supportive husband but not his hasty departure to Highgrove. The Prince of Wales showed little concern about the loss his sons might have felt at the death of their grandfather Earl Spencer. It almost echoes the death of his own grandfather, George VI, in 1952 when Charles was four and his parents were in Kenya and unavailable to him.

To maintain her high profile Diana adopted the most fashionable haircuts, the most sensational outfits and the latest fashions (a wardrobe on which she is said to have spent £1 million over twelve years), while at the same time touchingly maintaining her 'street cred'. In all this she is photographed, copied and reported. 'I am lovely', *ergo* 'I am loved.' She may be trying to please the camera by looking glamorous and enchanting in the same way that, as a child, she had hoped to please her mother and latterly her husband. Her strongest desire, after caring for her sons, was to be pleasing and dutiful. She had been brought up to expect only conditional love, which was further reinforced by her schooling. The ethos of boarding-school is based on performance and competitiveness, both of which are rewarded. Diana would have worked hard for approval in the early days of her marriage: that she was not to receive it must have led to frustration and a sense of helplessness. Charles, ever in search of recognition of his own worth, had learned to look for it from other women. Diana soon came to realize that the person from whom she had expected the rewards of obedience and duty was too involved with his own needs to recognize hers. Once again she found herself being cheated of the ultimate reward from the care-giver to whom she had committed herself. 'Nursery puddings' once more became her consolation, and, in her frustration, she again blamed herself for love having been withdrawn, self-harming herself frequently. It was several years before she could rid herself of her guilt and depression by turning her anger outwards and blaming Charles whom, she now knew, had rejected her.

Both Charles and Diana are said to have sought advice and perhaps consolation from marginal advisers. Both looked for some meaning in the stars, yet it is not in our stars but in ourselves that we find the answers. Her hoped-for destiny, which should have developed out of love, proved to be based on indifference and hostility. While Charles continued to re-enact his anger with Diana – the 'mother' who neglected him – she attempted to find some satisfaction in caring for those whose circumstances were worse than her own. As part of a self-fulfilling prophecy Charles seemed to have created a situation in which she could not be other than indifferent to him.

Diana, one of life's victims, found it easy to identify with other victims. Her concern for AIDS sufferers and leprosy research underlined this. She saw herself as an outcast, the victim of one of the socio-sexual diseases of our times, in her case parental divorce. She hoped that she could influence others by her example, to empathize with those who suffered from these antisocial disorders.

Her work for Barnardo's, Birthright and other children's charities reflected a concern for the disadvantaged child. As a disadvantaged child herself she could understand the feelings of children from broken homes. She worked with them enthusiastically and with compassion, tuning into their needs and feeling at one with them. Her work as patron of Relate (formerly the Marriage Guidance Council) reflected another problem with which she was familiar: the failed relationship.

Diana would readily order a new outfit – although she was at pains to point out that most of her clothes were altered, adapted, recycled and worn time and again, as if self-adornment made her feel guilty – if a photograph of herself in an eye-catching dress would help to raise awareness for child victims, sexual victims or marital victims.

No one would deny that Diana was genuinely caring and devoted, but it is common for those who believe they have been given insufficient maternal affection themselves to redress the balance by being especially giving of love when they have children of their own. Alternatively, early patterns of emotional neglect may be passed on to the next generation. William and Harry are fortunate in having one parent at least who was anxious to ensure that they did not lack for love. William was taken as a small baby to Australia with the Prince and Princess of Wales in 1983. Nothing was more important to Diana than her new baby. When he was old enough to go to school his nanny, Barbara Barnes, wanted to stay and look after him and his younger brother Harry. But it seems that Miss Barnes was dismissed because the Prince of Wales believed that she had not been strict enough with William, as if he wanted his sons to suffer withdrawal of affection as he himself had. Diana disliked Charles's attitude to their children: his mother had not been able to give him enough of her time and he envied the boys Diana's attention, presumably because they were faring so much better than he had done.

Diana had a wide range of personal interests. She not only enjoyed popular music and dancing, shopping and lunching with her girlfriends, but painted, took photographs, went to the ballet, made tapestries and played bridge.

Tensions existed within the royal marriage from the very beginning. Diana was blamed because members of Charles's household were said to have resigned because of her demands. By the mid-1980s royal-watchers were counting the number of days the couple had spent together, finding them to be few and already hinting at a rift. Birthdays and anniversaries were spent apart, holidays taken separately, and Charles and Diana did not look happy or comfortable when photographed in public together. During the fifteen years of their marriage Diana's character had developed while Charles seemed to become ever more set in his ways.

Diana was thought not to have had the best of relationships with the Queen Mother. Although the Queen Mother was particularly close to Charles, she was said to have done little to promote understanding between her grandson and his wife. A friend of Diana's told Andrew Morton that the Queen Mother 'drove a wedge' between the couple to help sustain the special closeness that had always existed between her and her grandson.

Another friend confirmed that Diana had no friends within what she called 'the Firm'. 'The whole royal business terrified her. They gave her no confidence or support.' Both the Queen Mother and Diana were 'commoners'. Clearly, by long association, the Queen Mother had become royal while Diana, like any newcomer to a closed society, was resented.

While Charles supported many causes and campaigns, enjoyed polo and his gardens and his friendships, Diana had her charities and her children, the adoration of her public and the occasional arousal that fast driving brings. When behind the wheel of a car she felt, at least for a moment, in control of her journey through life, but this was not to be for long on the road that she and Charles had set out on together and never less so than on her final journey in 1997 when she put her faith in a driver who had drunkenly decided to change her destiny. Forms of risk-taking such as illicit sex and dangerous games had previously been unavailable to her, but during the late 1980s, possibly as a retaliatory gesture, she had made token phone calls to admirers possibly to satisfy her expectation that her lovers – like her mother – were geographically distant. There was little to relieve her obvious sadness.

In June 1984 Prince Charles and Princess Diana appeared to have it all. Diana had blossomed into a beautiful and fashionable woman. Her photograph on the front of fashion magazines or in newspapers was guaranteed to increase circulation. They had one beautiful son, William, and Diana was six months pregnant. They looked happy enough in the photographs and newsreels of the time, but their contentment was to be short-lived. Once their second son, Harry, was born a different story began to unfold. Visiting Diana in hospital to see his newborn son for the first time, Prince Charles derogatory remark about the ginger hue of Harry's hair before he left to play polo seemed to have been the last straw. Later on, once the extent of Diana's infidelities became known, it was rumoured that a young cavalry officer, James Hewitt, was Harry's biological father. This was robustly denied by Hewitt who, in an interview with the *Sunday Mirror*, stated, 'I can understand the interest, but Harry was already walking by the time my relationship with Diana began', and 'Although I was with Diana for a long time I must state once and for all that I'm not Harry's father.' In a book *Diana: Closely Guarded Secret* written by her former protection officer Ken Wharfe, the author wrote, 'The nonsense should be scotched here and now. Harry was born on September 15, 1984. Diana did not meet James until the summer of 1986, and the red hair the gossips so love to cite as proof is, of course, a Spencer trait.' Whatever the truth of the matter and however many photographs and however few DNA tests, if any, later, the colour of Harry's hair provoked an explosive reaction from Charles.

According to Peter Donnelly, author of *The People's Princess* published in 1997, shortly after the birth of Harry Prince Charles began to demoralize the Princess with words and actions resulting in renewed psychological problems. This manifested itself in episodic binge eating, followed by feelings of guilt and self-condemnation. According to Donnelly, the Royal Family's expectations forced her to appear reserved, sombre and stodgy. They expected her to look like the royal image they had all come to represent. Rejected by her husband and marginalized by his family, she knew she needed to find the life she craved in which she could be her own person, loved for herself rather than for whom she had become. Once she knew that her husband no longer desired her she embarked on a series of extra-marital and post-divorce relationships, almost all with consequences that ultimately disappointed her.

The first of these extra-marital affairs is said to have been with one of her bodyguards and a married man, Barry Mannakee. When Prince Charles learned of the relationship Mannakee was fired and sent to work in the Diplomatic Protection Squad. He died in a motorcycle accident in 1987. Other alleged former lovers of Princess Diana whose names were linked to hers by the press are said to include David Waterhouse, James Gilbey, Oliver Hoare, Will Carling, Bryan Adams, Dodi Fayed and Hasnat Khan, the cardiac surgeon who loved Diana for two years. This relationship ended only a few weeks before her death.

Emad El-Din Mohamed Abdel Moneim Fayed, known as Dodi, was born on 15 April 1955. He was the eldest son of Egyptian billionaire Mohamed Al-Fayed and died alongside Diana Princess of Wales in the car crash on 31 August 1997. Their courtship was brief. He became romantically involved with Diana in July 1997. At the time of their deaths they had just enjoyed a nine-day holiday together in the French and Italian Riviera. Princes William and Harry had joined them but were not happy. Harry reputedly got into an argument with Omar, the youngest son of Mohamed Al-Fayed. William and Harry are reported to have disliked Dodi and did not care for the glitzy lifestyle and the publicity that accompanied it.

On the day of their mother's death William and Harry had been due to fly from Balmoral to London with their chaperone Tiggy Legge-Bourke who had been employed by Prince Charles to act *in loco parentis* to the boys at Highgrove. At twenty-eight she was a bundle of fun – a cross between a loving, liberal mother and a slightly wild big sister. Diana was jealous. She felt usurped and started a rumour that Tiggy and Charles were having an affair, although there was never any proof of this. Diana was due to fly back from Paris to spend the last few days of the school holidays with her boys in London. The first call alerting the Royal Family to Diana's accident came to Balmoral at 1 a.m. on Sunday, 31 August

1997. The Queen was advised not to wake William and Harry until their mother's death was confirmed. Strangely, William woke up many times during that night. He said he knew that 'something awful was going to happen'.

While he struggled to take in the fact that his mother had died, twelve year-old William went for long walks alone through the acres of heather and wild moorland. He appeared to internalize his grief, and no one saw him cry. At the funeral the boys made a decision to walk behind their mother's coffin. Her brother Earl Spencer had wanted to be the only one to do so, and he is reported to have slammed the phone down when he was told that his brother-in-law Prince Charles would also walk behind the casket.

It has been noted widely that William has the Windsor ability to keep his emotions hidden. The two Princes are very close perhaps because when they were growing up they did not know whom they could trust. After their mother's death the bond between them became their lifeline. William's personality is complex, while that of Harry seems more straightforward.

At the age of thirty-six Diana Princess of Wales and her 42-year-old friend Dodi Fayed were dead. On the day of her funeral on Saturday, 6 September 1997 millions of mourners lined the streets of London to pay their respects. The nation came to a halt. More than two billion people round the world watched the funeral service at Westminster Abbey unable to accept that this vibrant, beautiful and misunderstood woman had died in the most bizarre circumstances. In his eulogy Charles Spencer castigated the Royal Family for its behaviour towards his beloved sister and savaged the press for seemingly hounding her to her death. Addressing his dead sister, he said, 'There is a temptation to rush to canonize your memory. There is no need to do so. You stand tall enough as a human being of unique qualities not to need to be seen as a saint.'

12

PRINCESS ANNE

'I've always accepted the role of being second in everything from quite an early age. You adopt that position as part of your experience. You start off in life very much a tail-end Charlie, at the back of the line.' – Princess Anne

Princess Anne, born on 15 August 1950 and christened Anne Elizabeth Alice Louise, has seldom been a trendsetter. Despite journalistic attempts to associate her with the 'swinging London' of the 1960s, her half-hearted attempts to adopt the mini-skirt, her backcombed hair and the sporty caps she adopted as a teenager were ridiculed by the fashion pundits and other young women of her generation.

During her teenage years Princess Anne was expected by the public to identify with the mores of her contemporaries, as was her older brother Charles, but this did not come easily for either of them.

Like her grandfather and aunt before her, Anne married a commoner. Her marriage to Captain Mark Phillips took place in November 1973. The couple lived at first in married quarters near Sandhurst, to which Anne's husband was attached, and four years later the Queen presented them with Gatcombe Park in Gloucestershire, a large house surrounded by lands that were to be successfully farmed by Captain Phillips. By contrast the Prince of Wales had earlier been given a house in Sussex, followed, after his marriage in 1981, by Highgrove in Gloucestershire.

Princess Anne and Captain Phillips had two children, Peter and Zara, but separated in 1989 and were subsequently divorced. Princess Anne's divorce, having been preceded in 1978 by that of her aunt Princess Margaret from Lord Snowdon, was not the first within the present Royal Family, but the manner in which it was handled reflected the changing times. How was it that Anne, a princess of the Blood Royal, came to contract such a marriage in the first place?

To be a second or subsequent child in any aristocratic family is to occupy a second-class position. In the Royal Family this distinction is magnified. Princess Margaret experienced the same disadvantages as other second-born royals, but Anne's was a special case in that her invidious position as 'the spare' – and a female one at that – was exacerbated by the later arrival of her two younger brothers. Even before Princes Andrew and Edward were born Anne was acutely aware of her status within the family, particularly in the light of the affectionate bond that had developed between her older brother and their grandmother the Queen Mother. 'There is a rather special relationship', she said, perhaps ruefully, 'between the eldest grandson and a grandmother, I think, which is not true of granddaughters.'

Holding fast, perhaps, to her one claim to distinction within the family, Anne said that she was delighted that she did not have a sister and later declared that she had no sympathy with 'women's lib'. She clearly felt she was both the odd one out and underprivileged in that as a girl she was denied the special love her brother received from their grandmother. Her unconscious envy of her brother might have led her to devalue the contribution of women to society.

As the only girl among three brothers, and constitutionally the least important of the siblings, Anne might have felt the need to distinguish herself so that it looked as if her 'separate' and 'different' position was self-imposed rather than dictated. This may explain her decision to marry a commoner and may have been her resolution to deprive her children of the titles that would have been conferred on them had she permitted it. Perhaps she was passing on to them the lack of privilege she may have felt was characteristic of her childhood.

As Anne's constitutional importance dwindled, she made a statement – through her competitiveness as a world-class horsewoman – about her worth and her gender. She has spoken with admiration of the Amazon women who were able to demonstrate on horseback their 'virility', worth and power. 'It's the one thing that the world can see I do well that's got nothing whatsoever to do with my position or money or anything else. If I'm good at it, I'm good at it – and not because I'm Princess Anne.' Her determination and courage in this field – as well as her competitive spirit – suggest that she would have been a success from whichever stable she emerged.

Princess Anne's close relationship with horses and children can perhaps be traced back to her childhood. While she was free to lend her support to any charity, her choice of Save the Children indicates an empathy with children. Looking at the causes with which they identify, other members of the Royal Family (Princess Margaret and the Migraine Trust, the Princess of Wales and Birthright) also revealed something of themselves. Princess Anne's work for deprived children may appear altruistic, but is it not possible to see her statement that 'If you don't invest in people at the earliest point of their lives you miss an opportunity – and you never get the chance again' as an unconscious side-swipe at what she perceives as her own treatment by her parents? Was this also an intuitive understanding of what children really need? Nevertheless, like her own parents Princess Anne has spent a great deal of time away from her offspring.

When Anne was asked what she would have done with her life had she not been born a royal Princess, she said that she would have chosen to be a long-distance lorry driver. Although evidently a lighthearted response, a more revealing remark about herself could scarcely have been made: the image of the long-distance lorry driver, isolated in his cab, proceeding from point to point with his heavy load, is essentially a masculine one. While he relies on the instruction of others, he has the freedom of the road, the ability to set his own pace and independence as well as retain a sense of control and adventure. The lorry, with its illusion of freedom, is paralleled by the Princess's horse, the control of whose destiny, strength, power and energy is in the hands of its rider.

As a baby Anne had reason to feel short-changed by her mother and was forced to seek the approval and attention of her father. She was successful to the extent that Prince Philip responded to her needs and appreciated her qualities more readily than did her mother. But his devotion to her was qualified, and his absences were frequent. It is Anne's spirit that has enabled her to take the upper hand, to control her horse in response to the limited paternal attention she might perceive herself to have received. Like many another small girl she was in love – entirely appropriately – with her horses, and of course the horse has a strong masculine image.

Princess Anne has been romantically associated with one of her bodyguards – again a protective father figure – and in December 1992 married her second husband, a former equerry to the Queen and a naval officer clearly identifiable with Prince Philip, Vice-Admiral Tim Laurence. Commander Laurence is five years Anne's junior. That Anne chooses men of rank inferior to her own may be seen a a reflection of how she sees her own status within the Royal Family.

Princess Anne was born in August 1950, fifty years after her grandmother, twenty years after her aunt and when Charles was a little under two. While Anne enjoyed a better relationship with their father, Charles's uneasy relationship with Philip was probably exacerbated by his position of greater constitutional importance than his father would ever have and conceivably by the Oedipal rivalry felt by all sons with their fathers. No such restraints prevented Anne from forming an early alliance and bond of mutual admiration with her father, particularly since she was endowed with many of the characteristics Philip would have liked to see in her brother. After an unsuccessful attempt to kidnap Anne, in 1974, Prince Philip said admiringly, 'If the man had succeeded in abducting Anne she would have given him a hell of a time in captivity.' Both father and daughter possibly thought of themselves as outsiders: Prince Philip as a foreigner and consort, Princess Anne as second in the family and a girl who acted like the boy he would have preferred. Pressure on Anne to excel was always less than that which was imposed on Charles. To attract the attention she had earlier lacked, she was impelled to succeed at something of which her father would approve. Perhaps, too, it is easier to succeed if pressure is not exerted.

Despite not having a mother who was around all the time, a father who was absent on naval duties for much of her early childhood, the lack of a 'devoted' grandparent, and her unenviable place in the family pecking order, Anne appears comfortable in herself and in her uncompromising attitude to her public and private lives. Force of circumstance has made it necessary for her to plough her own furrow, develop self-reliance early and to depend on few people. 'I don't reckon I've many good friends, but that's partly the life one leads – one doesn't stay still for terribly long,' she once remarked. Her self-sufficiency, her suspicious nature and the barrier she has erected between herself and the world have contributed to her image of being cool, remote and sometimes antisocial.

Anne fitted in well at her school, Benenden, but made no special friends while she was there. She considered doing a degree at the University of East Anglia but shared neither Charles's intellectual bent nor his awkward interest in student diversions. She had been held back by him in the nursery, and, sharing lessons with her slower brother, she developed less of an interest in learning than she might otherwise have done and set out to prove herself in ways different from his. In 1960, when Anne was nine, she was faced with the arrival of her second brother, Andrew, to be followed by a third, Edward, four years later. That she was a girl was her only claim to distinction within her immediate family. With her two younger brothers the focus of media attention, Anne had to think of other ways to make her mark.

She had always been encouraged to excel physically, particularly by her father, who taught her to shoot and to drive – albeit on private land – before she was ten. It probably pleased him that his daughter appeared to have more aptitude for such skills than his eldest son. Princess Anne was a competent sailor at an early age and was coached in tennis by the late Dan Maskell. She was given her first pony when she was three, at a time when her parents set off on one of their lengthy tours abroad. Her equestrian skills may also reflect a desire to gain the approval of her mother who has always been keen on horses. Anne's attachment to horses became more hands-on than that of her mother and grandmother who are primarily associated with breeding, training and racing. Anne's achievements as a horsewoman – at Burghley, in the Olympics and in European championships – have proved her mastery of her sport and indicated the intensity of her desire as an individual to shine, to win and, most of all, to be applauded. The pressure on all children, particularly royal ones, to be obedient is strong. It was only on horseback that Anne knew she literally had the whip hand.

Princess Anne has inherited more from her father than his restless energy. She shares his volatile, impulsive, blunt nature, and, like him, she has endured long spells of unpopularity with the press. Determined not to conform to the image of 'fairy-tale princess' that the media were at one time keen to confer on her, Anne came to be regarded as graceless and churlish. 'I didn't match up to the public's idea of a fairy princess in the first place. The Princess of Wales has obviously filled a void in the media's life which I had not filled, but

I never had any intentions of filling it. I had already made a decision that it wasn't me in any way.' Anne was protesting too much, but in this case she was not troubled by the glamour and overwhelming popularity of her new sister-in-law Diana. Anne's difficulties with the press were apparent in the frequent and acrimonious brushes she had with them during the 1970s and 1980s. Her most celebrated public remark, 'Naff off', was directed at some journalists whose intrusions she resented at a horse show. For whatever reasons Anne has ensured that her children grow up with the minimum of the media attention she so despises. When told of the birth of her grand-nephew Prince George in July 2013 she declared, 'Nothing to do with me, but it's very good news.'

Anne has, of course, been able to enjoy the privileges of being royal, but at the same time she has shown little sign of wanting to be fêted simply because of the accident of her birth. The lonely child within her still craves solitude as an adult, probably on the principle that 'if you can't beat them join them'. Onlookers may also wonder whether the Princess is expressing her anger and resentment in her support of blood sports. Does the same violent impulse that inspires a competitive rider impel others to follow the hounds?

Even though Gatcombe Park is close to Highgrove, Princess Anne is not thought to be close to Charles. Diana usurped her sister-in-law's position as the foremost young woman in the Royal Family, and, although Anne has shunned publicity as much as Diana embraced it, it seems likely that some rivalry existed between them – Anne did not attend Prince Harry's christening. She knows that she will always remain in the background except within the context of her work and sporting achievements where her natural aggression and competitiveness stand her in good stead.

In 1987, when she was created Princess Royal by the Queen, Anne seemed finally to have gained recognition and reward from her mother, and in recent years she has begun to receive a more favourable press. Her charitable work has been recognized and applauded, and the dignified way in which her marriage to Mark Phillips was dissolved was greeted with approval.

By virtue of her upbringing Anne has found it hard to demon-strate the softer side of her nature. She was obliged to become independent at an unusually early age. Care-givers often encourage 'do-it-yourself' activities in their charges by emphasizing and rewarding these virtues long before the children are ready for them. An arrogant self-sufficiency – 'I can do it myself, thank you' – replaces the interdependency on which mature and mutually satisfying adult relationships depend. Anne's relationship with her elderly father may now be a fond and relaxed one – indeed, it probably always was – but his eking out of attention and his frequent absences when she was young ensured that as an adult she was destined to seek father substitutes.

The loneliness of her childhood must be continually re-enacted. She may be less concerned these days with performance-related displays of self-worth and competitive activity, and a greater level of public acceptance will have bolstered her self-esteem. But early conflicts are not easily resolved and those who pursue blood sports may be unconsciously re-enacting childhood hostility that can never be fully assuaged. On a number of occasions Princess Anne has made unequivocal, if unconscious, comments about how her treatment by her parents made her feel when she was a child. Her early jealousies and disappointments are revealed time and again in her adult behaviour, from the peasant-style headscarf she adopts when visiting famine or disaster areas (in contrast to her mother's 'county' knotting of the scarf under the chin) to the choice of a relatively understated wedding dress designed by the firm of Susan Small. She has always felt belittled, and whether on official duties abroad or dressed for her marriage she has made unconscious statements that confirm this.

When she said, 'I am the Queen's daughter, and as a daughter I get less involved than the boys. I doubt if the next generation will be involved at all', Princess Anne was being both prophetic and wistful, expressing once more her resentment at her relative neglect. Like her aunt Princess Margaret she has been labelled as 'difficult' by the press and by royal watchers. Both Princess Anne and the late Princess Margaret have had much to overcome. Princess Margaret achieved some emotional respite in her later life, and Princess Anne deserves the same. With the dissolution of her marriage, long before that of the Prince and Princess of Wales came under serious threat, Princess Anne detached herself from the dictates of a monarchy that may, as she has done, have to adapt to survive.

On 29 December 2010 Princess Anne became a grandmother when a daughter Savannah was born to her son Peter and his wife

Autumn. Another daughter, Isla, was born to the couple in March 2012. Her daughter Zara Phillips is married to a former international rugby player, Mike Tindall, and is expecting her first child.

Anne has developed her full potential and has not relied on the Royal Family and her place within it to meet her needs or to provide her with the support that her family failed to give her.

13

PRINCE ANDREW, HIS DUCHESS AND PRINCE EDWARD

'It takes two to destroy a marriage.' – Margaret Trudeau

Andrew, Duke of York, Queen Elizabeth's and Prince Philip's second son, married Sarah Ferguson in 1986. Six years later, amid rumour and scandal, the marriage came to an end.

Prince Andrew Albert Christian Edward was born in February 1960. His mother was by this time coping with her royal duties with a calm and expertise that could hardly have been anticipated in 1952 when as a recently bereaved young mother, with two small babies she acceded to the throne. Prince Philip had long since given up his full-time naval command but did not devote much time to his second son.

Andrew grew up with older and more tolerant parents than his brother and sister. The near ten-year age-gap between Andrew and Anne meant that he was less involved in nursery rivalry and enjoyed a more informal upbringing. He was allowed to watch television and to socialize with children his own age. His parents spent less time away than they had when the two older children were growing up, communication was easier and their absences shorter and less disruptive.

In view of Charles's unhappiness at his prep school Cheam the Queen and Prince Philip sent Andrew to Heatherdown. Later, taking Gordonstoun in his stride, Andrew met the physical and intellectual demands that were made on him more easily than had his brother. He graduated with reasonably good A levels in English, history, economics and political science but did not want to go to university. After having enjoyed a brief period at Lakefield College, Ontario, during his schooldays, where emphasis was placed on outdoor activity, he began his naval training at Dartmouth.

Andrew was lucky enough to grow up with several advantages. His father's athletic and leadership abilities came naturally to him, so there was little need for him to make a special effort to win Philip's approval. He was not under the same constitutional pressures as Charles. He was better-looking than his brother, and he found it easier to make friends; he was liked by the public and popular with the press.

Although it has never been suggested that there is any animosity between Andrew and Charles, it is possible that during his upbringing Andrew suffered from 'second son' syndrome. The good-humoured remark with which he greeted the discovery that he was an inch taller than was Charles at a similar age as 'the happiest day of my life' may conceal an underlying rivalry with his older brother. He later remarked, 'When I'm at sea I feel about six inches taller.'

There were few constraints on Andrew, and he was free to follow his chosen career of naval pilot. Brief but well-publicized partici-pation in manoeuvres during the 1982 Falklands conflict enhanced his popularity, and in view of his macho image and lifestyle, with which people identified more easily than with his brother's cerebral interests, they were prepared to forgive the occasional social lapse. There was much interest in Andrew's love life, which was followed keenly by the tabloids and which he did little to discourage. Although other members of his family have had premarital relationships, none advertised them as freely as Andrew. He seemed to have been making a clear and unequivocal statement about his image.

Andrew's naval obligations spared him the heavy burden of state responsibilities and enabled him to travel the world as a serving officer on duty and as a 'playboy prince' off duty. In the wardroom of his ship he was known as 'H', an abbreviation of HRH. (It was tempting to wonder, in view of the collapse of his marriage, to what extent he had been married to the wardroom rather than to his wife.) A portrait of a well-adjusted, unpretentious and personable young man emerged.

But Andrew's youthful flings, his choice of bride and the subsequent problems within his marriage suggested that, despite apparent advantages, he may be – in the long shadow cast by Queen Victoria, his great-grandfather and his grandfather – another victim of emotional deprivation. The Queen's first duty is to the Crown, her second is to its heir. While Andrew's mother was able to spend more time with him than many previous royal mothers had spent with their sons, he was not so high on her list of priorities that state commitments could be suspended or postponed, and, like his brother and sister before him, he saw more of his nannies than of his mother. Andrew was not, as was Charles, particularly favoured by the Queen Mother, and he saw little of Prince Philip's mother. Princess Andrew of Greece died in 1969 aged eighty-four, and her life had been devoted for many years to a Christian mission in Athens. Andrew's sister Anne was nine years his senior and too old to be much of a companion for him in his childhood. When his brother Edward was born in 1964, and lessons began with Catherine Peebles, Andrew's reign in the royal nursery was over, and he was forced to make way for the new arrival. His later attention-seeking activities – particularly those with his apparently inexhaustible supply of willing girlfriends – and the flamboyant lifestyle he later adopted were faithfully recorded on camera.

Andrew probably craved attention and admiration to fill the emptiness of an earlier vacuum. Andrew was, in effect, an only child until the age of four. Had his needs been satisfied during this period, he would have felt no need to gratify them before the cameras or see them reflected in the eyes of those he hoped would love him.

Like Lord Snowdon and Lord Lichfield, Andrew enjoyed being behind a camera lens and often photographed his girlfriends. Koo Stark, who had starred in soft-porn films and was by then herself a professional photographer, was Andrew's most high-profile consort. He may have hoped that their relationship might continue, but although Koo was intelligent as well as beautiful and the Queen liked her, revelations about her past made this impossible. Katie Rabett, another actress, was not to last. He also had an affair with Vicki Hodge, a model some years older than he, but the relationship came to an end when her account of their friendship was published in a tabloid newspaper. Andrew's remark 'My only vice is women' indicates a strange equating of women with corruption when what he might have thought he was saying was that his sole vice was sexual promiscuity.

Although it is fair to say that the Royal Family disapproved of many of Andrew's female friends, and that he was clearly encouraged to give them up, his choice of partner was invariably unsuitable. It was difficult to be persuaded that Andrew liked women since he had always loved them and left them.

His philanderings, which earned him the nickname 'Randy Andy', were at first eagerly and rather admiringly recorded by the popular press. When he overstepped boundaries, however, his popularity waned and the sobriquet assumed more pejorative overtones.

Sarah Margaret Ferguson was extrovert, upper-middle class and well connected. She was approved by the Royal Family as a girlfriend for Andrew, and their courtship and subsequent marriage were greeted with relief. Sarah, born in 1959, was a few months older than the Prince. She had had previous relationships with men, but since the birth of two sons to the Waleses meant that her children were unlikely to succeed to the throne this was not seen as a serious obstacle. Her father had known Prince Philip for many years and managed the Prince of Wales's polo ponies. It was at Cowdray Park that his daughter was first introduced to Prince Andrew by her friend the Princess of Wales.

The existence of Prince William and Prince Harry seemed to provide the Yorks with an excuse to behave, both together and separately, in ways not at all in keeping with the tradition and dignity of the Royal Family. Andrew had detected in Sarah exhibitionistic tendencies that mirrored his own. They were attracted not so much to each other as to what each saw of him or herself in the other. Andrew appreciated Sarah's good humour, her playfulness and perhaps the apparent maternalism inherent in her physique, which reflected aspects of nurturing of which he might have felt deprived. Sarah, from a broken home and needing reassurance, was similarly attention-seeking. She realized that in marrying Andrew she would seldom be out of his sight – and, by extension, the public eye. It was not until she became a mother that the promise that had drawn them to each other in the first place was revealed as false.

Sarah was twelve when her parents divorced. Her father, Major Ronald Ferguson, whose traditional upbringing of nanny, prep school, public school, Sandhurst and nineteen years in the Army left little time for close relationships with women, remained in the Life Guards until his daughter was nine, and he was unlikely to have been around much during her childhood. Major Ferguson remarried but died suddenly in 2003. Sarah has an older sister, Jane. Her mother remarried, to Hector Barrantes, an Argentinian polo player, who died in 1990. Her life was disrupted, too, by several changes of school. She attended private schools in Berkshire, near the family home, but finished without even the basic intellectual achievements of her future husband. As in the case of Andrew, she grew up largely among her own sex, and, like him, she preferred outdoor pursuits such as horse-riding and skiing.

When Sarah left school she undertook a secretarial course, which was followed by a succession of undemanding jobs appropriate to an upper-middle-class girl with private means. There is little to suggest that she genuinely hankered after a career, but she worked in public relations, publishing and an art gallery, jobs reflecting the same need for exposure and approval that drew her to Andrew. Their relationship foundered because their unconscious requirements – like Queen Victoria and Prince Albert, they looked to each other to make up for the losses of childhood – were identical, rather than complementary. An exhibitionist would have much to offer a voyeuristic partner. Two exhibitionists would be unable to satisfy each other's needs since they were competing with each other for approval.

Sarah enjoyed winter sports and followed the motor-racing Grand Prix, especially when her former boyfriend Paddy McNally was a competitor. She was generally attracted to older men. Given her background this was not surprising, and she seemed to be making up for lost time by enjoying a close relationship with her father that she did not have as a child before his early death. Her much-publicized, infantile behaviour while travelling by plane with him – such as, throwing bread-rolls around and placing a sick-bag on her head – suggests the attention-seeking antics of an infant.

Sarah had a distanced relationship with her mother. Sarah was twelve when her mother left her marriage without saying goodbye to her daughters, leaving their father to break the news to them. Mrs Barrantes made some supportive statements about her daughter during the Yorks' marital crisis in 1992, but it is doubtful whether they were of much help to Sarah.[1] The manner in which her mother was obliged to leave would not have encouraged trust between them, and it is unremarkable that Sarah preferred the company of her father, who was at least visible during her childhood. Ronald Ferguson himself once remarked, 'It doesn't matter what the father is like or how much he takes upon himself or what he does, there is no substitute whatever for a mother at that age.'

Sarah found some comfort in food. At the time of her engagement she was quite overweight. Although she lost weight before the wedding the new Duchess of York was still a large woman.

Like the Princess of Wales – who also lost weight before her wedding and even more after the births of her sons – Sarah is now as slim as she has ever been, in spite of having had two children.

Fergie's exuberance, her 'hilarious' social gaffes (about which she is unrepentant), her touching lack of dress sense and her obvious enjoyment of a good time at first endeared her to the public. She was fallible, overweight, unpretentious, reassuringly human and good-humoured. She even weathered a potential storm when the publication of her two children's books was greeted with some criticism and hostility. Her stories about a helicopter called Budgie displayed an uncomfortable similarity to ones published earlier by a less prominent author. Suggestions of plagiarism were quietly dampened, and the episode was apparently forgotten. Even the suggestion that the Duchess was keeping her royalties for herself, rather than directing them to the children's charities to which they were said to have been donated, failed to make a permanent dent in her popularity. She was forgiven because her 'crimes' appeared human and because it was still thought that she was a working girl from a broken home and could use a few lucky breaks. This goodwill on the part of her public helped her to breeze through the scandal that ensued in 1988 when her father was reported to have been seen in the Wigmore Club, a health club and massage parlour where male members were entertained by young women. But though she did not realize it at the time she was sailing close to the wind.

The Duchess of York's popularity began to wane after the birth of her first daughter, Princess Beatrice, the same year, when she was criticized for leaving the baby at home while she joined her husband in Australia. Although Andrew had failed to get leave of absence to be with his wife after the birth, it was Sarah who was pilloried for being a poor mother and not Andrew for putting duty before family. Sarah could well have gone to Australia, perhaps made anxious by his apparent neglect, in an effort to save what she may have perceived as her failing marriage. But even the birth of a second daughter, Eugenie, a year and a half later failed to redeem the marriage. If anything, it must have made it worse, for Sarah was becoming even more of a mother figure with whom her husband could no longer identify sexually. She was the mother of two daughters who were fifth and sixth in line to the throne. In the late 1980s the behaviour of the Yorks became the target for much criticism of which the Duchess bore the brunt. Her official workload was compared unfavourably with that of the Princess Royal, and there is no denying that she had only one public engagement for every four of her sister-in-law's, although it could be argued that her children were still very young and should have taken priority.

Sarah's 'Dallas-style' plans for a new home in Berkshire, followed by pictures of the interiors in *Hello* magazine, were openly derided as vulgar, ostentatious and an erosion of green-belt land. Although the Queen had given her permission for the house, the planners had allowed the Duke and Duchess to construct their home on previously protected land. The responsibility for affronting public taste was as much the Queen's and the Duke of York's as Sarah Ferguson's.

In the spring of 1992, when Sarah took Princess Beatrice skiing in Switzerland while she still had a rash but was in the non-infectious stage of chickenpox, she was criticized yet again. Every false move engendered a new barrage of comment, and it seemed that the Duchess could do nothing right. Her holiday with Steve Wyatt, a Texan millionaire, while the Duke was at sea, coupled with some innocent group snapshots, became widely publicized and another furore blew up. The Queen insisted that the Duchess cancel her engagements and remain out of the limelight for several months. Rumours began to circulate, and in the early summer of 1992 it was announced that the couple were to separate.

Sarah's marriage, like that of the Waleses, had been solemnized amid a fanfare of goodwill, optimism and affection. Even the Royal Family had welcomed her enthusiastically. 'My brother', said the Princess Royal, 'is a very lucky man.' 'I think she's wonderful,' agreed the Prince of Wales. When the marriage fell apart, however, the family closed ranks. Well before Sarah's liaison with John Bryan, her 'financial adviser', the family's attitude shifted from amused tolerance to frosty recrimination. Her relationship with the press was now intolerable, and the extrovert personality that had once been part of her charm now militated against her. When photographs of her on holiday in North Africa with her Texan male friend among the party were released, even her public were reproving: they had had enough. The Duchess was 'grounded' by the Queen, and her end was in sight as a member of the Royal Family.

It is likely that the rot set in with the televised showing of the undignified high jinks of *It's a Royal Knockout*, masterminded by Prince Edward. As far as the public was concerned, once she had proved to them by her juvenile antics that she was no different from them she lost her right to hide behind her halo or even to wear a coronet. In the past other members of the Royal Family have proved themselves equally human, but Sarah Ferguson did not have the absolution of royal birth. She was a commoner and disappointed her admirers by behaving like one. She became a scapegoat not only for the troubles within her family but for those who had placed her on a pedestal.

It cannot be said that Sarah Ferguson was anything but honest. On the day of her engagement she announced, 'I'm not going to change. Why should I?' A little later she said, 'I will just have to think slightly more, but I will not change when I go out. I'm just going to be me.' It was some time before either her public or her new family objected.

In the absence of outstanding British economic or intellectual achievement until recently, the monarchy remained the one area in which Great Britain still led the world. The Duchess of York and then later the Princess of Wales drew attention to the flaws in their respective marriages, which were the first steps towards highlighting cracks that were becoming all too obvious. While pomp and ceremony, visible extravagance and regal behaviour are tolerated, even encouraged, the Royal Family must never be vulgar. The Duchess of York was unable to make this distinction, and the direct result of her unthinking behaviour ('a silly girl' was a comment attributed to Princess Anne but later denied) is that the Royal Family had been dragged down to an uncomfortably low level.

Sarah acted recklessly, testing, as it were, the security of her position by sunbathing topless with a man friend in the South of France. The same recklessness informed her utterances, her choice of clothes for state occasions and her determination to fly. She even risked making public the announcement, in the early days of their marriage, that 'Andrew comes home on Friday, absolutely tired out. On Saturday we have a row. On Sunday we make it up, but by then he has to go back to base again.' Her comments were honest but reveal a degree of naïveté and tactlessness that did not endear her to her in-laws.

There have been three Duchesses of York this century, all of whom have been remarkable women. Queen Mary embodied the dignities and constraints of the past, while achieving a certain 'modern' outlook. She was in favour, for instance, of birth control. Queen Elizabeth the Queen Mother personified the warm and human face of royalty. Sarah Ferguson is a late-twentieth-century woman who tried – and failed – to reconcile duty and motherhood with a self-seeking determination and an inflated ego. Her career as a duchess was short and anything but sweet. She and Andrew divorced in 1996 but continued to live in Royal Lodge, the late Queen Mother's former country home in Berkshire. She is still relatively young, though, and it is possible that, having learned her lesson she will make a success of a future relationship which may, however, be something of an anti-climax unless the rumours of reconciliation with her former husband Prince Andrew turn out to be valid.

Both previous Dukes of York came to the throne unexpectedly. It might be interesting to speculate on what kind of Queen Consort Sarah would have made had circumstances been different. She has certainly shown little evidence of a sense of responsibility. She might, of course, have risen to the challenge and surprised her detractors, but it seems unlikely. While the monarchy will always in this day and age be challenged as an institution, it is hard to imagine that the tax-payer would ever tolerate Sarah Ferguson as Queen.

Its detractors have claimed that illusion is one of the many factors that have allowed the Royal Family to survive – some would say to throw stardust in our eyes – for as long as it has. The Yorks were at first thought to have dissipated that magic and left us with a rather ordinary family of fallible human beings who have contributed to the demystification that in recent years has been the greatest threat to the survival of the monarchy in its present form. Up to a point a section of the public were pleased to witness the human face of royalty. Beyond that point they were not prepared to go. Every ill-chosen remark uttered by Sarah Ferguson, and by extension the Yorks, was paid for to some extent by the Waleses. While Fergie was allowed to get away with murder, the Princess of Wales redressed the balance through her dignity and discretion, until the Morton revelations when she felt that she could no longer play her part. Times have changed, however, and now the greater concern is for the welfare of the children of the divorced rather than the behaviour of the parents. Although Andrew and Sarah divorced nine years after their marriage, they live in Royal Lodge at Windsor, bringing up their two girls, Beatrice and Eugenie, together and remain on good terms. Media reports, from time to time, suggest that they may be considering remarriage.

Sarah's loyalty to her father – when Major Ferguson's association with the Wigmore Club was the subject of speculation and criticism – displays a wish to retain the approval of a father whose Army duties necessitated absences in her childhood. It is to be hoped that, for the sake of their daughters, the Duke and Duchess of York will remain on good terms and be able to achieve the apparently civilized friendship that was maintained by Princess Margaret with Lord Snowdon.

Like earlier royal risk-takers Andrew and Sarah shared a passion for action and physical challenge. While they were married they were aroused by high speed, flying and social risk-taking. The most important flight for both of them was from each other. They sought the challenge of new horizons they hoped would provide them with the happiness they were unable to find together.

The Duchess of York, who will probably retain her title unless she remarries, is likely to remain in the public eye. This will bring her the attention she craves, combined with freedom from the responsibilities of being royal. It allows her the best of both worlds.

With the decline of the Yorks' popularity, the public appetite switched from a wish to applaud them for their common touch to a similar desire to berate them for it. Overnight Sarah and Andrew changed from being good news to being bad news, and it was the Duchess – not always deservedly – who was castigated. If it was thought that the Fergie débâcle would buy time for the Prince and Princess of Wales, Andrew Morton's timely *Diana: Her True Story*, which blew the whistle on the Waleses' marriage, put paid to any such idea.

Prince Edward, the Queen's youngest son, escaped public scrutiny until 1987 when at the age of twenty-three he resigned his commission in the Royal Marines. Prince Philip's anger at this was well documented, as was Edward's decision shortly afterwards to join Andrew Lloyd Webber's Really Useful Theatre Company as a production assistant where he was sometimes referred to as 'Barbara' Windsor. Edward later formed his own theatre production company and became totally committed to his work, as well as to his royal duties and his family. If scandal has as yet barely touched his private life, it is not for want of journalistic prying.

Edward was born in 1964, and other than gravitating towards the public domain of the theatre he has avoided personal publicity. Until the birth of Prince William in 1982 and his son Prince George in 2013 Edward was third in line of succession to the throne, and his childhood was respected. His liking for privacy is genuine, and in unassumingly performing his official duties and his work in the theatre he found little to engage him wholeheartedly or to attract attention to himself until his marriage to Sophie Rhys-Jones in 1999 and the birth of his two children Lady Louise Windsor and James, Viscount Severn. Known as the Earl of Wessex since his marriage, Edward's wish was to pass on an Earldom to his children rather than a royal title. He gave up his work in the theatre to devote himself to charitable causes.

The present balance of the Royal Family is delicate. It may be unable to survive in the absence of the limelight, but it may wither and die if the glare is too focused or too strong. If the monarchy continues to survive, it seems likely to be in the shadow left by Queen Victoria: still firmly attached to the heels of the young royals. But for about a generation it possessed neither the charm of Edward VII and Queen Alexandra, nor the dignity of Queen Mary and George V, and did not proclaim the family virtues extolled by George VI and Queen Elizabeth.

Will the future life of Sarah Ferguson inspire the speculation and gossip that dogged the Duchess of Windsor before her death in 1997? If Prince Andrew finds another woman, or returns to Sarah as has been frequently rumoured, will it hit the headlines? There are, for the moment, no more unbloodied young royals to satisfy the appetites of the tabloid editors or of their readers. William and Kate, Harry, Zara and Peter, Beatrice and Eugenie are old enough to be considered fair game for the press. How the curious will survive the absence of speculation and misinformation about the Royal Family has yet to be seen.

14

THE DUKE AND DUCHESS
OF CORNWALL

'Her loveliness I never knew
Until she smiled on me.'
– Hartley Coleridge, 'She Is Not Fair to Outward View'

Camilla Parker Bowles was born Camilla Shand on 17 July 1947.
Her life was to be one of immense social privilege, but it would have
taken a very powerful crystal ball to predict that she might one day
be the Queen of England. If it had been her ambition to marry a
Prince, she achieved it on her marriage on 9 April 2005 to Prince
Charles, the Prince of Wales and heir to the throne of England. It
was eight years after the sudden death in a road traffic accident of
Charles's estranged first wife Diana, Princess of Wales, the mother
of his two sons Prince William and Prince Harry and ten years after
Camilla's divorce from Andrew Parker Bowles.

When Camilla and Charles were first introduced in 1972 on the
polo field at Windsor Great Park Camilla was twenty-five and the elder
of two daughters born to Bruce Shand, a sometime Vice Lord Lieutenant of East Sussex and his wife Rosalie. The family lived an
upper-class life on a country estate in Plumpton, Sussex. Camilla was
sent to a fashionable private school, Queen's Gate in South Kensington, where she attained one O level. From there finishing schools
in France and Switzerland brought her formal education to an end. A
cocktail party in Kensington in 1965 hosted by her parents, at which
seventeen-year-old Milla Shand was photographed in elegant black
silk and chiffon, marked Camilla coming out as a débutante. Understandably she was not considered outstandingly beautiful by her school
friends. It was more likely to be her healthy appearance, love of sport
and her penchant for telling risqué jokes that appealed to her friends.

She is known to have had a number of boyfriends before she fell
for the charms of Cavalry Officer Andrew Parker Bowles, seven
years her senior. It was said by some that she was besotted with him
but by others that she married him because he brought her closer to
the royals. Parker Bowles's father was a racing friend of the Queen
Mother, and he had dated Princess Anne for a short time. Camilla's

relationship with him was an on–off one. It was during an 'off' period that she met Prince Charles. It is said that she introduced herself with the remark, 'You know, sir, my great-grandmother was the mistress of your great-great-grandfather – so how about it?'

It was an obvious reference to Edward VII and his mistress, Alice Keppel. Camilla, presumably finding Charles attractive, would have been worried about what to say to a high-ranking celebrity. That she chose to announce who she was and where she stood would not only have impressed him but would have been intended to do so. It is likely that a powerful chemistry between the shy Prince and the warm, mature-looking young woman who spoke proudly of her great-grandmother's sexual adventures would have developed very quickly. Charles was brought up to model himself on his extrovert father. He may well have been overwhelmed by a woman talking to him about love.

It would be many years before Charles allowed himself to consider that what he really needed was not the uniforms and rigid authority expected of him by his disciplinarian father but something softer and more caring and in the gift of his mother. But the Queen's duties and obligations demanded by her royal status took her out of his comfort zone and into one that pleased her subjects more than it pleased him.

Despite having found in Camilla someone like his mother, Charles embarked on a fruitless search. Years later, following military training, which ended with high ranking in all three services and a marriage in which he had to compete with someone with needs similar to his own, he decided to work at making the world a healthier and more fulfilling place.

In the meantime, Camilla's hope for possible commitment was out of the question. Charles was in the Navy. Six months after they had begun meeting in secret he went to sea as an officer on the frigate *Minerva*. In 1973 while he was away 25-year-old Camilla and 34-year-old Andrew Parker Bowles became engaged. They subsequently married and went on to have two children, Tom, born in the year following their marriage, and Laura.

According to Charles's biographer Penny Junor, Camilla was deeply in love with Charles from the outset and he was probably in love with her. If this was the case, then the comment he made just prior to his marriage to Diana, implying that being in love was a state with which he was unfamiliar, was perhaps more truthful than he meant it to be. Unable to make up a mind confused by drifting along unrealistic pathways, he dithered, hedged his bets and dated other girls. It was only when Camilla had given up on him and married Andrew Parker Bowles that Charles realized what he had lost. It also suggested that the unavailability of contact with a loved one was attractive. It was what he had been brought up to expect. Camilla and Andrew were married for twenty-two years before their divorce in 1995. It was reported that Andrew had had a long-term married mistress whom he subsequently married.

Charles, evidently thinking that nothing would ever come of his love for Camilla – a situation that echoed his relationship with his mother, several nannies and various girlfriends – waited another two years before ending his marriage to Diana. It was only then that they were free to formalize a relationship that other people seemed to know more about than he.

There is some suggestion that Charles and Camilla had been romantically involved for twenty-five years, the entire period of their respective marriages. There was, however, one incident, shortly after his marriage to Diana, that gives reason to believe that their relationship had ended, at least for the time being. Diana had discovered a gold bracelet Charles was planning to send to Camilla. It had a blue enamel disc set in gold with the initials GF standing for 'Girl Friday' engraved on it– his nickname for her. Diana was convinced the entwined initials stood for Fred and Gladys, their pet names for one another. She was probably correct in her thinking but was eventually convinced that it was one of several pieces of jewellery he had bought for friends to thank them for looking after him during his bachelor years. Naïvely it did not occur to Charles that Diana might have a problem with a former girlfriend remaining in his circle of friends. When she made it plain that she did he claimed to have severed all contact with Camilla, but Diana's suspicions continued to trouble her, and years later she was proved right. Her husband was back with his old flame. The 'Camillagate' tape that emerged in January 1993, apparently consisting of intimate conversations with his mistress, was the ultimate humiliation – not so much that Charles spoke about his wish always to be with the woman he adored but by the public reaction provoked by the broadcasting of a tape of pillow-talk intimacies in his hope of achieving this.

In June 1984 Prince Charles and Princess Diana appeared to have everything. Diana had blossomed into a beautiful and fashionable woman whose photograph on the front of any newspaper or magazine was guaranteed to increase circulation figures. They had one beautiful son, William, and Diana was six months pregnant. They looked happy and content in the photographs and television images of the time, but once their second son Harry was born it was a different story. Visiting Diana to see his new son Charles made a derogatory remark about the colour of the baby's hair and then left to play polo. It was only later that she may have wondered whether he was questioning the child's paternity.

It was now an open secret that Camilla and Charles had rekindled their relationship. Camilla had supported Charles after the death of his beloved uncle Lord Louis Mountbatten in an IRA terrorist attack. He had looked upon his uncle as a father figure, very much more available than his own father and easier to talk to. Camilla was the person to whom he turned when feelings of sadness overcame him.

The only one person who did not know of the renewal of their relationship appeared to be Diana. Her insecurities, already heightened by her parents' divorce, were reinforced by Charles's coldness following the birth of their second son. Diana needed to feel loved.

Charles's lack of sexual interest could have been due to seeing her in a new role. She was now the mother he had been looking for. She was in his bed and had come between them. Any sexual contact with his wife would have run into the incest barrier.

Diana referred to her home in Kensington Palace as her 'palace prison'. She saw it as an enclosure that offered her everything apart from the one thing she wanted, proof of her husband's love for her. During the BBC *Panorama* programme in which she was interviewed by Martin Bashir she said, 'Well, there were three of us in this marriage, so it was a bit crowded.' These words informed the world of her husband's infidelity, and the third party she referred to was, of course, Camilla. Diana could not have guessed that the person who had come between them was, in fact, the shadowy image of his mother. Had Charles's mother been there for him when she was needed more than forty years earlier it would not have been necessary for him to invent her at a time and in a place where she was definitely not wanted. Successful eradication of his mother's image would have allowed Charles and Diana to see one another as they really were and might have changed the course of history.

Diana was asked to authorize the publication of a biography that gave an account of her life. This was initiated by the journalist Andrew Morton and was published in 1992 under the title *Diana: Her True Story*. The book stunned the world. Diana had crossed the royal line by exposing her husband's adultery.

Two months after Diana's death Charles told his sons about Camilla. Although his children must have had some inkling of the relationship, he explained to them how Camilla had re-entered his life after a youthful love affair and had made him deeply happy. William, who was fifteen at the time, is reputed to have said he 'didn't want to know'.

Diana's name for Camilla was 'the Rottweiler', which probably referred to her tenacity, fearlessness and tendency to behave like a guard dog with respect to Charles. Charles and Camilla had frequently stayed together either at Charles's marital home Highgrove or at the Parker Bowleses' Bodehyde Manor. It is said that their affair was well known to both their spouses as well as to Queen Elizabeth and the Queen Mother. Camilla seemed to have felt little resentment at her husband Andrew's infidelities. They have remained on good terms and after the death of Andrew's second wife, she attended her funeral as did Princess Anne. Perhaps the infidelity of Andrew Parker Bowles gave Camilla the freedom to continue her relationship with Charles without the burden of guilt.

It was not until 2005, eight years after Diana's death and ten years after Camilla's divorce, that Charles and Camilla finally came together as husband and wife. She was not popular with the British people. In the aftermath of Diana's death she was perceived as the 'wicked witch' who had destroyed the fairy-tale princess. However, the Prince was far from being the 'handsome prince' of the fairy stories. Charles has always appeared to have low self-esteem as far as his looks are concerned, and he never appeared comfortable in the role of 'handsome prince'.

In order to live up to his father's expectations of him Charles joined the Navy and rose rapidly through the ranks to become a high-ranking officer. Military service was never on his agenda, despite his being toughened up at Gordonstoun in anticipation of it. His career preferences and natural inclinations were to create good ecological systems and wholesome food products. His nurturing of leadership qualities, through the Prince's Trust, was a far cry from his father's aspirations for his son to live a military life as he had himself. It was Camilla who appeared to accept him as the person he wanted to be – not suave and sophisticated but a man who, in his own way, would fight for better nutrition, a healthier lifestyle and an architecturally pleasing landscape. Diana appeared neither to share nor care about his needs in so far as they could be identified – so intent had she been in carving out a niche for herself and her own brand of caring.

Stunned by hostile public opinion after Diana's death – Camilla was pelted with bread rolls in a supermarket – she decided to maintain a low profile. She has since referred to the media spotlight as 'putting her head above the parapet'.

It would need a targeted media campaign to ensure Camilla's acceptance as the future wife of the heir to the throne. Her public appearances, charities and personal appearance had to be carefully orchestrated in the period leading to her marriage to Prince Charles in April 2005.

In an article in the *Observer* from 2002 by Ben Summerskill, he refers to the grooming of CPB, as she is apparently known by Prince Charles's office staff. A spin doctor, Mark Bolland, had been engaged by Charles in 1995 to restore his reputation. Mark Bolland set about reinventing Camilla as a suitable 'companion' for Prince Charles. She became President of the National Osteoporosis Society – a natural choice since her mother had this condition and later died from it.

Camilla even appeared on Radio 4's soap opera *The Archers* to help promote interest in osteoporosis in a fictitious charity visit to Ambridge. There was a planned series of 'casual appearances' including her attendance at a Golden Jubilee Concert where she was seated discreetly behind the Queen. Gradually and almost imperceptibly Camilla was becoming the Prince of Wales's regular consort. In 2002 the General Synod voted to permit those who were divorced to remarry in church. The picture used to illustrate this story in the world's media was one of Charles and Camilla. It was clear that it was only a matter of time before the couple would marry and be expected to live happily ever after.

There is every reason to believe that they will do so. Until their wedding in 2005 marriage had been a struggle. Each had married a partner whose personality and outlook was similar to their own. Both of them had been raised in the shadow of 'the parade ground', and both realized that, although their respective families were steeped in military history and tradition, the demands and expectations made of them were not those with which either felt comfortable. Charles with his idealistic aspirations and Camilla with her less than well-ordered lifestyle met at a point when they felt harmonious and appreciated by one another. The Prince's Trust provided Charles with armies not of men waiting to go into battle but of grateful young people who, having benefited from the Prince's endorsement, gave him admiration, respect and affection. It was the endorsement he never received from his father. The call of duty for Charles and Camilla to marry 'appropriately' had been answered, badly researched traditional expectations had come and gone, and it had become obvious to both of them that they had loved one another for most of their adult lives. Their marital needs had evolved out of their upbringing, although neither of them realized it. Charles from the moment of birth had been attended to by those whose job it was to service his needs. He was not so much brought up as directed along a path which in royal terms might have been appropriate but in terms of his psychological needs was ill advised. Uniforms and uniformity, instruction and obedience did not appeal to him. Wearing the uniform of an admiral after five years in the Navy, that of an air chief marshal in the RAF and a general in the Army did not attract him. The softer side of social interaction was more appealing. He needed a woman, but none of the ones who attracted him were Queen material. They were more likely to be nursery-maid material, in his eyes at least, although not in their own. They were the women to whom he had been close as a child.

Diana was attractive, much in demand and drew the crowds not so much to both of them as to herself. She was Queen material, but she was stealing his thunder before he had had an opportunity to use some of it for himself. Noisy fireworks seemed to push him into damp-squib mode and made him resentful. He did not like it. He had already had to choose between uniform and medals and the soft touch. He thought enviously of his father who had achieved both. He had all the accoutrements but none of the responsibilities. It was Queen Victoria and Prince Albert over again. It was not until he met Camilla that what he had been waiting for since infancy finally swam into focus. Of course the Palace did not like it. His parents loved uniforms and the ceremonies and the horses and the stately homes; particularly the horses. If horses did not do what was expected of them they soon got to know who was in the saddle. His father was less keen on horses. He preferred canoes. He had been paddling his own throughout his life and was happy continuing to do so.

Has Camilla's quest to achieve in her own right been successful? She is Patron of the National Literacy Trust and Book Trust; in presenting the Man Booker Prize in 2013 she spoke of the 'astonishing breadth, depth and beauty of the written word'. As Patron of the National Osteoporosis Society she is helping to create more awareness of the illness that prematurely killed her mother and grandmother. After her long and complex relationship with Charles she can stand in the garden at Highgrove, deadheading the roses and contemplating her future as Queen.

Charles, on the other hand, is helping to create the environment he has sought all his life – the pure, fresh, unpolluted air that nurtures and protects; the supply of organic unadulterated foods that support healthy living and the absolute banning, not only in his home but also on his land, of one of the 'evils' of life – cigarettes. It was good news to him when Camilla gave up her habit of smoking ten cigarettes a day.

He is patron of more than 400 organizations, including the British Hedge Laying Society. It is known that he is something of an expert in repairing natural fencing, perhaps finally realizing the importance of mending fences rather than breaking them down. They appear a happy late-middle-aged couple perhaps hoping that the monarchy will be left as their inheritance for their heir Prince William and, in the course of time, his heir Prince George. Whether the latter will think this a good idea is too early to predict.

15

THE DUKE AND DUCHESS
OF CAMBRIDGE

'And kiss me, Kate, we will be married . . .'
– William Shakespeare, *The Taming of the Shrew*

On 29 July 1981 Carole Middleton, who was in the early months of pregnancy, and her husband Michael would most likely have been two of the millions of people throughout the world who watched the spectacular wedding of HRH Prince Charles, the Prince of Wales, to the beautiful and aristocratic Lady Diana Spencer in St Paul's Cathedral. It is unlikely that in their wildest dreams they would have imagined that the child Carole was carrying, as she followed the ceremony on television, might one day become the Queen of England.

Catherine Elizabeth Middleton was born at the Royal Berkshire Hospital, Reading, on 9 January 1982 to the 27-year-old Carole Middleton and Michael, her husband of thirteen months. At the time the couple were living in the village of Bradfield, thirty miles from Windsor. Michael was seven months younger than the Prince of Wales and Carole six years older than the twenty-year-old Lady Diana Spencer.

Bradfield was conveniently situated for Heathrow Airport where Michael Middleton, following in his father's footsteps, had undergone training as an airline pilot. Before completing his training, however, he switched to ground crew and worked as an aircraft dispatcher. Smartly dressed in his brass-buttoned blue uniform, Michael Middleton attracted the attention of air hostess Carole Goldsmith who was enjoying her career with British Airways. She loved her work, and Michael was her first serious boyfriend. While she was descended from strong northern working-class stock, Michael had a solid middle-class background. Carole's mother was delighted when the couple announced their engagement.

Eleven months after the royal wedding the succession to the throne was ensured when Prince William Arthur Philip Louis was born at St Mary's Hospital, Paddington, to the Prince of Wales and

Princess Diana. One day earlier, on 20 June 1982, Catherine Middleton was christened in a small ceremony for family and friends at the local church of St Andrew's, a flint and chalk building on the banks of the River Pang.

While the media was camped outside the Lindo Wing of St Mary's Hospital in London awaiting the birth of the heir apparent to Charles and Diana, no one could have imagined that thirty years later the Middleton baby, now the Duchess of Cambridge, and her husband Prince William, the Duke of Cambridge, would emerge from the same hospital cradling the third in line of succession, HRH Prince George Alexander Louis born on 22 July 2013.

Shortly after the birth of the new Prince, William's commission with the RAF came to an end. It was reported that he was leaving his military career to concentrate on the furtherance of his royal duties and charitable work.

William and Kate were aware that, in effect, they had taken on two new responsibilities – Prince George and the future of the monarchy. As would any new parents, they naturally prioritized the needs of baby George, and the early photographs of him with his parents leave us in no doubt of their feelings for him. The fact that they not only made use of the royal christening gown but took on the royal nanny – Prince William's former nanny Jessie Webb who came out of retirement – points to the responsibility they now assumed for the continuity of the House of Windsor. While the Princess of Wales went on to have a second son in 1984, Prince Henry Charles Albert David (Prince Harry), Carole Middleton had two more children, Philippa (Pippa) born 6 September 1983 and James born 15 April 1987.

By now Carole Middleton had given up her job with British Airways and the family were living on Michael's salary. It was not a vast sum but sufficient to live reasonably well in the English countryside. Carole was ambitious and wanted the best for her children. She became involved with the social life of the village and joined the mothers and toddlers playgroup and later the pre-school group. Her daughters Kate and Pippa were later nicknamed 'the Wisteria Sisters' because they were intertwined, decorative and fragrant with an insatiable appetite to climb.

Bradfield was home to many young upwardly mobile couples with small children who held regular children's parties. At these parties the 'going home' goodie bag would include the traditional slice of birthday cake, a balloon and a small toy. Spotting a niche in the market Carole Middleton began to make her own original party bags that she sold to the other parents. This satisfied her need not only to make children happy but to provide some extra cash for her family. In the early years of the internet she had the business acumen to register the name 'Party Pieces' and to create her own website. Today this site offers a range of themed parties for all occasions as well as souvenirs for national celebrations, the wedding of her daughter Kate to the Duke of Cambridge being one of them.

By all accounts Carole never shirked from dealing with the less glamorous side of life in the village. She took her turn in helping with the playgroup, changed nappies and mopped up puddles. At the time many families employed mothers' helps, au pairs or nannies, but Carole wanted to spend time with her children and was determined to do so. The popularity of 'Party Pieces' grew, with increased turnover and profit margins. When at the age of twenty-nine Catherine Elizabeth Middleton married Prince William, Duke of Cambridge, the eldest son of Charles, Prince of Wales, on 29 April 2011 a new chapter in British history began to unfold. It is reported in the biography *Kate: The Future Queen*, written by Katie Nicholl of the *Daily Mail*, that the paths of Kate Middleton and Prince William first crossed in 1999 at Highgrove. At the time Kate was a pupil at Marlborough College, and it is thought that one of her fellow students introduced her to William. Kate was seventeen, and she had the required academic grades to study at her first choice of university, Edinburgh. Once it was announced, however, that Prince William had opted for St Andrew's University in Scotland Kate decided to apply there as well, although to be on the same course as William meant that she would have to take a gap year.

She was not without competition for William's attention. According to Catherine Ostler writing in March 2011 in the *Daily Mail*, it would seem that in the run-up to making a commitment to Kate William was involved in several brief relationships. From early adult life he had not been unaware that the heavy burden of history might one day settle on his shoulders. He was conscious that there were many young girls around who were more than willing to share that burden with him. During his gap year he was rumoured to have had a holiday romance with Jessica Craig at her parents' ranch in

Kenya. The summer before going up to St Andrews saw him dating Arabella Musgrave whose father was a friend of Prince Charles. In 2004, when he was visiting Tennessee, he had a fling with American interior designer Anna Sloan whose business partner Emilia is one of Kate's closest friends. His first 'girlfriend', when he arrived at St Andrews, was said to have be Carly Massy-Birch, an aspiring actress who has lately gone to ground in the South of France.

According to Claudia Joseph writing in *Kate Middleton: Princess in Waiting*, the break-up with Carly might have been a catalyst for some soul-searching on the Prince's part. In the small, remote town of St Andrews he felt isolated from his friends in London and Gloucestershire. American students were particularly fascinated by him and were constantly following him around. His father counselled his son against giving up university, telling him it would be detrimental to his public image. It is generally Kate Middleton, however, who is credited with being the person who not only persuaded him to stay on but to change his degree course from a study of history of art to geography.

Kate appears to have had fewer involvements than William before they became romantically linked. Journalist Willem Marx was said to be her first love and her boyfriend at Marlborough where the *Daily Mail* in March 2011 dubbed her 'tediously well behaved'. She is also said to have dated Rupert Finch, a law student and a gifted cricketer, who was in his final year at St Andrews when Kate turned up in 2001. They went out for less than a year. Rupert has never spoken of his relationship with her and says he intends never to do so. He is now married to Lady Natasha Rufus Isaacs, a friend of Prince William.

Kate and William immersed themselves in student life. They were often spotted together at bars and would occasionally attend the theatre together. William joined the university athletics club, playing rugby and football in a Sunday league and, in the family tradition, became a member of the St Andrews polo team. He enjoyed water-skiing and surfing in the North Sea. To keep fit he started a regime of early-morning runs along the sea wall.

At this point William and Kate were living in St Salvator's Hall of Residence. There was clearly a burgeoning romance because, for their second year, they had become close enough to share a flat in the centre of the town with two of their friends. Although Kate was now dating the second in line to the throne she still had practical matters to attend to, one of these being the repayment of her student loan. To earn extra cash she served drinks at the Henley Regatta for an upmarket catering contractor. The owner of the company is reported to have said 'she's a pretty girl, so she takes home plenty of tips'. Kate thus demonstrated to the world her ability to balance the two aspects of her life, 'princess-in-waiting' and 'hard-up student'. This combination of sophistication and ordinariness would in time mirror Princess Diana's ability to communicate equally well with the 'great and good' and with ordinary people.

Prince William, too, had his fair share of mundane tasks. He is reported to have said, 'I do a lot of shopping – I enjoy shopping actually. I get very carried away, you know, just food shopping. I buy lots of things and then go back to the house and see the fridge is full of all the stuff I've just bought . . . We all get on very well and started off having rotas, but of course it just broke down into complete chaos. Everyone helps out when they can. I try to help out when I can, and they do the same for me, but usually you just fend for yourself.'

From late 2002 it was generally accepted that William and Kate were an item. It was around this time that Carole and Michael Middleton bought a flat in Chelsea, a convenient location for society gatherings. Kate was invited to a shooting party in Sandringham where six young women and ten young men , including Prince William, shared a six-bedroom cottage. Prince Charles was hosting his own event in the Queen's Edwardian mansion, also in Sandringham, and it is thought that he organized an upmarket 'takeaway' for his son and his guests at their nearby shooting lodge.

By then William and Kate were spending a great deal of time together. They were frequently to be seen in deep conversation and appeared comfortable in each other's company. At the beginning of 2003 Kate had her twenty-first birthday party, celebrating with a group of her closest friends including Prince William. William's own party was held a few months later at Windsor Castle, which was converted for the occasion into an African jungle. Two giant elephants towered over the guests with their trunks intertwined to form an archway, and more than three hundred guests in fancy dress danced the night away. Two of William's uncles, Prince Andrew and Charles Spencer, were dressed as big-game hunters. Prince Charles wore a safari suit and hunting hat. Kate's appearance, when she arrived with her St Andrews friends, was overshadowed by the arrest of an intruder who, dressed as Osama bin Laden, gatecrashed the castle and grabbed the microphone from Prince William as he was thanking the Queen and Prince Charles for the party. Also somewhat overshadowing Kate's presence was the attendance of Jessica Craig. Did William still harbour feelings for her? Why else had she flown from Kenya for his 'Out of Africa' party? William was at pains to quash the rumour by issuing a public statement denying any romance with Jessica. Not only did he deny having a relationship with her but denied having a girlfriend at all, saying, 'There's been a lot of speculation about every single girl I'm with, and it actually does quite irritate me after a while, more so because it's a complete pain for the girls. These poor girls, whom I've either just met or who are friends of mine, suddenly get thrown into the limelight and their parents get rung up and so on. I think it's a little unfair on them really. I'm used to it, because it happens quite a lot now. But it's very difficult for them, and I don't like that at all.' He appeared to be telling the world that he was single – but was it just a smokescreen to draw attention away from his friendship with Kate?

In March 2004 on the ski slopes of Klosters, a regular playground of the Royal Family, William and Kate were photographed together and the picture was then published in the *Sun* newspaper. They were four days into their holiday in the Swiss Alps, and the gossip and conjecture of the last eighteen months seemed to be bearing fruit. It seemed that William and Kate, now in their third year at St Andrews, were indeed in a serious relationship.

In the autumn of the same year, after the summer vacation, Kate and William decided to move into a farmhouse on the outskirts of St Andrews to ensure greater privacy. They were to remain there until they left university. The cottage was discreetly placed and totally secure; it had a £1.5m security system, was bombproof, under surveillance with CCTV and had panic buttons installed. They were more discreet than ever about the nature of their relationship. They left the cottage at different times and showed no overt affection towards one another in public. It is believed that they had romantic evenings at a former home of William's great-grandmother the Queen Mother. Birkhall, a fourteen-bedroom mansion on the banks of the River Muick near Balmoral, had been inherited by Prince Charles on the death of his grandmother. It is thought that this is where Kate met her future father-in-law Prince Charles for the first time. It is known that Charles and Camilla Parker Bowles frequently stayed together at Birkhall for their own trysts. Kate and William would often drive there in William's black Volkwagen Golf for hunting and shooting weekends.

In 2005, a year after the famous photograph on the ski slopes of Klosters, the couple now became openly affectionate towards each other. Kate joined William on a family holiday in Klosters, and this was seen as a signal that their relationship was serious and unlikely to end when they left university.

William and Kate graduated on 23 June 2005. The Queen and Prince Philip were in attendance, as were Kate's parents, William's father and his new stepmother the former Camilla Parker Bowles. Both William and Kate received upper-second-class degrees. In his speech to the graduates the university's Vice-Chancellor Dr Brian Lang said, 'You will have made lifelong friends. I say this to all new graduates: "You may have met your husband or wife." Our title as the top matchmaking university in Britain signifies so much that is good about St Andrews, so we rely on you to go forth and multiply – but in the positive sense that I earlier urged you to adopt.' A shrewd speech that would doubtless carry a strong message to those contemplating applying to St Andrews.

Thus it was that on 29 April, nine years after their first meeting, the wedding of Prince William, Duke of Cambridge, and Catherine Middleton took place at Westminster Abbey. Of the two thousand guests many were family and friends of the couple, although there were a significant number of Commonwealth leaders, leaders of religious organizations, military officials and representatives of the charities supported by William. The cost of the wedding itself, said to be in the region of £20 million including the most expensive security event in history, was borne by the Royal Family and the Middletons. The wheel had turned full circle and the wedding was watched by viewers in more than 180 countries – as the wedding of Prince Charles and Princess Diana had been.

Immediately after the wedding Prince William, putting duty first, returned to his work as a search-and-rescue pilot, and it was not until 9 May, eleven days later, that the couple left for a ten-day honeymoon in a villa on a private island in the Seychelles. The length of the honeymoon was limited by William's RAF duties and a scheduled official tour to Canada and the United States.

After their honeymoon the couple returned to their secluded rented farmhouse in Anglesey conveniently located close to the RAF base at which Prince William was based. After the birth of George it was announced that the couple with their newborn son would move to Kensington Palace and William would give up his career as a search-and-rescue pilot.

So we have the modern royal heir who was free to make his own choices. He chose Kate, a demure, beautiful and intelligent girl who was prepared to change her first choice of university and to wait patiently in the background for her Prince during his long absences. In so doing did Catherine Middleton, like anyone else who had found the love of her life, demonstrate steely determination? She is certainly proving a popular choice, and like Princess Diana before her she has already won the hearts of the British public. Has William chosen a wife in the image of his mother? The marriage certainly bears all the hallmarks of a genuine love match with a balance of duty and family life. Prince George will know three of his grandparents and, in all likelihood, two of his great-grandparents. His future seems solidly set. The nation will follow with great interest the progress of their future King.

16

HIS ROYAL HIGHNESS
PRINCE GEORGE OF CAMBRIDGE

'Georgie Porgie, puddin' and pie,
Kissed the girls and make them cry.'
– English nursery rhyme

The day has long passed since King Henry VIII disposed of Anne Boleyn when she failed to provide him with an heir. As her husband arranged for her to be executed – for offences that she could not possibly have committed – Anne was well aware, that six months earlier, had she given birth to a live rather than a stillborn son the future King would have been 'her saviour'.

Having produced not only a live but a bonny male child, the Duchess of Cambridge has nothing to fear. As the mother of a future King she has rapidly achieved new status in the royal household and is at liberty to bring up her child free from the constraints imposed by previous monarchs. There are already indications that times are changing. While tradition is accepted – royal nannies and christening-gowns are handed down from previous generations – there are portents of modernity and of a more hands-on maternal approach.

These signs can only be surmised and the Duchess's intentions merely guessed at: the new addition to the Royal Family is closely guarded, and brief incursions into its members' privacy by the paparazzi are granted only on occasions such as Prince George's christening and during his brief appearances on state occasions overseas.

Although hearsay has it that the protocol of changing clothes several times a day while spending Christmas at Sandringham was not to the Duchess's liking – she was breastfeeding the future monarch at the time – we do know that she is exponentially growing in popularity and that she seems to be setting the tone for a monarchy appropriate to the twenty-first century

The Duke and Duchess of Cambridge seem willing not only to form a happyand loving family unit in a cottage but also do their own washing-up. Their more relaxed lifestyle provides a template for those looking to a new royal generation whose members will be brought up surrounded by parental love and affection, rather than by the bullying and unhappiness endemic in the Victorian household in which children were reared, largely by servants, to be seen and not heard. In such an environment there is little chance that 'Georgie Porgie' will grow up to make 'the girls cry' or that his mother will lose her head.

EPILOGUE

Shedding light on the Royal Family, with its high public profile, enables us to understand its members and, by extension, some of our own family dynamics. The long lenses of the paparazzi have replaced the keyhole and provided us with significant information. A good mother allows her child to develop in a happy, structured and secure environment in which care and understanding are not confused with discipline and restraint. Her child will grow up feeling grateful and appreciative, a continuing re-enactment of what was provided in infancy. By remaining in touch with these good and positive feelings such a child's inner resources allow him or her to develop genuine independence and as an adult to make commitments. A 'neglectful' mother provokes hostility that her child is obliged to suppress until it surfaces in later relationships.

Until recently a royal mother has had to choose between the duties imposed upon her by the Crown and the needs of her children. The demands placed upon her to travel, often for weeks or months at a time, necessitating the engagement of nurses and governesses, have taken precedence over the nursery. Victoria, Mary and Elizabeth II all emphasized their royal duties at the expense of their duty to their sons who have grown up either to reject their mothers – as they themselves were rejected – or to scapegoat other women. Edward VII's apparent love for women covered his hostility to them, as he turned from one to another, rejecting the previous one in the process. Edward VIII's behaviour was similar until eventually he found a woman whom he believed would compensate him for the love denied him in the nursery. His hostility then switched from women to the Crown.

Prince George of Cambridge, the most recent addition to the royal household, will benefit from having a father who is well aware of the dangers of parental disharmony and neglect. A male child learns security and trust in his relationship with his mother. If he feels safe with her he will acquire self-confidence, self-worth and self-esteem. If he knows he can trust her he will be able to love other women and to entrust them with his feelings. If his mother has been strong, supportive and faithful to him he will be able to be strong, supportive and faithful to his partner in later life. When siblings arrive he will need to believe that he is loved, uniquely – as if they did not exist – just as they will also need to feel that they are loved, uniquely, as if he did not exist. Meanwhile in the absence of a good relationship with her father a daughter will seek a father in all men.

When a child becomes aware that others are sharing his or her mother's love, jealousy may surface. If breastfeeding is terminated too early he may believe that something of value is being withheld. If he or she is allowed to express these jealous feelings at the time they will soon be replaced by the ability to share. As 'mother' of her people, the Queen might have invited greater envy than most parents, because her children had to share her not only with their siblings but with millions. Love should be freely available to infants. If it is not, they may grow up to believe that symbols of love that do not belong to them are theirs by right. Queen Mary's compulsion to acquire the prized possessions of others is a sad echo of her feelings of worthlessness in her childhood when she was denied the love that should have been hers.

Had Sarah Ferguson at the age of twelve not been the victim of a broken home she might have learned to rely on and trust an opposite-sex partner. The one-on-one relationship with her father, which she was entitled to expect, could not, in her case, have been completely fulfilling. Since her father was a regular soldier until she was nine years old it was probable that even before her parents divorced she saw very little of him. Both Sarah and her mother suffered from the consequences of the lifestyle of her father's Army background. Like her father, Sarah's husband Prince Andrew was away from home for long periods of time. In the course of his naval duties he became a constant reminder of her absent father, precipitating the search for a better and more available male figure outside the marriage. Both her father and her husband served their country well at the expense of their wives' needs. Did the Duchess of York feel that Andrew loved the Navy (as her father had loved the Army) more than he loved her?

Unlike Sarah Ferguson, her sister-in-law, the late Princess Diana was not deprived of a father when her parents divorced. On the contrary, it was her mother who went away, reluctantly leaving her daughter's upbringing to her ex-husband. Diana, it seems, was doubly disadvantaged. Her mother had, to all intents and purposes, loved her and left her, while her father had to fill the role of both parents and found this impossible to achieve. As an adult it was natural for Diana to look for love from an older man. A Prince and future King, and the potential father of his people, seemed the ideal candidate. What Diana was unaware of was her need for the nurturing on which she had missed out. This need was unlikely to be satisfied by Prince Charles whose own mother had been insufficiently available to him. By the time Charles and Diana realized that it was mothering *and* fathering they needed it was too late. The maternal absence in their childhoods meant that neither was able fully to satisfy the needs of the other.

If only pleasing behaviour is permitted in childhood, a male adult is likely to develop as self-effacing and with little or no self-esteem. He may, in his turn, be able only to offer 'conditional' love to his children, to whom he will look for the love he was himself denied. This of course applies to females brought up similarly. It is the child's good relationship with the opposite-sex parent that will enable the individual to make successful commitments later in life, such as marriage. When such a role model has been unavailable or seems uninterested, resentment, rage, disappointment and retaliation may be inappropriately acted out with the adult partner. A partner with similar childhood experiences to one's own will often be unconsciously chosen, and with that person the rejections experienced in childhood will be both re-enacted and perpetuated.

Someone prone to fall repeatedly in love will recognize the miraculous feeling that each new partner has been 'known' to him all his life. He is unaware that what attracts him to these 'soulmates' is the identification in them of aspects of himself. The sense of 'oneness' and 'sameness' that results is frequently mistaken for true transactional love. It is more likely to be self-gratificatory. A permanent relationship formed on this inadequate basis may soon break down. Both partners will realize that what each is seeking in the other is something neither of them has had in the first place, something for which they may spend their lives looking.

A man who has been deprived of his mother's love will be

condemned to search for it in future relationships. Making one conquest after another, his hostility towards his mother will lead him to disappoint and reject all women as he was disappointed and rejected by his first love. His hostility towards women may take the form of sexual coldness, sometimes leading to potency problems.

Queen Victoria is an example of the 'neglectful' mother. Of her nine children none – except possibly Vicky who was doted on by Albert – experienced maternal love. It was possibly this neglect that led Edward, her heir, to spend his adult life in promiscuous sexual activity as he sought vainly the approval, attention and reassurance denied him by his mother. Queen Mary, too, had little or no time for her children and was happy to leave them with nursemaids. It is hardly surprising that her heir Edward VIII, while Prince of Wales, had one affair after another with married women as he sought compensation for what his mother had denied him. In a supreme and final act of revenge he chose to turn his back on his mother country.

A woman whose father has been unavailable at critical times in her development will similarly seek a substitute for him in her mate. An unconscious wish to punish the father who had never loved her may lead her to turn her back on her husband once he has become a father. She may form extramarital relationships with other father figures in an attempt to satisfy her unfulfilled needs for paternal love and attention. Hostility to the new partner will inevitably occur as this partner once again becomes the scapegoat for the absent parent. Signals are given off by the 'unloved', which others with similar feelings may readily home in on. As with Victoria and Albert, a woman neglected by one or other parent in infancy will find herself drawn to a similarly deprived man and vice versa.

Identification, or feeling at one with another person, is a powerful defence against fear of separation. If a child's separation from the mother has been gradual this will have prepared him or her to cope with inevitable losses in later life. The degree of independence the individual ultimately achieves will depend on the quality of the mothering he or she has formerly received. The Duchess of Kent certainly failed Victoria as far as quality love was concerned. Victoria remained so reliant upon her mother that she was unable to separate from her. She could not sleep alone and shared the Duchess's bedroom until, at the age of eighteen, she became Queen. Her desperate need for a caring partner led her to confuse her dependence on her husband – whose need to be of use she was unable to fulfil – with true unconstrained love.

A smothering mother who is unable to let go of her son may prevent him later on from making a commitment to another woman, as mother and son remain perpetually in love with one another. If her son does reject her for another woman, she experiences this as an act of infidelity, and the guilt that this engenders may result in her son turning away from women altogether. Albert Victor, Duke of Clarence, Queen Alexandra's eldest and favourite son, died at the age of twenty-eight probably from an opportunistic infection, having spent his short adult life promiscuously in search of a same-sex partner. Alexandra's second son, later George V, affected by his mother's possessiveness, turned in on himself with his lonely habits and hobbies and survived a marriage to Mary who may have enjoyed ceremony more than she did sex.

A bad mother is insensitive to the messages her infant sends out that convey a need for attention. The interaction so essential to the child's healthy development is aborted. The child fails to receive the responses he or she needs for intellectual growth, becomes discouraged and learns to send out only the more obvious signals such as crying (a reaction to pain or hunger) that can be picked up by the most insensitive and non-stimulating mother. There are many ways in which gratification is sought to compensate for an unsatisfactory childhood. If there has been lack of stimulation in early life that has been experienced as regimented and routine, excitement – such as that which is found in gambling or dangerous sports – may be sought later. Feelings of deprivation may also be covered up and denied under the influence of addictive drugs. Both George VI and his brother Edward VIII turned to alcohol as an illusory substitute for the mother love neither perceived himself to have received. Edward VII found some consolation in gambling, but any activity compulsively carried out to compensate for deprivation may lead only to further feelings of loss. To lose out becomes a self-fulfilling prophecy fulfilled at the gaming tables.

Gratification may also be sought in sexual activity or in the acquisition of possessions more commonly found in the nursery. These transitional objects, a piece of cloth, a beloved toy, a teddy bear (Prince Charles) or a reliance on 'Lady Luck' (Edward VII), from which solace is derived, are unconsciously experienced as being a part of the mother which the child cannot let go. They are an extension of his need to be at one with her. Possessions such as cars and boats are compulsively acquired by the bored and lonely adult who, as he did in the nursery, rapidly tires of them. Promiscuous sexual activity may serve a dual purpose. There is a need for conquest – winning love to compensate for its absence from carers – but at the same time one partner is rejected for another in retaliation against earlier parental renunciation. Edward VII chose as mistresses women who had children. Thus he was able to delude himself unconsciously that he had found a mother's love. He could, at the same time, take a form of revenge on the cuckolded husband and fathers in retaliation for what he saw as the purloining of the mother-love, rightly his, by his own father.

Family life, heavily dependent on the role played by the nurturing mother, is complemented by a powerful, upright and just father who will make his own contribution to it. As the male with whom his daughter forms her first relationship, a father influences the expectations and attitudes that will colour her relationships with the opposite sex in later life. If her father reciprocates the love that she has for him in childhood, she will be able to let him go and transfer her love to another man. If he has failed to meet her loving expectations, she will be compelled to search in other men for that which she was denied. When she herself has a child she may regard her husband as the loving 'father' whom she never had. A cruel irony then overtakes her. Sexual activity with the replacement father, with whom until their child was born she has had a good relationship, may suddenly become repugnant as the psychological barrier of incest reappears. Her father's image, now superimposed on that of her husband, may bring the healthy relationship to an end.

A strong, caring and, above all, available father is as essential to the development of a male child as he is to a female. Fathers who are passive or absent at a crucial stage of their son's development may lead them to turn to alternative males by way of compensation as did the Duke of Clarence – elder brother of George V – whose father Edward VII, because of his own defective upbringing, was unable to provide him with positive paternal input.

It could be argued that the Royal Family, born to wealth and privilege, is a special case. It is the right of every infant, however, irrespective of rank and privilege, to be loved and cared for and to have his or her needs gratified, until such time as growing independence allows for a gradual anxiety-free separation from the parents. This love must be freely given and unconditional and should not be regarded as an investment on which the return will be the child's gratitude and obedience. To demand love from a child is the first step to child abuse. A girl who pleases her father by being good may one day be obliged to please him sexually. Counselling must be available for children whose appropriate feelings of rage, jealousy and other negative emotions have been cruelly, if unwittingly, repressed by parents to pre-empt their inappropriate recurrence in adult life. By the time that stealing the 'symbols of love' such as jewellery or money has offended society or the denial of deprivation through drug and alcohol abuse has been acted out, it is too late.

The rights of the child are paramount. The healthy family is a unit in which all members are equal, no one is victimized or scapegoated, and tyrannical paternalism does not exist. This has seldom been the case in the Royal Family where there has often been a combination of neglectful mothering and harsh fathering. Queen Victoria's long depression affected all her children, although none more so than Edward VII. Victoria envied her eldest son Edward the father she had been denied and later blamed him – unfairly – for contributing to his father's death. Edward's need for love and approval from his parents fell on deaf ears. Later he was to marry Alexandra, who was herself deaf, unable to hear either him or their children.

Edward's children, the Duke of Clarence and George V, had not only a deaf mother but an absentee father. Edward was to compensate for his own inadequate mothering by his sexual promiscuity, while his son George became introspective, heavily over-dependent on himself, cold, angry and lonely, and married his mirror image. George V and Queen Mary relived their experiences of childhood in their dealings with their sons Edward VIII and George VI. They were distant and formal towards them, failed to give them adequate emotional or intellectual stimulation and did not provide satisfactory care-givers. As a result, their eldest son Edward later found the idea of commitment to a woman frightening until he eventually met a nanny figure in the form of Wallis Simpson in whom he could trust, whereupon he left the stage to his younger brother.

George VI played the 'favourites' game with his elder daughter Elizabeth, just as Albert had done with Vicky. Both sought to replace the love they had been denied by their mothers with love from their daughters. Elizabeth's younger sister Margaret Rose, disadvantaged as a child in her relationship with her father, was to repeat her disappointment with men as an adult. At this point the family's recurring patterns might well have changed. Elizabeth had felt loved and wanted. She was her parents' golden girl and could have provided the right kind of caring for her own four children. But this time fate intervened. Elizabeth's uncle abdicated, her father died, and she became Queen. The available Prince was a man with a fragmented background whose narcissism and inability to acknowledge the effect of his disturbed past led him to turn away from the emotional and spiritual to the material and physical.

Neither Elizabeth nor Philip was able to provide constancy of care to their four children. Elizabeth, as Queen, was preoccupied with affairs of state that led to frequent absences abroad without her children. Philip's emotional need to maintain a naval officer's sang-froid – a defence against his early losses – distanced him as a father. As a consequence of this unsatisfactory childhood both young women from broken homes, Anne divorced, and Edward experienced problems with his family status and took himself out of the loop by downgrading himself in 1999, at the time of his marriage to Sophie Rhys-Jones, to Earl of Wessex.

Many of the difficulties involved in bringing up children are well illustrated by the Royal Family. Although it is better to have absentee parents than cruel or negligent ones, the duties of royalty should, ideally, be correlated with the requirements of their children. The Queen fulfils an important role in Britain, and her time is taken up by the many demands made upon her by her public engagements both at home and abroad. In common with other working mothers she has had to find her own solution to the problems of child-rearing. Providing there is constancy of care, and the child is old enough to realize that when the mother leaves home she is not abandoning him or her and will reappear at the end of the day, a grandmother or a suitable nanny will often be the answer. These surrogates, however – no matter how good – do not provide the child with security; they can only reinforce what the child has already learned during the early bonding process with the mother. The working mother commonly takes maternity leave which entitles her to stay at home to look after her baby. The fatal flaw that appears to run through the monarchy might well be eradicated if royal mothers were permitted to do the same.

The publicity given to the Royal Family's marital problems and the realization that maternal bonding is vital to the well-being of children has already begun to influence the present generation of royal mothers. Both the Princess of Wales and the Duchess of York have been loving and caring towards their children, although their own needs were not fulfilled at home. In satisfying the needs of the young Princes and Princesses, however, and in considering their feelings, they will have gone a long way to ensure that these same healthy attitudes are handed down to their grandchildren.

NOTES

Chapter 1: Queen Victoria and Prince Albert
1. Princess Victoria had a half-brother, Charles, born in 1804, and a half-sister, Feodora, born in 1817. Her mother, Victoire, was the widow of Prince Erich Charles of Leiningen. She became Regent of that state when her husband died.
2. Germany was then a network of linked but independent principalities of which Prussia was the most powerful.

Chapter 4: Prince George and His Brother, the Duke of Clarence
1. Like Queen Victoria, Princess Mary Adelaide was a grandchild of George III, so the two women were cousins. Mary Adelaide's father was Adolphus, Duke of Cambridge, who married Augusta, Princess of Hesse-Cassel. Mary Adelaide married Francis, Duke of Teck, and had three sons after her daughter May.

Chapter 8: Queen Elizabeth II and Prince Philip
1. Mountbatten was elated to see his family name enter Britain's constitutional records, albeit briefly, when his nephew married Princess Elizabeth. Shortly after the marriage it was decided that the family name would be simply Windsor, but for a brief period it was Mountbatten-Windsor. Years later he hoped for a marriage between his granddaughter Amanda Knatchbull and Prince Charles, but this was not to be.

Chapter 13: Prince Andrew, His Duchess and Prince Edward
1. Susan Barrantes was killed in a car accident in 1998.

SELECT BIBLIOGRAPHY

In the preparation of this volume many books have proved invaluable sources of reference, and I am indebted to all their authors and publishers. In particular I would like to acknowledge the debt owed to the following:

Allison, Ronald and Sarah Riddell (eds), *The Royal Encyclopaedia*, Macmillan, London, 1991

Crawford, Marion, *The Little Princesses*, Cassell, London, 1950

Donaldson, Frances, *Edward VIII*, Weidenfeld and Nicolson, London, 1974

Edwards, Anne, *Matriarch*, Hodder and Stoughton, London, 1984

Joseph, Claudia, *Kate Middleton, Princess in Waiting*, Mainstream Publishing, Edinburgh, 2009

Lacey, Robert, *Majesty*, Hutchinson, London, 1977

Longford, Elizabeth, *Victoria RI*, Weidenfeld and Nicolson, London, 1964

Magnus, Philip, *King Edward VII*, John Murray, London, 1964

Morton, Andrew, *Diana: Her True Story*, Michael O'Mara Books, London, 1992

Nicholl, Katie, *Kate: The Future Queen*, Weinstein Books, New York, 2013

Rose, Kenneth, *King George V*, Weidenfeld and Nicolson, London, 1987

St Aubyn, Giles, *Queen Victoria*, Christopher Sinclair-Stephenson, London, 1991

Ziegler, Philip, *King Edward VIII*, William Collins, London, 1990

OTHER SIGNIFICANT SOURCES

Battiscombe, Georgina, *Queen Alexandra*, Constable, London, 1969

Benson, A.C. (ed.), *Letters of Queen Victoria, Vol. I*, John Murray, London, 1908

Bloch, Michael, *The Secret File of the Duke of Windsor*, Bantam Books, London, 1988

Carlton, Charles, *Royal Mistresses*, Routledge, London, 1990

Chandos, John, *Boys Together*, Hutchinson, London, 1984

Chester, Lewis, David Leitch and Colin Simpson, *The Cleveland Street Affair*, Weidenfeld and Nicolson, London, 1976

Cooper, Jilly, *Class*, Eyre Methuen, London, 1979

Darby, Elisabeth and Nicola Smith, *The Cult of the Prince Consort*, Yale University Press, New Haven and London, 1983

Ebbetts, Leslie, *The Royal Style Wars*, Sidgwick and Jackson, London, 1988

Encyclopaedia Britannica, 14th edition, London, 1957

Gathorne-Hardy, Jonathan, *The Rise and Fall of the British Nanny*, Hodder and Stoughton, London, 1972

Heald, Tim, *The Duke*, Hodder and Stoughton, London, 1991

Heald, Tim, *Networks*, Hodder and Stoughton, London, 1983

Hibbert, Christopher, *The Court at Windsor*, Longman, London, 1964

Higham, Charles and Roy Moseley, *Elizabeth and Philip*, Sidgwick and Jackson, London, 1991

Holden, Anthony, *Prince Charles*, Weidenfeld and Nicolson, London, 1979

James, Paul, *Margaret*, Sidgwick and Jackson, London, 1990

Johnston, Susanna and Anne Tennant, *The Picnic Papers*, Hutchinson, London, 1983

Judd, Denis, *The Life and Times of George V*, Weidenfeld and Nicolson, London, 1973

Junor, Penny, *Charles*, Sidgwick and Jackson, London, 1987

Junor, Penny, *Prince William: Born to Be King: An Intimate Portrait*, Hodder and Stoughton, London, 2012

Longford, Elizabeth (ed.), *The Oxford Book of Royal Anecdotes*, Oxford University Press, Oxford, 1989

Macalpine, Ida and Richard Hunter, *George III and the Mad Business*, Allen Lane, London, 1969

Mitchell, Juliet, *The Selected Melanie Klein*, Penguin Books, Harmondsworth, 1986

Miller, Alice, *Prisoners of Childhood*, Basic Books, New York, 1981

Moore, Sally, *The Definitive Diana*, Sidgwick and Jackson, London, 1991

Morrow, Ann, *The Queen*, Granada Publishing, London, 1983

Mortimer, Penelope, *Queen Elizabeth*, Viking, London, 1986

Mosley, Diana, *The Duchess of Windsor*, Sidgwick and Jackson, London, 1980

Parker, John, *Prince Philip*, Sidgwick and Jackson, London, 1990

Princess Alice, *Duchess of Gloucester, Memories of Ninety Years*, Collins and Brown, London, 1991

Selway, Lance, *Queen Victoria's Grandchildren*, Collins and Brown, London, 1991

SELECT BIBLIOGRAPHY

Schatzman, Morton, *Soul Murder*, Random House, New York, 1973

Schreber, D.G.M., *The Harmful Body Positions of Children, Including a Statement of Counteracting Measures*, Fleischer, Leipzig, 1853

Van der Kiste, John, *Edward VII's Children*, Alan Sutton, Stroud, 1989

Van der Kiste, John, *George V's Children*, Alan Sutton, Stroud, 1991

Vanggaard, Thorkil, *Phallos: A Symbol and Its History in the Male World*, Jonathan Cape, London, 1969

Viorst, Judith, *Necessary Losses*, Simon and Schuster, London, 1988

Warwick, Christopher, *The Abdication*, Sidgwick and Jackson, London, 1986

Wharfe, Ken with Robert Jobson, *Diana, Closely Guarded Secret*, Michael O'Mara, London, 2003

Whiting, Audrey, *The Kents*, Hutchinson, London, 1985

Zec, Donald, *The Queen Mother*, Sidgwick and Jackson, London, 1990

INDEX

Adams, Bryan, 189

Adeane, Sir Edward, 172

Aird, John, 172

Airlie, Mabell, Lady, 102, 111–12, 152

Albert, Prince: birth/childhood, 19–20; death, 25–6, 37, 39, 56; difficulty fitting into English society, 32, 35–6; distanced behaviour, 32, 36, 47; emotional deprivation, 19, 31–2, 37; harshness of parenting, 47–8, 52, 54–5, 71; hypochondria, 31; leisure interests, 31–2; physical appearance, 32–3; relationship with eldest daughter, 33–4, 36, 46, 123; resentment of Lehzen, 24, 35, 45; response to Edward's sexual liaisons, 55–6; sexual indifference, 34; shyness, 32; subsidiary role, 34–5

alcohol, problems with, 19, 114, 233

Alexander III, Tsar, 87

Alexandra, Tsarina, 87, 114

Alexandra of Denmark, Queen (of Edward VII), 59–69; deafness, 37, 62, 65, 235; family background, 59–60; manipulativeness, 40, 65; physical appearance, 61–2; plans for

marriage, 54, 55, 56–7; pregnancies, 63; relationship with husband, 63–4, 66–7; relationship with Victoria, 61, 67; relationships with children, 65–6, 72–3, 76, 78–9, 80; relationships with grandchildren, 88; social acomplishments, 62–3, 64–5; wedding, 57; widowhood, 65

Alfred, Prince (son of Victoria), 50–51, 131, 133

Alice, Princess (daughter of Victoria), 38, 46–7

Alice of Battenberg (Princess Andrew of Greece), 133–4, 201

Allen, Gertrude, 175, 176

Altrincham, Lord, 142

Andrew, Prince see York, Duke of

Andrew, Prince, of Greece (father of Philip), 133

Anne, Princess Royal, 123, 191–8, 206, 211, 215; birth/childhood, 137, 138–9, 191, 194; charity work, 192–3; education, 194–5; equestrian achievements, 192, 193, 195; marriages, 191, 193–4, 236; position within family, 191–2, 194, 195, 197; public image, 195–6, 197; relationship with father, 139, 140, 164, 193, 194, 195–6

Rocca, Fiametta, 138
Roose, Nurse, 134
Rose, Kenneth, 86
Royal Family: relationship with
media, 159–60, 165, 209; as
'special case', 234–5, 236–7

Saxe-Coburg-Gotha, Ernst, Duke
of (brother of Albert), 31
Saxe-Coburg-Gotha, Ernst, Duke
of (father of Albert), 19
Saxe-Coburg-Saalfeld, Louise,
Duchess of (mother of Albert),
19, 31–2
Schleswig/Holstein, disputes over, 67
Schreber, D.G.M., 47–8
Shakespeare, William, 59, 111, 125,
219
Shand, Bruce, 211
Shand, Rosalie, 211
Shand Kydd, Frances (née Roche,
formerly Spencer), 175, 176–7
Shand Kydd, Peter, 175
Simpson, Ernest, 106
Simpson, Wallis, 15, 17, 40;
Edward's infatuation with, 106–8;
jewellery given to, 99, 106–7; as
mother figure, 95, 107–8
Sloan, Anna, 222
Snowdon, Earl of (Antony
Armstrong-Jones), 143, 150, 154,
160, 191, 208
Somerset, Lady Geraldine, 78
Spencer, Charles, 9th Earl, 175,
190, 223
Spencer, Edward John, 8th Earl,
175, 184–5
Spencer, Raine, 176, 179, 190
Spock, Benjamin, 164

St Laurent, Julie de, 20
Stark, Koo, 201
Stephen, James, 74–5
Stevens, Jocelyn, 156
Stockmar, Baron von, 21, 35, 36,
45, 48–9
Stonor, Julie, 77
Strathmore and Kinghorne,
Countess of, 116, 118
Strathmore and Kinghorne, Earl
of, 104, 116
Stuart, James, 120
Summerskill, Ben, 216
Sutherland, Duchess of, 29

Taylor, Elizabeth, 157
Teck, Duke of, 83
Teck, May of see Mary, Queen
Temple, Shirley, 126
Tennyson, Alfred, Lord, 45, 60
Thatcher, Margaret, 143
Tindall, Zara, née Phillips, 191, 198
Tolstoy, Leo, 80
Townsend, Peter, Group Captain,
141, 143, 150, 152–4, 163
Trollope, Anthony, 159
Trudeau, Margaret, 199

Vacani, Betty, 130
van der Post, Sir Laurens, 168,
172
Victoria, 19–44; artistic tastes, 26,
117; attitudes to childbirth/
motherhood, 23, 34; birth, 13,
19–20; childhood, 15, 20–21, 22–3;
comfort eating, 28; contemplation
of suicide, 27; dependence, 25–6;
early meetings with Albert, 29–31;
emotional deprivation, 19, 22–3,